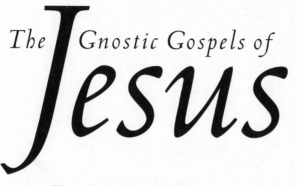

The Gnostic Gospels of *Jesus*

THE DEFINITIVE COLLECTION OF MYSTICAL GOSPELS AND SECRET BOOKS ABOUT JESUS OF NAZARETH

Marvin Meyer

HarperSanFrancisco

A Division of HarperCollins*Publishers*

I wish to express my gratitude to Chapman University and the Griset Chair
in Bible and Christian Studies for the generous support of my research.
A number of people at Harper San Francisco have been very helpful in producing
this book, among them Eric Brandt, John Loudon, Kris Ashley, and Lisa Zuniga.
To my wife and children I offer my special thanks. They have been patient with
my preoccupations and have encouraged me with their wisdom.

Text design by rlf design

Library of Congress Cataloging-in-Publication Data
        The gnostic Gospels of Jesus : the definitive collection of mystical gospels and secret books about Jesus of Nazareth / [edited by] Marvin Meyer.—1st ed.
        p.   cm.
        Includes bibliographical references.
        ISBN-13: 978–0-06-076208-7
        ISBN-10: 0-06-076208-X
        1. Gnosticism.   2. Jesus Christ—Gnostic interpretations.   3. Nag Hammadi codices.   I. Meyer, Marvin W.
        BT1390.G4938   2005
        299'.932—dc22   2004054324

        07 08 09 RRD(H) 10 9 8

The Gnostic Gospels of
Jesus

Contents

Introduction   *vii*

PART ONE

The Gospel of Thomas with the Greek Gospel of Thomas fragments

I

PART TWO

The Gospel of Mary

31

PART THREE

The Gospel of Philip

43

PART FOUR

The Gospel of Truth by Valentinus

89

PART FIVE

The Holy Book of the Great Invisible Spirit or the Egyptian Gospel

113

PART SIX

The Secret Book of John

143

PART SEVEN

The Secret Book of James

185

PART EIGHT

The Book of Thomas

203

PART NINE

The Dialogue of the Savior

219

PART TEN

The Second Discourse of Great Seth

241

PART ELEVEN

The Book of Baruch by Justin

261

PART TWELVE

The Round Dance of the Cross

277

Notes   287

Bibliography   329

Introduction

Discoveries of Gnostic Gospels

The gnostic gospels and related texts published in this volume are providing remarkable new ways of understanding Jesus and the beginnings of Christianity, but none of this would be possible were it not for recent discoveries of papyrus manuscripts buried in the sands of Egypt.

In December 1945, as Muhammad Ali of the al-Samman clan has told his story, several Egyptian fellahin, including Muhammad Ali himself, were riding their camels near the Jabal al-Tarif, a prominent cliff that flanks the Nile River in Upper Egypt near the modern city of Nag Hammadi.[1] The fellahin hobbled their camels at the foot of the Jabal al-Tarif and proceeded to dig around a large boulder that had fallen onto the talus, the slope of debris against the face of the cliff. They were looking for sabakh, natural fertilizer that may be gathered in such places, but to their surprise they discovered something else: a large storage jar, buried by the boulder, with a bowl sealed on the mouth of the jar as a lid. Muhammad Ali has noted that he paused before removing the lid, since he was concerned that the jar might contain a jinni, or spirit, that could do harm if released from the jar. Yet Muhammad Ali apparently also recalled stories about treasures hidden in the ground in that region, and his love of gold overcame his fear of jinn. As he has reported, he smashed the jar with his mattock, and something golden came out of the jar and disappeared into the air.

What Muhammad Ali saw, we now conclude, was not gold but rather papyrus fragments, golden in color, which were released from the confines of the jar into the sunlight. When he looked inside the jar, he was disappointed that there was no more gold remaining, but he found what scholars judge to be worth more than gold. There, in the jar, was a collection of ancient texts, thirteen codices of what we now call the Nag Hammadi library.[2] All the texts are written in Coptic, a late form of the Egyptian language. Within this small library are most of the gnostic gospels and related texts presented in this volume: the Gospel of Thomas, the Gospel of Philip, the Gospel of Truth, the Holy Book of the Great Invisible Spirit (also known as the Egyptian Gospel), the Secret Book of John, the Secret Book of James, the Book of Thomas, the Dialogue of the Savior, and the Second Discourse of Great Seth.

A few decades earlier, in January 1896, a dealer in manuscripts in Cairo had offered to sell a papyrus codex to a German scholar named Carl Reinhardt.[3] The book, like the dealer, may have come from Akhmim, Egypt, but precisely where the codex was discovered remains uncertain. It may have been buried in a cemetery or somewhere else near Akhmim, if the book's editor, Carl Schmidt, is correct. Reinhardt bought the codex in Cairo and took it to Berlin, where it was housed in the Ägyptisches Museum. Today it is frequently called BG 8502, for Codex Berolinensis Gnosticus 8502, or Berlin Gnostic Codex 8502.

Carl Schmidt was prepared to publish this papyrus book in

1912, but curses fit for the legendary stories of Egyptian magic began to afflict the lives of those working on the codex. A water pipe burst at the print shop in Leipzig and destroyed the pages being prepared for publication. World War I broke out and delayed the publication of the book. Carl Schmidt died. World War II further hindered the book's appearance. And the Nag Hammadi library was discovered in 1945 and distracted scholars from their work on the Berlin codex. At last, in 1955, Walter C. Till, who assumed editorial responsibility for the Berlin codex after the death of Carl Schmidt, saw the German critical edition of BG 8502 through the press, and finally the book was made available.

Within Berlin Gnostic Codex 8502 are four texts, also written in Coptic. The first text is the incomplete but fascinating Gospel of Mary, which is included in this volume. The other texts are the Secret Book of John (the shorter version), the Wisdom of Jesus Christ (also found in the Nag Hammadi library), and the Act of Peter (compare the Acts of Peter).[4]

Other ancient texts have also contributed to the collection of gnostic gospels and related texts presented in this volume. From a rubbish heap at ancient Oxyrhynchus (modern Bahnasa) in Egypt archaeologists have uncovered thousands of papyri, among them Greek fragments of the Gospel of Thomas (Papyrus Oxyrhynchus [P. Oxy.] 1, 654, 655) and the Gospel of Mary (Papyrus Oxyrhynchus [P. Oxy.] 3525 and Papyrus Rylands [P. Ryl.] 463). Within the Refutation of All Heresies of Hippolytus of Rome, scholars have identified quotations from a version of the Gospel of Thomas[5] and long passages from the Book of Baruch, a gnostic text authored by a certain Justin. And in the Acts of John there is a section, termed the Round Dance of the Cross (or, the Hymn of

Jesus), that provides a gnostic interpretation of Jesus, the nature of suffering, and the destiny of people.

What Is Gnosticism?

More than any other publication, I would suggest, it was Elaine H. Pagels's book *The Gnostic Gospels* that brought to our attention the phrase "gnostic gospels," and the same phrase is used in the title of this present volume. But what is gnosticism?

"Gnosticism" currently is a most compelling and controversial term. The word "gnosticism" was apparently coined in the seventeenth century, and it was employed for anti-Catholic polemical purposes.[6] However, the Greek words *gnōsis*, "knowledge," and *gnōstikos*, "knower" or "gnostic," were used much earlier. The word *gnōsis* is a common term in texts from antiquity and late antiquity, and both *gnōsis* and *gnōstikos* are found throughout the writings of the heresiologists, who set out to combat and expose as heresy what they perceived to be inappropriate thought and action.

Hence, because of the polemical purposes inherent in most of the discussions of *gnōsis*, gnostics, and gnosticism, some scholars have recommended that we abandon these terms altogether. Leading the charge in the attack on these terms are Michael A. Williams and Karen L. King, and the arguments of both of these scholars merit serious consideration.

In his book *Rethinking "Gnosticism,"* Michael Williams argues that he intends to dismantle "a dubious category," that category being gnosticism itself. Williams surveys a wide variety of attempts on the part of scholars to define and describe gnosticism, and he finds all the attempts to be wanting. "The term 'gnosticism,'" Williams observes, "has indeed ultimately brought more confusion than clarification."⁷ In the wake of scholarly confusion and obfuscation regarding gnosticism, Williams proposes a new category to replace gnosticism: biblical demiurgical traditions. He writes,

> By "demiurgical" traditions I mean all those that ascribe the creation and management of the cosmos to some lower entity or entities, distinct from the highest God. This would include most of ancient Platonism, of course. But if we add the adjective "biblical," to denote demiurgical traditions that also incorporate or adopt traditions from Jewish or Christian Scripture, the category is narrowed significantly.⁸

Karen King, in her book *What Is Gnosticism?* agrees with Michael Williams that the term "gnosticism" is problematic and may well be set aside, but her approach is somewhat different. King notes problems with definitions in general ("Definitions tend to produce static and reified entities and hide the rhetorical and ideological interests of their fabricators"),⁹ but in the case of the term "gnosticism" the problems of definition are compounded. The term "gnosticism" and related terms, King states, are only rhetorical constructs used, from the days of the heresiologists to the present, to designate "the other" and to describe it as heresy, and these designations have been shaped by anti-Catholic, anti-Jewish, colonialist, and evolutionary interests. King suggests that we need new and different discussions of gnosticism in our pluralistic and postmodern world:

> The analysis I propose here aims to get at practice rather than at origins and essence. It offers no larger connected totality but rather a set of episodes no longer linked in any causal-linear frame of origins and development. . . . These twenty-first-century historical practices would without doubt result

in more than one possible, legitimate narrative of Christianity, based as they
would be not only in the different perspectives of scholars and the communi-
ties to which they are accountable, but also in different ethical orientations.[10]

These thoughtful contributions by Michael Williams and Karen
King should make us pause to acknowledge the polemical baggage
that accompanies the discussion of gnosticism. After Williams
and King, the study of gnosticism must be undertaken with a new
perspective, and we are indebted to them for their contributions.

Nevertheless, I remain confident that the terms *gnōsis,* "gnostic,"
and "gnosticism" may still be used in a meaningful way to designate a series of religious movements that have existed since ancient
times. After all, the word *gnōsis* is commonly attested in gnostic
and heresiological texts, and heresiological references to such expressions as "falsely so-called knowledge (*gnōsis*)" in Irenaeus of
Lyon and elsewhere make it clear that a battle was being waged
over whose knowledge is *true* knowledge. The word "gnostic" is
also used in heresiological sources, often with polemical intent, as
we have seen, but occasionally Irenaeus seems to concede in his
work Against Heresies that some of his opponents, particularly
Sethians (or, Barbelognostics) and followers of a certain female
teacher named Marcellina, referred to themselves as gnostics.[11]

If the Sethians, who are represented by at least two texts in this
volume (the Holy Book of the Great Invisible Spirit and the Secret Book of John), used "gnostic" as a term of self-designation,
this may function as the historical foundation for the legitimate
and meaningful use of *gnōsis,* gnostic, and gnosticism. It turns
out that we are in possession of what is a classic text of Sethian
gnōsis, the Secret Book of John,[12] and when we identify the leading
themes of that text, we may dare to describe them as gnostic

themes. Further, since Sethian texts appear to be linked to other texts historically (for example, Valentinian texts) and resemble still other traditions phenomenologically (that is, in terms of themes and characteristics), the term "gnostic" may be extended beyond Sethian texts to Valentinian and other texts. The precise extent to which any particular text reflects gnostic themes and characteristics may be determined through a careful study of the text.[13]

From the Secret Book of John, then, I suggest several themes to be indicative of the traits of gnostic religions, and I propose the following description of gnosticism:

> *Gnosticism is a religious tradition that emphasizes the primary place of* gnōsis, *or mystical knowledge, understood through aspects of wisdom (often personified wisdom) presented in creation stories, particularly stories based on the Genesis accounts, and interpreted by means of a variety of religious and philosophical traditions, including Platonism, in order to proclaim a radically enlightened way and life of knowledge.*[14]

In this volume, gnostic gospels and related texts are understood to be literary works that fit, to some extent, this description of gnosticism. The extent to which they are gnostic is discussed here in the general Introduction and in the introductions to the individual texts.

The Composition of the Gospels

Five of the texts included in this volume are explicitly referred to as gospels in the manuscripts themselves. The Gospel of Thomas, the Gospel of Mary, the Gospel of Philip, the Gospel of Truth, and the Holy Book of the Great Invisible Spirit (or the Egyptian

Gospel) are called gospels, though the Gospel of Thomas is also identified in its incipit, or opening section, as a collection of "hidden sayings" of Jesus, the Gospel of Truth is so entitled on the basis of its incipit, and the Holy Book of the Great Invisible Spirit is said to be a gospel only secondarily, in a copyist's note at the conclusion of the text.[15]

These five texts are all entitled, in one way or another, gospels, as an indication that they are works of "good news" or "proclamation." The modern English word "gospel" derives from the Old English "godspel," a translation of the Latin *evangelium* and Greek *euangelion*, "good news." The earliest known use of the Greek term in early Christian literature is in the writings of Paul. In Galatians 1:11–12 Paul explains the good news or gospel he preaches, and he maintains that it came from a revelation of Christ. Paul's gospel is the content of Paul's preaching, and from what he writes elsewhere (for instance, 1 Corinthians 15), his gospel is a gospel of the cross.[16]

Of the four New Testament gospels, the Gospel of Mark is almost certainly the earliest composition. It presents the term "gospel" in its incipit ("The beginning of the gospel of Jesus Christ . . ."), and from the incipit the term eventually found its way into the later title, the Gospel According to Mark. Since the other two synoptic gospels,[17] Matthew and Luke, depend literarily upon Mark, and there is also some sort of relationship between Mark and John, the term "gospel" eventually was applied to the titles of the other three gospels as well. All four New Testament gospels focus attention upon the crucifixion of Jesus, and in all four gospels the passion narratives are the culmination of the gospel story.

If Paul preached a gospel of the cross, the New Testament gospel authors each composed a gospel of the cross, so that, as one scholarly commentator observed, the New Testament gospels are passion narratives with long introductions.[18]

Some scholars have sought to define the Christian genre of gospel exclusively with reference to the New Testament gospels of the cross, but such texts as the gnostic gospels included in this volume indicate that a wider diversity of Christian texts can be called gospels or proclamations of good news. In this volume a collection of sayings of Jesus, a dialogue featuring Mary of Magdala, an anthology of meditations about Jesus and the Christian life, a Christian sermon on salvation through knowledge, and a mythological and mystical handbook on baptism may all equally be called gospels. They are not gospels of the cross, but they are gospels nonetheless, and as Christian gospels they show the rich variety of ways a Christian message can be articulated. There were, and there still are, multiple gospels, multiple proclamations of good news, multiple ways of understanding Jesus.

In addition to the five texts in this volume that are *named* gospels, seven more texts, not given the title of gospel but similar in content to gnostic gospels, merit inclusion. The Secret Book of John, the classic of Sethian spirituality, was apparently composed as a Jewish gnostic text and subsequently Christianized as a revelation that Jesus taught to his disciple John, son of Zebedee. This text helps to clarify the perspective of the Holy Book of the Great Invisible Spirit, and it has been interpreted by Karen King, in a Society of Biblical Literature presentation, to be understood as the second part of the Gospel of John.[19] The Secret Book of James—that is, of James the righteous, brother of Jesus and leader of the church in Jerusalem—describes itself as a book comparable to other books, perhaps gospel books, attributed to the twelve disciples. The Book of Thomas is closely related to the Gospel of

Thomas, as is the Dialogue of the Savior. The Second Discourse of Great Seth is ostensibly an interpretation of gnostic salvation provided by Jesus himself, who utters his message in first-person singular ("I") about the word, baptism, and the true meaning of the crucifixion. Jesus criticizes those people who (like those who preach a gospel of the cross) "proclaim the doctrine of a dead man"—namely, the crucified Christ—instead of the truth of the living savior. The Book of Baruch, disentangled from the pages of the heresiologist Hippolytus, may be one of the earliest gnostic texts. Its hierarchy of angels seems to anticipate the fuller ranks of angels and powers in texts like the Holy Book of the Great Invisible Spirit and the Secret Book of John, and its plot climaxes in the account of the angel Baruch coming to Jesus of Nazareth, who remains faithful to Baruch and ascends to the Good. Finally, the Round Dance of the Cross, taken from the Acts of John, depicts the liturgical song Jesus taught his disciples in order to explain what suffering is and how to escape it.

The twelve gnostic gospels and related texts in this volume provide a broad spectrum of gnostic perspectives. The texts fall roughly into four groups.

The first group of texts includes the Gospel of Thomas and the other texts in the Thomas tradition, the Book of Thomas and the Dialogue of the Savior. The Gospel of Thomas is a collection of sayings of Jesus that may be compared with the sayings gospel Q[20] and that presents Jesus as a proclaimer of wisdom. Some of the sayings of Jesus in the Gospel of Thomas, like those in Q, may come from the historical Jesus himself, while others are expansions of Jesus traditions. In my opinion, the Gospel of Thomas cannot be called a gnostic text without considerable qualification.

I prefer to describe it as a text with an incipient gnostic perspective. The Book of Thomas and the Dialogue of the Savior incorporate some of the sayings materials from the Thomas tradition, and they make use of them in a more gnosticizing manner within a framework that involves the questions and answers characteristic of a dialogue of Jesus with his disciples.

The second group of texts in this volume consists of Sethian texts, particularly the Holy Book of the Great Invisible Spirit and the Secret Book of John. Sethian texts frequently portray the glorious fullness (*plērōma*) of the divine in graphic detail, and they highlight the fall of the divine, through wisdom's folly, as the source of the creation, fall, and redemption of the world of humankind. Such Sethian texts make good use of the creation accounts in Genesis, and they interpret these creation stories in an innovative fashion and blend their revolutionary interpretations with Greek philosophical ideas. The result is a combination of Jewish and Greek (and especially Platonic) themes. Sethian texts build on reflections upon Seth, son of Adam and Eve, as a paradigmatic human being. In these texts Seth is the primal human being above who reveals saving knowledge below. Where, in the Holy Book of the Great Invisible Spirit and the (slightly Christianized) Secret Book of John, the Sethian message is given as Christian wisdom, Jesus becomes a revealer of knowledge and a manifestation of Seth. The Second Discourse of Great Seth may also be influenced by Sethian ideas (though, conversely, the title may be the most obvious Sethian aspect of the text).[21]

The third group of texts published here are Valentinian texts: the Gospel of Truth, the Gospel of Philip, the Secret Book of James, and perhaps the Round Dance of the Cross. Valentinian

gnostics were followers of the great teacher Valentinus (ca. 100–
ca. 175), an Egyptian convert to Christianity who became a bril-
liant teacher and author. Valentinus went to Rome, and it is said
that he hoped to become bishop of Rome—that is to say, in contemporary terms, the pope of the Christian church. Valentinus
himself may well be the author of the Gospel of Truth, and Valentinian meditations on Jesus and Christian wisdom comprise the
Gospel of Philip. Valentinian gnostics apparently relied upon insights from New Testament traditions, Thomas materials, and
Sethian texts, and they composed gospels, biblical commentaries,
letters, and other works. The Valentinians loved pleromatic speculation about the fullness of the divine no less than the Sethians,
and they were also able to bring such speculation down to earth
to speak to the lives of everyday Christians, as in the Gospel of
Truth.[22]

Two other texts in this volume form a fourth group, a group of
texts that defy classification. The Gospel of Mary is fragmentary
and fascinating, and whether it is gnostic is disputed by scholars.
It may be assigned an early date, and it follows Mary of Magdala,
the disciple close to Jesus, as she reveals her understanding of the
meaning and message of Jesus. The Book of Baruch is thoroughly
Jewish in its approach to *gnōsis,* yet it also finds room for Heracles
as a prophet from the gentiles and Jesus as the final messenger of
Baruch and revealer of the Good.

Jesus in Gnostic Gospels and Related Texts

In the texts in this volume Jesus emerges as a teacher of wisdom
and a revealer of knowledge. The figure of Jesus in gnostic
gospels and related texts is developed from earlier materials about

Jesus, and some of the features of Jesus in gnostic gospels may be linked to the historical Jesus. The historical Jesus, in my understanding, was a Jewish teacher and storyteller, in the tradition of Jewish wisdom, who used parables, aphorisms, and other utterances to tell of God's presence and God's reign. The earliest evidence for sayings of Jesus is to be found in Q, the New Testament gospels, and the Gospel of Thomas. Representative of Jewish wisdom, the sayings of Jesus relate well to themes in Jewish wisdom literature; and upon occasion, even in the earliest sources, Jesus is associated with wisdom.

In the Jewish world wisdom frequently refers to the personified wisdom of God: Hokhmah or Sophia.[23] Already in Q there are reflections upon Jesus and personified wisdom. According to the Lukan version of Q 11:49, the wisdom of God offers a saying about those sent forth; in the Matthean version it is Jesus who speaks. Again, according to the Lukan version of Q 7:35, Jesus refers to wisdom being vindicated by her children, John the baptizer and Jesus; in the Matthean version wisdom is vindicated by her deeds. And in Paul, in 1 Corinthians 2, wisdom and the rulers of this aeon are portrayed within the context of true wisdom, which Paul calls the wisdom of God.

Within gnostic gospels and related texts, especially in the Secret Book of John, Sophia plays a prominent role as the personified wisdom of God, but in gnostic texts she is radicalized. In these texts she creates, reveals, falls, and is restored. Divine wisdom saves and is saved, and with her human beings are saved and restored. Yet, whether personified or not, wisdom plays a central role in gnostic accounts of salvation.

In gnostic gospels and related texts, Jesus reveals wisdom and knowledge. What I have written in *The Gospel of Thomas* about Jesus is applicable to a number of gnostic gospels. In the Gospel of Thomas Jesus performs no physical miracles, he discloses no fulfillment of prophecy, he announces no apocalyptic kingdom that will disrupt the world order, and he dies for no one's sins. Instead, he reveals wisdom and knowledge so that people may be enlightened.[24]

The wisdom and knowledge revealed by Jesus in the gnostic gospels is a mystical knowledge, an insight into the connectedness of Jesus the revealer with those to whom revelation is given, and ultimately the connectedness of the light and life of God with the light and life within people. Because such knowledge is the flash of enlightenment that sheds light on one's own being, Jesus in the Gospel of Thomas can even be made to deny that he is, properly speaking, a teacher. Jesus in the Gospel of Thomas is "the living Jesus" who lives through his sayings, his words. Nevertheless, Jesus says, "I am not your teacher. Because you have drunk, you have become intoxicated from the bubbling spring that I have tended" (13:5). Jesus is not a teacher in the conventional sense, according to the Gospel of Thomas, because people must come to knowledge themselves. Jesus is more like a bartender, in that he serves the intoxicating drink of knowledge, but people must drink for themselves.[25]

Thus, the Gospel of Thomas and other gnostic texts often call upon readers to know themselves. In gnostic texts, unlike gospels of the cross, knowledge is more important than faith, and knowledge of oneself leads to salvation. In the Gospel of Thomas 3:4 Jesus says, "When you know yourselves, then you will be known, and you will understand that you are children of the living father"; in the Book of Thomas 138 Thomas himself is described as "one who knows oneself." The imperative *gnōthi sauton*, "Know yourself," was among the Greek inscriptions at the oracular center dedicated to Apollo at Delphi, and this saying is discussed by Plato in Al-cibiades I and by Plutarch in his essay On the E at Delphi. The Gospel of Philip also reflects upon this saying (76). In the Secret Book of James, Jesus tells the disciples to know themselves (12), and he adds that they should save themselves (11). For if knowl-edge in gnostic thought is salvation, then knowing oneself is com-ing to salvation through oneself. That is the *gnōsis* of Jesus.

In these gnostic gospels and related texts, the human problem that is addressed is not sin but rather ignorance, and hence Jesus does not save people from their sins but rather communicates knowledge to address human ignorance and bring about enlight-enment. People in this world of mortality—this underworld—are confused, and they have grown forgetful, have fallen asleep, have been seduced by the deceptive pleasures and pains of the world. People have become mixed up in this world of death, and they no longer remember who they are: they have forgotten that they are children of the divine, with the light of the divine within.[26] As the Gospel of Mary has Jesus tell the disciples, "There is no such thing as sin, but you create sin when you mingle as in adultery, and this is called sin" (7). In this and other gnostic gospels, people are called upon to recall who they are, open their minds, and think, and in this way they can experience salvation.

This is the good news of the gnostic texts. These gospels are gospels of wisdom, not gospels of the cross; the Jesus of this good news is the source of wisdom and knowledge, not first and fore-most the crucified savior; and people come to salvation through insight and creative thought, not primarily through faith.

Elaine Pagels, in *Beyond Belief,* emphasizes the centrality of such insight and creative thinking in gnostic texts by discussing the role of *epinoia,* which may be translated "insight," "afterthought," "creativity," or the like, in the Secret Book of John. In the Secret Book of John Jesus reveals the story of *epinoia*. Jesus describes *epinoia* personified as an aspect of the divine mind that comes to expression within humankind and enables people to engage in creative thinking, and he interprets the Genesis story of Eve coming out of Adam as the story of *epinoia* coming to aid humankind. The Secret Book of John reads,

> *So with its benevolent and most merciful spirit the mother-father sent a*
> *helper to Adam, an enlightened insight* (epinoia) *who is from the mother-*
> *father and who was called life. She helped the whole creature, laboring with*
> *it, restoring it to its fullness, teaching it about the descent of the seed, teaching*
> *it about the way of ascent, which is the way of descent. (II, 20)*

Pagels responds to this story by suggesting, "The Secret Book intends this story to show that we have a latent capacity within our hearts and minds that links us to the divine—not in our ordinary state of mind but when this hidden capacity awakens."[27]

This human—and divine—capacity for thought is what enables people to encounter the wisdom and knowledge of Jesus in an insightful and creative manner.

According to the gnostic gospels and related texts, the knowledge communicated through the sayings of Jesus with his disciples is often explicitly mystical. In the Gospel of Thomas Jesus says, "Whoever drinks from my mouth will become like me; I myself shall become that person, and the hidden things will be revealed to that person" (108). In the Gospel of Philip it is claimed that in the realm of truth "you have seen Christ and have become Christ, you have seen the [father] and will become father" (61), and the person who receives the name of God in the chrism is said no longer to be a Christian "but is Christ" (67). In the Second Discourse of Great Seth, Jesus himself announces, in a word from scripture, "I am in you and you are in me, just as the father is in me <and in> you, with no guile at all" (49–50).

At the same time, the knowledge Jesus communicates in the gnostic gospels and related texts is a knowledge both of what is outside and of what is inside. The more mythological texts included in this volume (for example, the Gospel of Mary, the Holy Book of the Great Invisible Spirit, and the Secret Book of John) provide cosmological speculations on the universe outside us and provocative interpretations of the creation stories of Genesis. These mythological and cosmological passages are reflective of ancient and late antique metaphysics and astronomy, and they describe the nature, origin, and extent of the cosmos in order to explain the place of human beings in the larger scheme of things. While these accounts may present challenges to modern readers, they are not fundamentally different from contemporary metaphysical and astronomical reflections upon the stars, the universe, and the ultimate limit—or limitlessness—of things.

These more mythological gnostic texts discuss cosmic realities outside us, but they may show, simultaneously, an interest in how what is outside may also be within. In the Gospel of Thomas Jesus says that the kingdom is inside and outside (3:3), and the inner may be like the outer and the outer like the inner (22:4). Mary of Magdala recounts her vision in the Gospel of Mary, and it is apparent that the cosmic powers through which the soul must pass on her[28] celestial journey are also the inner dispositions that a person must overcome: darkness, desire, ignorance, wrath. In the Holy Book of the Great Invisible Spirit and the Secret Book of John, the emanations and expressions of the divine One are mental characteristics and capabilities, mind (*nous*), forethought (*pronoia*), thought (*ennoia*), insight (*epinoia*), wisdom (*sophia*), even mindlessness (*aponoia*). Hence, the story of the unfolding of the divine One is as much a story about psychology as it is about mythology and metaphysics. Additionally, in the Gospel of Truth, many of the technical terms commonly used to portray aeons and entities in the realm of divine fullness and characters involved in the story of the cosmic fall (fullness, depth, thought, grace, mind, truth, word, error) are incorporated into a sermon that proclaims salvation and life in the everyday world of Valentinian Christians.

Another Valentinian gospel, the Gospel of Philip, gives a meditation on the outer and the inner. Based on an utterance of Jesus very much like Gospel of Thomas 22:4, this meditation maintains it is actually more fitting to focus attention upon what is within, what is innermost. The world of the *plērōma*, the fullness of God, thought by many to be the divine realm above, truly is within. In the words of the Gospel of Philip, "What is innermost is the fullness, and there is nothing further within" (68). If the fullness is within, so, in the Gospel of Thomas, is the kingdom within, or spread out upon the earth, unseen by people (3:3; 113:4), and so also, in the Gospel of Mary, is the child of humankind (or son of man) within. As Jesus says to the disciples in the Gospel of Mary, "Follow that. Those who seek it will find it" (8).[29]

The gnostic gospels and related texts may not be gospels of the cross, but the historical tradition of the crucifixion of Jesus does not go completely unnoticed in these texts. How the gnostic gospels deal with the crucifixion, however, is another matter. Some of these texts, like the Gospel of Thomas, pay little or no attention to the cross; the sole reference to the cross in the Gospel of Thomas occurs in saying 55, where the image of one bearing a cross seems to be used in a metaphorical sense.

Other gnostic texts, particularly Valentinian texts, incorporate significant references to the crucifixion of Jesus and reiterate more familiar Christological and soteriological formulations, but they often interpret the crucifixion in a more symbolic fashion. In these texts the emphasis is not upon a doctrine of atonement through the death of Jesus on the cross, and there is no sacrifice of Jesus for the sins of the world. A statement in the Gospel of Truth declares that in reality the crucifixion means the public disclosure of the will of the father and the revelation of the incorruptibility of the savior:

> *Jesus appeared,*
> *put on that book,*
> *was nailed to a tree,*
> *and published the father's edict on the cross.*
> *Oh, what a great teaching!*
> *He humbled himself even unto death,*
> *though clothed in eternal life.*
> *He stripped off the perishable rags*
> *and clothed himself in incorruptibility,*
> *which no one can take from him. (20)*

This is so, the Gospel of Truth explains, because Jesus "encompasses knowledge and perfection." A meditation in the Gospel of Philip cites the words of Jesus on the cross, taken from Psalm 22:1, "My God, my God, why, lord, have you forsaken me?" and immediately observes that Jesus "spoke these words on the cross, for he (the divine person within) had left that place" (68).

Still other gnostic texts, like the Second Discourse of Great
Seth, may deny the reality of the crucifixion of Christ in graphic
terms. This text asserts that the true Christ did not suffer at all,
for the powers of the world are blind, and they made a mistake.
They got the wrong person. As for the living Christ, he himself
states, "I was on high, poking fun at all the excesses of the rulers
and the fruit of their error and conceit. I was laughing at their
ignorance" (56). This tradition of the crucifixion that never
really happened to the true Christ is known from other sources as
well—for example, the Nag Hammadi Revelation of Peter,
Basilides according to Irenaeus of Lyon, and perhaps the Book of
Baruch—and Christ without the cross may also be present in the
Islamic heritage. When in Qur'an sura 4 it is said that 'Isa (Jesus)
was crucified only in appearance, the translation remains difficult,
but within the Muslim tradition it has commonly been suggested
that another person was crucified instead of Jesus.[30]

The suffering of Jesus and of all people is pursued further in
the Round Dance of the Cross. There Jesus sings and dances with
his disciples in a scene that is said to take place just before the crucifixion. Jesus utters paradoxical lines ("I will be wounded and
I will wound"), and the disciples respond by singing "Amen."
Thereafter Jesus proceeds to explain the passion that is at hand,
and he says, "Yours is the human passion I am to suffer." Jesus
goes on to explain the true meaning of suffering: to understand
suffering is to be free of it. Jesus concludes,

> *If you knew how to suffer*
> *you would be able not to suffer.*
> *Learn how to suffer*
> *and you will be able not to suffer.* (96)

The last words of Jesus in the Round Dance of the Cross reveal how to be free from suffering. As Elaine Pagels notes, here the wisdom of Jesus resembles the wisdom of the Buddha, and both Jesus and the Buddha teach that a true understanding of suffering leads to liberation from suffering.[31]

Finally, Jesus, or Christ, emerges in gnostic gospels and related texts as a heavenly redeemer who speaks to rouse people to knowledge and self-understanding. His is a divine voice, and his call is a wake-up call from God. The Gospel of Philip states that Christ brings bread from heaven to nourish people (55). The Gospel of Truth announces that Christ enlightens people who are in darkness on account of forgetfulness (18). As the son of the father, Christ has the name of the father, and he reveals the father's name and the father's will. In the Holy Book of the Great Invisible Spirit the living Jesus is a manifestation of heavenly Seth, and in the Secret Book of John Jesus is the one sent by the father from the perfect eternal realm to disclose eternal things. In the Second Discourse of Great Seth Christ comes from above, passes through the gates of the cosmic rulers, adopts a human body, and proceeds to disclose the nature of this world of impermanence over against the eternal world of the divine. Elsewhere in gnostic texts, the role of the revealer can be assumed by Seth, divine forethought (*pronoia*), or insight (*epinoia*) in Sethian texts; by Derdekeas ("the child") in the Paraphrase of Shem; by Manda dHayye (the personified "knowledge of life") in Mandaean traditions; even by the heavenly letter that becomes speech in the Hymn of the Pearl (in the Acts of Thomas). In gnostic gospels and Christian texts, the revealer is said to be Christ.

In these mystical texts that maintain the oneness of the divine outside a person with the divine within a person, the divine voice of Christ is the divine voice within, and the call from without is

the call from within. Whoever awakens to that call and listens to
that voice finds true life. As Jesus—and divine forethought—proclaim at the end of the Secret Book of John,

> *I am the forethought of pure light,*
> *I am the thought of the virgin spirit,*
> *who raises you to a place of honor.*
> *Arise, remember that you have heard*
> *and trace your root,*
> *which is I, the compassionate.*
> *Guard yourself against the angels of misery,*
> *the demons of chaos, and all who entrap you,*
> *and beware of deep sleep*
> *and the trap in the bowels of the underworld.*
>
> *I raised and sealed the person*
> *in luminous water with five seals,*
> *that death might not prevail over the person*
> *from that moment on. (II, 31)*

Gnostic Gospels and Related Texts in Translation

This volume is intended to make available fresh English translations
of twelve gnostic gospels and related texts.[32] The translations are
meant to be as accurate as possible, and at the same time I have tried
to present them in felicitous English. I have adopted several conven-
tions for these translations. I use inclusive language when such language communicates the spirit of the text (for example, I use "child
of humankind" for the title traditionally translated "son of man"),
though I have attempted to avoid compromising thereby the accu-
racy of the translations. Coptic texts from the Nag Hammadi library

are notorious for the ambiguity of pronouns and their antecedents, and I have resolved many such ambiguities by supplying the nouns that are the most likely antecedents of pronouns. Unlike many other translations, these translations make minimal use of capitalization, even in the case of personified mental attributes in the divine *plērōma*, in order to indicate the nature of such personified attributes as both mythic characters in a cosmic drama and mental capacities in the story of the origin and destiny of mind and thought.

Within the translations, relevant numbers of sections and Coptic manuscript pages, given within square brackets, are included for ease of reference. Square brackets also indicate textual restorations, and pointed brackets indicate textual emendations; I have tried, however, to be modest in the number of emendations adopted. When a textual restoration remains uncertain, a note indicates that the restoration is tentative. Ellipsis dots are employed to indicate an unrestored lacuna in the text or a gap in the flow of the text. The subheadings given in italics within the translations are not in the texts themselves but have been supplied by the translator. When multiple titles of texts are listed, the first title is the primary or preferred title and the other titles are secondary titles or titles used in the scholarly literature. Notes have been added to explain difficult passages and refer to parallel passages.

Most of the translations in this volume were undertaken within the context of a larger project on the Nag Hammadi library. The members of the advisory board of that project, Wolf-Peter Funk, Paul-Hubert Poirier, and James M. Robinson, along with two collaborators, Birger A. Pearson and John D. Turner, provided assistance in suggesting translational policies and offering comments on the translations themselves. To them I offer particular thanks for their valuable contributions.

PART ONE

The Gospel of Thomas

with

The Greek Gospel
of Thomas fragments

THE GOSPEL OF THOMAS, or the Hidden Sayings of Jesus, is a collection of sayings of Jesus, traditionally numbered by scholars at 114, which are said to communicate salvation and life. While the Gospel of Thomas has some features in common with gnostic gospels, it does not seem to fit the definition of gnosticism given in the Introduction to a significant extent. Thus I prefer to consider the Gospel of Thomas to be a gospel with an incipient gnostic perspective. According to the incipit (or prologue) of the Gospel of Thomas, the sayings are hidden or secret sayings spoken by the living Jesus and recorded by Judas Thomas the Twin. Judas Thomas was thought in some circles, particularly within Syriac Christianity, to be the twin brother of Jesus and as such the ideal person to function as guarantor of the Jesus tradition. The Gospel of John in the New Testament begs to differ with this positive assessment of Judas Thomas, however, and instead chooses to depict him as "doubting Thomas."

The sayings included in the Gospel of Thomas include a variety of aphorisms, parables, stories, and other utterances of Jesus, the interpretation of which, saying 1 announces, can lead to salvation and life. Saying 1 states, "Whoever discovers the interpretation of these sayings will not taste death," and saying 2 describes the epistemological process whereby one comes to knowledge and understanding: "Let one who seeks not stop seeking until one finds. When one finds, one will be troubled. When one is troubled, one will marvel and will reign over all." The Greek Gospel of Thomas adds an additional stage to the interpretive process: "and [having reigned], one will [rest]." In other words, the quest for an understanding of the sayings of Jesus is an enterprise to be undertaken with commitment, and although the way to knowledge may be difficult and even disturbing, those who persevere will discover God's reign and God's rest. And if God's reign, God's kingdom, is outside a person, it is also within (Gospel of Thomas 3:3).

As in Q and the New Testament gospels, especially the synoptic gospels of Mark, Matthew, and Luke, Jesus in the Gospel of Thomas asks his disciples to seek and find. In the Gospel of Thomas and other early texts, the sayings of Jesus are open to interpretation, so that disciples and readers are encouraged to search for the meaning of the sayings of Jesus and complete his thoughts after him. The Gospel of Thomas is an interactive gospel: wisdom and knowledge come when readers creatively encounter sayings of Jesus and respond to the sayings with insight. Such an interactive approach may go back to the historical Jesus, whose sayings and stories seem to have provided the opportunity for his disciples and others around him to react and respond. To that extent the Gospel of Thomas coheres well with much of the Jesus sayings tradition. A number of the sayings in the Gospel of Thomas, however, are especially cryptic and riddle-like, and the need for creative interpretation is obvious. Much is at stake. Those who find the meaning of Jesus's sayings find life, the Gospel of Thomas proclaims, and they come to realize that they are children of the living father. Or, as Jesus puts it in saying 108, those who drink from his mouth will be like him and he will be one with them, and they will understand what is hidden.

Jesus in the Gospel of Thomas confronts his disciples and readers of the gospel with powerful sayings, but he does not pull rank. In the Gospel of Thomas Jesus assumes very few Christological titles, and, as Stephen Patterson notes, Jesus in this gospel is just Jesus. Jesus in the Gospel of Thomas is not designated the Christ or the messiah, he is not acclaimed master or lord, and when he refers to himself once in the gospel, in saying 86, as child of humankind or son of man, he does so in the generic sense of referring to any person (or to himself) as a human being. If Jesus in the Gospel of Thomas is a child of humankind, so are other people called children of humankind (sayings 28 and 106). Jesus in the Gospel of Thomas is not presented as the unique or incarnate son of God, and nothing is said of a cross with saving significance or an empty tomb. Jesus is named the living Jesus, but God is also said to be a living one, and followers of Jesus are called living ones as well. Jesus the living one lives through his words and sayings.

The Gospel of Thomas is the second tractate in Codex II of the Nag Hammadi library, where it is preserved in Coptic translation. Three Greek fragments of the Gospel of Thomas also survive (Papyrus Oxyrhynchus 1, 654, and 655), as do testimonia in early Christian literature, especially in the writings of Hippolytus of Rome. Translations of the Nag Hammadi Coptic text, the Greek fragments, and two testimonia from Hippolytus are given below. Most likely the Gospel of Thomas was composed in Greek, probably in Syria, perhaps at Edessa, where Thomas was revered and his bones venerated. A reasonable case can be made for a first-century date for a first edition of the Gospel of Thomas, though some scholars prefer a second-century date.

For further reading: Helmut Koester, Bentley Layton, Thomas O. Lambdin, and Harold W. Attridge, "The Gospel According to Thomas"; Marvin Meyer, *The Gospel of Thomas*; Marvin Meyer, *Secret Gospels*; Elaine H. Pagels, *Beyond Belief*; Stephen J. Patterson, *The Gospel of Thomas and Jesus*; Stephen J. Patterson, James M. Robinson, and Hans-Gebhard Bethge, *The Fifth Gospel*; Gregory J. Riley, *Resurrection Reconsidered*; Jens Schröter and Hans-Gebhard Bethge, "Das Evangelium nach Thomas"; Risto Uro, ed., *Thomas at the Crossroads*; Richard Valantasis, *The Gospel of Thomas*.

The Gospel of Thomas

or

The Hidden Sayings of Jesus[1]

(NHC II,2)

Prologue

These are the hidden sayings that the living Jesus spoke and Judas Thomas the Twin[2] recorded.[3]

1   And he[4] said, "Whoever discovers the interpretation of these sayings will not taste death."[5]

2   1) Jesus said,[6] "Let one who seeks not stop seeking until one finds. 2) When one finds, one will be troubled. 3) When one is troubled, one will marvel 4) and will reign over all."[7]

3   1) Jesus said, "If your leaders say to you, 'Look, the kingdom is in heaven,' then the birds of heaven will precede you. 2) If they say to you, 'It is in the sea,'[8] then the fish will precede you. 3) Rather, the kingdom is inside you and it is outside you.[9]

   4) "When you know yourselves, then you will be known, [33] and you will understand that you are children of the living father. 5) But if you do not know yourselves, then you dwell in poverty, and you are poverty."[10]

4   1) Jesus said, "The person old in days will not hesitate to ask a little child seven days old[11] about the place of life, and that person will live.[12] 2) For many of the first will be last[13] 3) and will become a single one."

5   1) Jesus said, "Know what is in front of your face, and what is hidden from you will be disclosed to you.[14] 2) For there is nothing hidden that will not be revealed."[15]

6   1) His disciples asked him and said to him, "Do you want us to fast? How should we pray? Should we give to charity? What diet should we observe?"[16]

2) Jesus said, "Do not lie, 3) and do not do what you hate,[17] 4) because all things are disclosed before heaven.[18] 5) For there is nothing hidden that will not be revealed, 6) and there is nothing covered that will remain undisclosed."[19]

7   1) Jesus said, "Blessings on the lion that the human will eat, so that the lion becomes human. 2) And cursed[20] is the human that the lion will eat, and the lion will become human."[21]

8   1) And he said, "Humankind[22] is like a wise fisherman who cast his net into the sea and drew it up from the sea full of little fish. 2) Among them the wise fisherman discovered a fine large fish. 3) He threw all the little fish back [34] into the sea and with no difficulty chose the large fish. 4) Whoever has ears to hear should hear."[23]

9   1) Jesus said, "Look, the sower went out, took a handful of seeds, and scattered them. 2) Some fell on the road, and the birds came and pecked them up. 3) Others fell on rock, and they did not take root in the soil and did not produce heads of grain. 4) Others fell on thorns, and they choked the seeds and worms devoured them. 5) And others fell on good soil,

and it brought forth a good crop. It yielded sixty per measure and one hundred twenty per measure."[24]

10 Jesus said, "I have thrown fire upon the world, and look, I am watching it until it blazes."[25]

11 1) Jesus said, "This heaven will pass away, and the one above it will pass away.[26]

2) "The dead are not alive, and the living will not die.

3) "During the days when you ate what is dead, you made it alive. When you are in the light, what will you do?[27]

4) "On the day when you were one, you became two. But when you become two, what will you do?"

12 1) The disciples said to Jesus, "We know that you are going to leave us. Who will be our leader?"

2) Jesus said to them, "No matter where you have come from, you are to go to James the righteous, for whose sake heaven and earth came into being."[28]

13 1) Jesus said to his disciples, "Compare me to something and tell me what I am like."

2) Simon Peter said to him, "You are like a righteous messenger."[29]

3) Matthew said to him, [35] "You are like a wise philosopher."

4) Thomas said to him, "Teacher, my mouth is utterly unable to say what you are like."

5) Jesus said, "I am not your teacher. Because you have drunk, you have become intoxicated from the bubbling spring that I have tended."

6) And he took him, and withdrew, and spoke three sayings[30] to him.

7) When Thomas came back to his friends, they asked him, "What did Jesus say to you?"

8) Thomas said to them, "If I tell you one of the sayings he spoke to me, you will pick up rocks and stone me, and fire will come from the rocks and consume you."[31]

14   1) Jesus said to them, "If you fast, you will bring sin upon yourselves, 2) and if you pray, you will be condemned, 3) and if you give to charity, you will harm your spirits.[32]

4) "When you go into any region and walk through the countryside,[33] when people receive you, eat what they serve you and heal the sick among them.[34] 5) For what goes into your mouth will not defile you; rather, it is what comes out of your mouth that will defile you."[35]

15   Jesus said, "When you see one who was not born of woman, fall on your faces and worship. That is your father."[36]

16   1) Jesus said, "Perhaps people think that I have come to impose peace upon the world. 2) They do not know that I have come to impose conflicts upon the earth: fire, sword, war. 3) For there will be five [36] in a house: there will be three against two and two against three, father against son and son against father, 4) and they will stand alone."[37]

17   Jesus said, "I shall give you what no eye has seen, what no ear has heard, what no hand has touched, what has not arisen in the human heart."[38]

18   1) The disciples said to Jesus, "Tell us how our end will be."[39]

2) Jesus said, "Have you discovered the beginning, then, so that you are seeking the end? For where the beginning is the end will be. 3) Blessings on one who stands at the beginning: that one will know the end and will not taste death."[40]

19   1) Jesus said, "Blessings on one who came into being before coming into being.[41]

    2) "If you become my disciples and listen to my sayings, these stones will serve you.[42]

    3) "For there are five trees in paradise for you; they do not change, summer or winter, and their leaves do not fall. 4) Whoever knows them will not taste death."[43]

20   1) The disciples said to Jesus, "Tell us what heaven's kingdom is like."

    2) He said to them, "It is like a mustard seed. 3) <It>[44] is the smallest of all seeds, 4) but when it falls on prepared soil, it produces a large plant and becomes a shelter for birds of heaven."[45]

21   1) Mary said to Jesus, "What are your disciples like?"

    2) He said, "They are like [37] children living in a field that is not theirs.[46] 3) When the owners of the field come, they will say, 'Give our field back to us.' 4) They take off their clothes in front of them in order to give it back to them, and they return their field to them.[47]

    5) "For this reason I say, if the owner of a house knows that a thief is coming, he will be on guard before the thief arrives and will not let the thief break into the house of his estate and steal his possessions.[48] 6) As for you, then, be on guard against the world. 7) Arm yourselves with great strength, or the robbers might find a way to get to you, 8) for the trouble you expect will come.[49] 9) Let there be among you a person who understands.

    10) "When the crop ripened, the person came quickly with sickle in hand and harvested it.[50] 11) Whoever has ears to hear should hear."

22 1) Jesus saw some babies nursing. 2) He said to his disciples, "These nursing babies are like those who enter the kingdom."

3) They said to him, "Then shall we enter the kingdom as babies?"

4) Jesus said to them, "When you make the two into one, and when you make the inner like the outer and the outer like the inner, and the upper like the lower, 5) and when you make male and female into a single one, so that the male will not be male nor the female be female, 6) when you make eyes in place of an eye, a hand in place of a hand, a foot in place of a foot, an image in place of an image, 7) then you will enter [the kingdom]."[51] [38]

23 Jesus said, "I shall choose you, one from a thousand and two from ten thousand, and they will stand as a single one."[52]

24 1) His disciples said, "Show us the place where you are, for we must seek it."

2) He said to them, "Whoever has ears should hear. 3) There is light within a person of light, and it[53] shines on the whole world. If it does not shine, it is dark."[54]

25 1) Jesus said, "Love your sibling like your soul,[55] 2) protect that person like the pupil of your eye."[56]

26 1) Jesus said, "You see the speck that is in your sibling's eye, but you do not see the beam that is in your own eye. 2) When you take the beam out of your own eye, then you will see clearly to take the speck out of your sibling's eye."[57]

27 1) "If you do not fast from the world, you will not find the kingdom. 2) If you do not observe the sabbath as a sabbath, you will not see the father."[58]

28 1) Jesus said, "I took my stand in the midst of the world, and in flesh I appeared to them.[59] 2) I found them all drunk, and I

did not find any of them thirsty. 3) My soul ached for the children of humanity,[60] because they are blind in their hearts and do not see, for they came into the world empty, and they also seek to depart from the world empty. 4) But now they are drunk. When they shake off their wine, then they will repent."

29 1) Jesus said, "If the flesh came into being because of spirit, it is a marvel, 2) but if spirit came into being because of the body, it is a marvel of marvels. 3) Yet I marvel [39] at how this great wealth has come to dwell in this poverty."[61]

30 1) Jesus said, "Where there are three deities, they are divine. 2) Where there are two or one, I am with that one."[62]

31 1) Jesus said, "A prophet is not acceptable in the prophet's own town; 2) a doctor does not heal those who know the doctor."[63]

32 Jesus said, "A city built upon a high hill and fortified cannot fall, nor can it be hidden."[64]

33 1) Jesus said, "What you will hear in your ear, in the other ear[65] proclaim from your rooftops. 2) For no one lights a lamp and puts it under a basket, nor does one put it in a hidden place. 3) Rather, one puts it on a stand so that all who come and go will see its light."[66]

34 Jesus said, "If a blind person leads a blind person, both of them will fall into a hole."[67]

35 1) Jesus said, "You cannot enter the house of the strong and take it by force without tying the person's hands. 2) Then you can loot the person's house."[68]

36 Jesus said, "Do not worry, from morning to evening and from evening to morning, about what you will wear."[69]

37 1) His disciples said, "When will you appear to us and when shall we see you?"

2) Jesus said, "When you strip without being ashamed and you take your clothes and put them under your feet like little children and trample them, 3) then [you] will see [40] the child of the living one and you will not be afraid."[70]

38 1) Jesus said, "Often you have desired to hear these sayings that I am speaking to you, and you have no one else from whom to hear them. 2) There will be days when you will seek me and you will not find me."[71]

39 1) Jesus said, "The Pharisees and the scholars have taken[72] the keys of knowledge[73] and have hidden them. 2) They have not entered, nor have they allowed those who want to enter to do so.[74] 3) As for you, be as shrewd as snakes and as innocent as doves."[75]

40 1) Jesus said, "A grapevine has been planted away from the father. 2) Since it is not strong, it will be pulled up by its root and will perish."[76]

41 1) Jesus said, "Whoever has something in hand will be given more, 2) and whoever has nothing will be deprived of even the little that person has."[77]

42 Jesus said, "Be passersby."[78]

43 1) His disciples said to him, "Who are you to say these things to us?"

2) "You do not know who I am from what I say to you.[79] 3) Rather, you have become like the Jewish people, for they love the tree but hate its fruit, or they love the fruit but hate the tree."[80]

44 1) Jesus said, "Whoever blasphemes against the father will be forgiven, 2) and whoever blasphemes against the son will be forgiven, 3) but whoever blasphemes against the holy spirit will not be forgiven, either on earth or in heaven."[81]

45 1) Jesus said, "Grapes are not harvested from thornbushes, nor are figs gathered from thistles, for they yield no fruit. 2) A good person brings forth [41] good from the storehouse; 3) a bad person brings forth evil things from the corrupt storehouse in the heart and says evil things. 4) For from the abundance of the heart this person brings forth evil things."[82]

46 1) Jesus said, "From Adam to John the baptizer, among those born of women, there is no one greater than John the baptizer, so that his eyes[83] should not be averted.[84] 2) But I have said that whoever among you becomes a child will know the kingdom and will become greater than John."[85]

47 1) Jesus said, "A person cannot mount two horses or bend two bows. 2) And a servant cannot serve two masters, or that servant will honor the one and offend the other.[86] 3) No person drinks aged wine and immediately desires to drink new wine. 4) New wine is not poured into aged wineskins, or they might break, and aged wine is not poured into a new wineskin, or it might spoil.[87] 5) An old patch is not sewn onto a new garment, for there would be a tear."[88]

48 Jesus said, "If two make peace with each other in a single house, they will say to the mountain, 'Move from here,' and it will move."[89]

49 1) Jesus said, "Blessings on those who are alone[90] and chosen, for you will find the kingdom. 2) For you have come from it, and you will return there again."[91]

50 1) Jesus said, "If they say to you, 'Where have you come from?' say to them, 'We have come from the light, from the place where the light came into being by itself, established [itself], [42] and appeared in their image.' 2) If they say to you, 'Is it you?'[92] say, 'We are its children, and we are the chosen of the

living father.' 3) If they ask you, 'What is the evidence of your father in you?' say to them, 'It is motion and rest.' "[93]

51   1) His disciples said to him, "When will the rest[94] for the dead take place, and when will the new world come?"

2) He said to them, "What you look for has come, but you do not know it."[95]

52   1) His disciples said to him, "Twenty-four prophets[96] have spoken in Israel, and they all spoke of you."

2) He said to them, "You have disregarded the living one who is in your presence and have spoken of the dead."[97]

53   1) His disciples said to him, "Is circumcision useful or not?"

2) He said to them, "If it were useful, children's fathers would produce them already circumcised from their mothers. 3) Rather, the true circumcision in spirit has become valuable in every respect."[98]

54   Jesus said, "Blessings on the poor, for yours is heaven's kingdom."[99]

55   1) Jesus said, "Whoever does not hate father and mother cannot be a disciple of me, 2) and whoever does not hate brothers and sisters and bear the cross as I do will not be worthy of me."[100]

56   1) Jesus said, "Whoever has come to know the world has discovered a carcass, 2) and whoever has discovered a carcass, of that person the world is not worthy."[101]

57   1) Jesus said, "The father's kingdom is like a person who had [good] seed. 2) His enemy came at night [43] and sowed weeds among the good seed. 3) The person did not let them pull up the weeds, but said to them, 'No, or you might go to pull up the weeds and pull up the wheat along with them.'

4) For on the day of the harvest the weeds will be conspicuous and will be pulled up and burned."[102]

58 Jesus said, "Blessings on the person who has labored[103] and has found life."[104]

59 Jesus said, "Look to the living one as long as you live, or you might die and then try to see the living one, and you will be unable to see."[105]

60 1) <He saw>[106] a Samaritan carrying a lamb as he[107] was going to Judea.

2) He said to his disciples, "That person is carrying the lamb around."[108]

3) They said to him, "Then he may kill it and eat it."[109]

4) He said to them, "He will not eat it while it is alive, but only after he has killed it and it has become a carcass."

5) They said, "Otherwise he cannot do it."

6) He said to them, "So also with you, seek for yourselves a place for rest, or you might become a carcass and be eaten."[110]

61 1) Jesus said, "Two will rest on a couch; one will die, one will live."[111]

2) Salome said, "Who are you, mister? You have climbed onto my couch[112] and eaten from my table as if you are from someone."[113]

3) Jesus said to her, "I am the one who comes from what is whole. I was given from the things of my father."[114]

4) "I am your disciple."

5) "For this reason I say, if one is <whole>,[115] one will be filled with light,[116] but if one is divided, one will be filled with darkness."

62   1) Jesus said, "I disclose my mysteries to those [who are worthy] of [44] [my] mysteries.[117] 2) Do not let your left hand know what your right hand is doing."[118]

63   1) Jesus said, "There was a rich person who had a great deal of money. 2) He said, 'I shall invest my money so that I may sow, reap, plant, and fill my storehouses with produce, that I may lack nothing.' 3) These were the things he was thinking in his heart, but that very night he died. 4) Whoever has ears should hear."[119]

64   1) Jesus said, "A person was receiving guests. When he had prepared the dinner, he sent his servant to invite the guests.

2) "The servant went to the first and said to that one, 'My master invites you.'

3) "That person said, 'Some merchants owe me money; they are coming to me tonight. I must go and give them instructions. Please excuse me from dinner.'

4) "The servant went to another and said to that one, 'My master has invited you.'

5) "That person said to the servant, 'I have bought a house and I have been called away for a day. I shall have no time.'

6) "The servant went to another and said to that one, 'My master invites you.'

7) "That person said to the servant, 'My friend is to be married and I am to arrange the banquet. I shall not be able to come. Please excuse me from dinner.'

8) "The servant went to another and said to that one, 'My master invites you.'

9) "That person said to the servant, 'I have bought an estate and I am going to collect the rent. I shall not be able to come. Please excuse me.'

10) "The servant returned and said to his master, 'The people whom you invited to dinner have asked to be excused.'

11) "The master said to his servant, 'Go out on the streets and bring back whomever you find to have dinner.'[120]

12) "Buyers and merchants [will] not enter the places of my father."[121] [45]

65 1) He said, "A [usurer][122] owned a vineyard and rented it to some farmers, so that they might work it and he might collect its produce from them. 2) He sent his servant so that the farmers might give the servant the produce of the vineyard. 3) They seized, beat, and almost killed his servant, and the servant returned and told his master. 4) His master said, 'Perhaps he did not know them.'[123] 5) He sent another servant, and the farmers beat that one as well. 6) Then the master sent his son and said, 'Perhaps they will show my son some respect.' 7) Since the farmers knew that he was the heir to the vineyard, they seized him and killed him. 8) Whoever has ears should hear."[124]

66 Jesus said, "Show me the stone that the builders rejected: that is the cornerstone."[125]

67 Jesus said, "One who knows everything but lacks in oneself lacks everything."[126]

68 1) Jesus said, "Blessings on you when you are hated and persecuted, 2) and no place will be found, wherever you have been persecuted."[127]

69 1) Jesus said, "Blessings on those who have been persecuted in their hearts: they are the ones who have truly come to know the father.[128] 2) Blessings on those who are hungry, that the stomach of the person in want may be filled."[129]

70 1) Jesus said, "If you bring forth what is within you, what you have will save you. 2) If you do not have that within you, what you do not have within you [will] kill you."[130]

71 Jesus said, "I shall destroy [this] house, and no one will be able to build it [again]."[131] [46]

72 1) A [person said] to him, "Tell my brothers to divide my father's possessions with me."

2) He said to the person, "Mister, who made me a divider?"

3) He turned to his disciples and said to them, "I am not a divider, am I?"[132]

73 Jesus said, "The harvest is large but the workers are few. So beg the master[133] to send out workers to the harvest."[134]

74 Someone said,[135] "Master,[136] there are many around the drinking trough, but there is nothing[137] in the <well>."[138]

75 Jesus said, "There are many standing at the door, but those who are alone[139] will enter the wedding chamber."[140]

76 1) Jesus said, "The father's kingdom is like a merchant who had a supply of merchandise and then found a pearl. 2) That merchant was prudent; he sold the merchandise and bought the single pearl for himself.[141] 3) So also with you, seek his treasure that is unfailing, that is enduring, where no moth comes to devour and no worm destroys."[142]

77 1) Jesus said, "I am the light that is over all things.[143] I am all: from me all has come forth, and to me all has reached.[144] 2) Split a piece of wood; I am there. 3) Lift up the stone, and you will find me there."[145]

78 1) Jesus said, "Why have you come out to the countryside? To see a reed shaken by the wind? 2) And to see a person dressed

in soft clothes, [like your] rulers and your [47] powerful ones? 3) They are dressed in soft clothes, and they cannot understand truth."[146]

79 1) A woman in the crowd said to him, "Blessings on the womb that bore you and the breasts that fed you."[147]

2) He said to [her], "Blessings on those who have heard the word of the father and have truly kept it.[148] 3) For there will be days when you will say, 'Blessings on the womb that has not conceived and the breasts that have not given milk.'"[149]

80 1) Jesus said, "Whoever has come to know the world has discovered the body, 2) and whoever has discovered the body, of that person the world is not worthy."[150]

81 1) Jesus said, "Let one who has become wealthy reign, 2) and let one who has power renounce it."[151]

82 1) Jesus said, "Whoever is near me is near the fire, 2) and whoever is far from me is far from the kingdom."[152]

83 1) Jesus said, "Images are visible to people, but the light within them is hidden in the image of the father's light. 2) He will be disclosed, but his image is hidden by his light."

84 1) Jesus said, "When you see your likeness, you are happy. 2) But when you see your images that came into being before you and that neither die nor become visible, how much you will bear!"[153]

85 1) Jesus said, "Adam came from great power[154] and great wealth, but he was not worthy of you. 2) For had he been worthy, [he would] not [have tasted] death."

86 1) Jesus said, "[Foxes [48] have] their dens and birds have their nests, 2) but the child of humankind[155] has no place to lay his head and rest."[156]

87   1) Jesus said, "How miserable is the body that depends on a body, 2) and how miserable is the soul that depends on these two."[157]

88   1) Jesus said, "The messengers[158] and the prophets will come to you and give you what is yours. 2) You, in turn, give them what you have, and say to yourselves, 'When will they come and take what is theirs?' "[159]

89   1) Jesus said, "Why do you wash the outside of the cup? 2) Do you not understand that the one who made the inside is also the one who made the outside?"[160]

90   1) Jesus said, "Come to me, for my yoke is easy and my mastery[161] is gentle, 2) and you will find rest for yourselves."[162]

91   1) They said to him, "Tell us who you are so that we may believe in you."

2) He said to them, "You examine the face of heaven and earth, but you have not come to know the one who is in your presence, and you do not know how to examine this moment."[163]

92   1) Jesus said, "Seek and you will find.[164] 2) In the past, however, I did not tell you the things about which you asked me then. Now I am willing to tell them, but you are not seeking them."[165]

93   1) "Do not give what is holy to dogs, or they might throw them upon the manure pile. 2) Do not throw pearls [to] swine, or they might make [mud] of it."[166]

94   1) Jesus [said], "One who seeks will find; 2) for [one who knocks] it will be opened."[167]

95   1) [Jesus said], "If you have money, [49] do not lend it at interest. 2) Rather, give [it] to someone from whom you will not get it back."[168]

96 1) Jesus [said], "The father's kingdom is like [a] woman. 2) She took a little yeast, [hid] it in dough, and made it into large loaves of bread. 3) Whoever has ears should hear."[169]

97 1) Jesus said, "The [father's] kingdom is like a woman who was carrying a [jar] full of meal. 2) While she was walking along [a] distant road, the handle of the jar broke and the meal spilled behind her [along] the road. 3) She did not know it; she had not noticed a problem.[170] 4) When she reached her house, she put the jar down and discovered that it was empty."[171]

98 1) Jesus said, "The father's kingdom is like a person who wanted to put someone powerful to death. 2) While at home he drew his sword and thrust it into the wall to find out whether his hand would go in. 3) Then he killed the powerful one."[172]

99 1) The disciples said to him, "Your brothers and your mother are standing outside."

2) He said to them, "Those here who do the will of my father are my brothers and my mother. 3) They are the ones who will enter my father's kingdom."[173]

100 1) They showed Jesus a gold coin and said to him, "Caesar's people demand taxes from us."

2) He said to them, "Give Caesar the things that are Caesar's, 3) give God the things that are God's, 4) and give me what is mine."[174]

101 1) "Whoever does not hate [father] and mother as I do cannot be a [disciple] of me, 2) and whoever does [not] love [father and] mother as I do cannot be a [disciple of] me. 3) For my mother [gave me [50] falsehood],[175] but my true [mother][176] gave me life."[177]

102 Jesus said, "Shame on the Pharisees, for they are like a dog sleeping in the cattle manger, for it does not eat or [let] the cattle eat."[178]

103 Jesus said, "Blessings on the person who knows at what point[179] the robbers are going to enter, so that [he] may arise, bring together his estate, and arm himself before they enter."[180]

104 1) They said to Jesus, "Come, let us pray today and let us fast."
2) Jesus said, "What sin have I committed, or how have I been undone? 3) Rather, when the bridegroom leaves the wedding chamber, then let people fast and pray."[181]

105 Jesus said, "Whoever knows the father and the mother will be called the child of a whore."[182]

106 1) Jesus said, "When you make the two into one, you will become children of humankind,[183] 2) and when you say, 'Mountain, move from here,' it will move."[184]

107 1) Jesus said, "The kingdom is like a shepherd who had a hundred sheep. 2) One of them, the largest, went astray. He left the ninety-nine and sought the one until he found it. 3) After he had gone to this trouble, he said to the sheep, 'I love you more than the ninety-nine.' "[185]

108 1) Jesus said, "Whoever drinks from my mouth will become like me; 2) I myself shall become that person, 3) and the hidden things will be revealed to that person."[186]

109 1) Jesus said, "The kingdom is like a person who had a treasure hidden in his field but did not know it. 2) And [when] he died, he left it to his [son]. The son [did] not know about it. He took over [51] the field and sold it. 3) The buyer went plowing, [discovered] the treasure, and began to lend money at interest to whomever he wished."[187]

110 Jesus said, "Let someone who has found the world and has become wealthy renounce the world."[188]

111 1) Jesus said, "The heavens and the earth will roll up in your presence, 2) and whoever is living from the living one will not see death."[189]

3) Does not Jesus say, "Whoever has found oneself, of that person the world is not worthy"?[190]

112 1) Jesus said, "Shame on the flesh that depends on the soul. 2) Shame on the soul that depends on the flesh."[191]

113 1) His disciples said to him, "When will the kingdom come?"

2) "It will not come by watching for it. 3) It will not be said,[192] 'Look, here it is,' or 'Look, there it is.' 4) Rather, the father's kingdom is spread out upon the earth, and people do not see it."[193]

114 1) Simon Peter said to them, "Mary should leave us, for females are not worthy of life."

2) Jesus said, "Look, I shall guide her to make her male, so that she too may become a living spirit resembling you males. 3) For[194] every female who makes herself male will enter heaven's kingdom."[195]

The Gospel According to Thomas

The Greek Gospel
of Thomas

or

The Hidden Sayings
of Jesus[196]

(P. Oxy. 1, 654, 655; Hippolytus,
Refutation of All Heresies 5)

Prologue

These are the [hidden] sayings [that] the living Jesus spoke [and Judas, who is] also called Thomas, [recorded].

1   And he said, "[Whoever finds the interpretation] of these sayings will not taste [death]."[197]

2   1) [Jesus says], "Let one who [seeks] not stop [seeking until] one finds. 2) When one finds, [one will be astonished, 3) and having been] astonished, one will reign, 4) and [having reigned], one will [rest]."

3   1) Jesus says, "[If] your leaders [say to you, 'Look], the kingdom is in heaven,' the birds of [heaven will precede you. 2) If they say] that it is under the earth, the fish of the sea [will

enter, and will precede] you. 3) And [God's kingdom] is inside you [and outside you. 4) Whoever] knows [oneself] will find this. [And when you] know yourselves, [you will understand that] you are [children] of the [living] father. 5) [But if] you do [not] know yourselves, [you are] in [poverty], and you are [poverty]."

4   1) [Jesus says], "A [person old in] days will not hesitate to ask a [little child seven] days old about the place of [life, and] that person will [live]. 2) For many of the [first] will be [last, and] the last first, 3) and they [will become one]."

5   1) Jesus says, "[Know what is before] your face, and [what is hidden] from you will be disclosed [to you. 2) For there is nothing] hidden that [will] not [become] apparent, 3) and nothing buried that [will not be raised]."

6   1) [His disciples] ask him and say, "How [shall we] fast? [How shall] we [pray]? How [shall we give to charity]? What [diet] shall [we] observe?"

      2) Jesus says, "[Do not lie, 3) and] do not do [what] you [hate, 4) because all things are disclosed before] truth. 5) [For there is nothing] hidden [that will not be apparent]."

7   [*possible restoration*] 1) . . . "Blessings on [the lion that a human eats, and the] lion will be [human. 2) And cursed is the human] that [a lion eats . . .]."

24   [*possible restoration*] 3) ". . . There [is light within a person] of light, [and it shines on the whole] world. [If it does not shine, then] it is [dark]."

26   2) ". . . and then you will see clearly to take out the speck that is in your brother's eye."[198]

27 1) Jesus says, "If you do not fast from the world, you will not find God's kingdom. 2) And if you do not observe the sabbath as a sabbath, you will not see the father."

28 1) Jesus says, "I took my stand in the midst of the world, and in flesh I appeared to them. 2) I found them all drunk, and I found none of them thirsty. 3) My soul aches for the children of humanity, because they are blind in their hearts and [do not] see . . . ."

29 3) "[. . . comes to dwell in this] poverty."

30 1) [Jesus says], "Where there are [three, they are without] God, 2) and where there is only [one], I say, I am with that one.

77 2) "Lift up the stone, and you will find me there. 3) Split the piece of wood, and I am there."

31 1) Jesus says, "A prophet is not acceptable in the prophet's hometown, 2) nor does a doctor perform healings on those who know the doctor."

32 Jesus says, "A city built on top of a high hill and fortified can neither fall nor be hidden."

33 1) Jesus says, "<What> you hear in one ear of yours, [proclaim . . .]."

36 1) [Jesus says, "Do not worry], from morning [to nightfall nor] from evening [to] morning, either [about] your [food], what [you will] eat, [or] about [your robe], what clothing you [will] wear. 2) [You are much] better than the lilies, which do not card or [spin]. 3) And since you have one article of clothing, what[199] . . . you . . . ?[200] 4) Who might add to your stature? That is the one who will give you your clothing."[201]

37 1) His disciples say to him, "When will you be revealed to us
     and when shall we see you?"

     2) He says, "When you strip off your clothing and are not
     ashamed, 3) [. . . and you will not be afraid]."

38 1) [Jesus says, "Often you have desired to hear these sayings of
     mine], and [you have no one else from whom to hear them].
     2) And [there will come days when you will seek me and you
     will not find me]."

39 1) [Jesus says, "The Pharisees and the scholars] have [taken
     the keys] of [knowledge;[202] they themselves] have [hidden them.
     2) Neither] have [they] entered, [nor] have they [allowed
     those who are in the process of] entering [to enter. 3) As for
     you, be as shrewd] as [snakes and as] innocent [as doves]."

4   1) "One who seeks will find me in children from seven years,
     for there, hidden in the fourteenth age,[203] I am revealed."[204]

11 3) "If you ate dead things and made them living, what will you
     do if you eat living things?"[205]

PART TWO

*The Gospel
of Mary*

THE GOSPEL OF MARY is preserved in fragmentary form as a dialogue between Jesus and his disciples that features the disciple Mary—namely, Mary of Magdala or Mary Magdalene. Whether the Gospel of Mary is specifically a gnostic gospel is debated among scholars: Esther de Boer and Karen King suspect that it is not, while others maintain that it is. In the surviving sections of the gospel, Mary is described as a disciple loved by Jesus and a recipient of teachings that Jesus communicated to her. Andrew and Peter are dismayed about the special place Mary holds, and this hostility of Peter is reminiscent of his opposition to Mary in Gospel of Thomas 114 and the gnostic text Pistis Sophia ("Faith Wisdom"). In the Gospel of Mary, Levi concludes that the savior knows Mary very well, and that is the reason the savior loves Mary more than the other disciples.

The opening pages of the Gospel of Mary are lost, but the portions that survive present the savior Jesus explaining about the nature of salvation (7–9), the disciples and especially Mary responding to the words of the savior (9–10), and Mary recounting her vision of the soul's ascent (15–17) and dealing with the opposition of the other disciples (17–19). According to the savior, the real problem for people in the world is not committing sin but rather getting entangled in passion, in what is unnatural—that is, what is contrary to nature. In this explanation Jesus speaks of nature and natures and the resolution of natures to their roots in terms that echo Stoic philosophical themes. Jesus goes on to greet the disciples and offer his peace. As in Gospel of Thomas 3:3, where Jesus says that the kingdom is within a person, here in the Gospel of Mary Jesus announces that the child of humankind, or the son of man, is within. To follow the child of humankind, then, is to undertake an inner journey of seeking and finding within oneself. What one finds within is the child of humankind, which is one's true self, or it is Jesus, with whom one is joined. This good news, Jesus proclaims, is not a matter of law or commandment. Soon after this proclamation Mary herself delivers the same message in her discussion with the other disciples: the good news is a message about finding one's own humanity and becoming truly human (9).

Mary indicates that she saw the master Jesus in a vision, and she gives an account of the vision to the other disciples. She recollects that Jesus told her that such a vision is neither a purely emotional experience of the soul nor a purely spiritual inspiration from outside. A true vision involves insight of the mind. Much of Mary's account of her vision is now lost (pages 11–14), but in what remains she describes the soul's ascent past the cosmic powers in such a way as to bring to mind the inner journey of the soul as it leaves behind what may imprison it—darkness, desire, ignorance, wrath. Freed at last, the soul exclaims,

> *What binds me is slain; what surrounds me is destroyed; my desire is gone; ignorance is dead. In a world I was freed through another world, and in an image I was freed through a heavenly image. The fetter of forgetfulness is temporary. From now on I shall rest, through the course of the time of the age, in silence. (16–17)*

Near the end of the Gospel of Mary, Andrew and Peter protest against the proclamation of Mary, but Levi comes to her defense, and finally the disciples (or only Levi, in Papyrus Rylands 463) go forth to preach. The question raised about Mary of Magdala by an angry Peter, "Should we all turn and listen to her?" is answered, though only by implication. Yes, disciples should all turn and listen to the teaching and preaching of Mary of Magdala.

The Gospel of Mary is known from the Coptic version in Berlin Gnostic Codex 8502, in which it is the first tractate, and from two Greek fragments (Papyrus Oxyrhynchus 3525 and Papyrus Rylands 463). The Coptic version is the most complete text, although it is missing six manuscript pages at the beginning and four in the middle, and that version is translated below. Presumably the Gospel of Mary was originally composed in Greek, but the date and place of composition are unknown. Karen King has suggested that the original Gospel of Mary may have been written in the late first or early second century, perhaps in Syria or Egypt.

For further reading: Esther A. de Boer, *The Gospel of Mary*; Judith Hartenstein, "Das Evangelium nach Maria"; Karen L. King, *The Gospel of Mary of Magdala*; Karen L. King, "The Gospel of Mary"; Marvin Meyer, *The Gospels of Mary*; Anne Pasquier, *L'Évangile selon Marie*; R. McL. Wilson and George W. MacRae, "The Gospel According to Mary."

The Gospel of Mary[1]

(BG 8502,1; P. Oxy. 3525; P.Ryl. 463)

The Disciples Dialogue with the Savior

". . . Will matter be destroyed or not?"[2]

The savior replied, "All natures, all formed things, all creatures exist in and with each other, and they will dissolve into their own root. The nature of matter is dissolved into the root of its nature. Whoever has ears to hear should hear."[3]

Peter said to him, "You have explained everything to us. Tell us also, what is the sin of the world?"

The savior replied, "There is no such thing as sin, but you create sin when you mingle as in adultery,[4] and this is called sin.[5] For this reason the good came among you, to those of every nature, in order to restore every nature to its root."

He continued, "That is why you become sick and die, for [you love] [8] what [deceives you].[6] Whoever has a mind should understand.

"Matter gave birth to passion that is without form, because it comes from what is contrary to nature, and then confusion arose in the whole body. That is why I told you, Be of good courage.[7] And if you are discouraged, be encouraged in the presence of the diversity of forms of nature.[8] Whoever has ears to hear should hear."

When the blessed one said this, he greeted all of them and said, "Peace be with you. Receive my peace.[9] Be careful that no one leads you astray by saying, 'Look here' or 'Look there.' The child of humankind[10] is within you.[11] Follow that.[12] Those who seek it will find it. Go and preach the good news of the kingdom. Do not [9] lay down any rules other than what I have given you, and do not establish law, as the lawgiver did, or you will be bound by it."

When he said this, he left them.[13]

Mary Consoles the Disciples and Recalls a Vision

The disciples were grieved. They wept profoundly and said, "How can we go to the gentiles and preach the good news of the kingdom of the child of humankind? If they did not spare him, how will we be spared?"

Mary[14] stood up, greeted them all,[15] and said to her brothers,[16] "Do not weep or grieve or be in doubt, for his grace will be with you all and will protect you. Rather, let us praise his greatness, for he has prepared us and made us truly human."

When Mary said this, she turned their hearts to the good, and they began to discuss the words of the [savior]. [10]

Peter said to Mary, "Sister, we know the savior loved you more than any other woman.[17] Tell us the words of the savior that you remember, which you know but we do not, because we have not heard them."

Mary answered and said, "What is hidden from you I shall reveal to you."

She began to speak these words to them.

She said, "I saw the master[18] in a vision and I said to him, 'Master, today I saw you in a vision.'[19]

"He answered and said to me, 'Blessings on you, since you did not waver at the sight of me. For where the mind is, the treasure is.'[20]

"I said to him, 'Master, how does a person see a vision, with the soul or with the spirit?'

"The savior answered and said, 'A person sees neither with the soul nor with the spirit. The mind, which is between the two, sees the vision . . . .' "[21]

Mary Recounts Her Vision of the Soul's Ascent

"Desire said,[22] 'I did not see you descending, but now I see you ascending. Why are you lying, since you belong to me?'

"The soul answered and said, 'I saw you, but you did not see me or know me. To you I was only a garment,[23] and you did not recognize me.'

"After the soul said this, she left, rejoicing greatly.

"The soul approached the third power, called ignorance. The power questioned the soul, saying, 'Where are you going? You are bound by wickedness; you are bound, so do not pass judgment.'

"The soul said, 'Why do you pass judgment on me, though I have not passed judgment? I was bound, but I have not bound. I was not recognized, but I have recognized that all is to be dissolved, both what is earthly [16] and what is heavenly.'

"When the soul overcame the third power, she ascended and saw the fourth power. It took seven forms:

> The first form is darkness,
> the second, desire,
> the third, ignorance,
> the fourth, death wish,

the fifth, fleshly kingdom,
the sixth, foolish fleshly wisdom,
the seventh, angry person's wisdom.

These are the seven powers of wrath.[24]

"The powers asked the soul, 'Where are you coming from, slayer of humans, and where are you going, destroyer of realms?'

"The soul answered and said, 'What binds me is slain; what surrounds me is destroyed; my desire is gone; ignorance is dead. In a world I was freed [17] through[25] another world, and in an image I was freed through a heavenly image. The fetter of forgetfulness is temporary. From now on I shall rest, through the course of the time of the age, in silence.'"

Peter and Andrew Doubt Mary's Word

When Mary said this, she became silent, since the savior had spoken this much to her.

Andrew answered and said to the brothers, "Say what you think about what she said, but I do not believe the savior said this. These teachings certainly are strange ideas."

Peter voiced similar concerns. He asked the others about the savior: "Did he really speak with a woman in private, without our knowledge? Should we all turn and listen to her? Did he prefer her to us?"[26] [18]

Levi Speaks on Behalf of Mary

Then Mary wept and said to Peter, "My brother Peter, what do you think? Do you think that I made this up by myself or that I am lying about the savior?"

Levi[27] answered and said to Peter, "Peter, you always are angry. Now I see you arguing against this woman like an adversary. If the savior made her worthy, who are you to reject her? Surely the savior knows her well. That is why he has loved her more than us.[28]

"So, we should be ashamed and put on perfect humanity and acquire[29] it, as he commanded us, and preach the good news, not making any rule or law other than what the savior indicated."

When [19] [Levi said] this, they[30] began to leave [in order to] teach and preach.

The Gospel According to Mary

PART THREE

The Gospel
of Philip

THE GOSPEL OF PHILIP is a Valentinian anthology of meditations on a variety of themes, including the sacraments and the biblical figures of Adam and Eve. Philip is mentioned by name in the text at Gospel of Philip 73, and this may be the reason the authorship of the gospel is attributed to Philip. The meditations in the Gospel of Philip seem to be arranged in a more or less random order, although at times they seem to be connected to each other by means of catchwords or the juxtaposition of similar ideas. The meditations may derive from different sources, and Bentley Layton leaves open the possibility that some may come from Valentinus himself.

A major theme in the Gospel of Philip is the nature of the sacraments, especially the sacrament of the bridal chamber. Gospel of Philip 67 seems to list five sacraments, each called a "mystery": "The master [did] everything in a mystery: baptism, chrism, eucharist, redemption, and bridal chamber." The meaning of these five sacraments is not entirely clear. They may be rituals for the passages in one's life (for example, baptism and chrism for initiation, eucharist for the holy meal, redemption and bridal chamber for the transition to death), they may be stages in a more complicated ritual of religious initiation, or they may simply be five separate sacraments.

Of these five sacraments, the bridal chamber receives special attention in the Gospel of Philip. Whether the sacrament of the bridal chamber was acted out in some way or was simply understood spiritually is not known, but the text does say, concerning marriage,

> No [one can] know when [a husband] and wife have sex except those two, for marriage in this world is a mystery for those married. If defiled marriage is hidden, how much more is undefiled marriage a true mystery! It is not fleshly but pure. It belongs not to desire but to will. It belongs not to darkness or night but to the day and the light. (81–82)

The bridal chamber in this world is considered to be a mystery, and the pure bridal chamber is said to be that much greater. The Gospel of Philip also acknowledges the role of kissing: the text states, "The perfect conceive and give birth through a kiss" (59). This wording may connote a ceremonial kiss, it may designate how life or spirit is communicated, or it may refer to sexual intercourse. These considerations have led April D. DeConick to assume that Valentinian Christians embraced sexual activity in their lives:

> Sexual intercourse between Valentinian spouses was to continue until the last spiritual seed was embodied and harvested. On that great day, the Bridal Chamber would open and their spirits would reunite with God. How important was sex to the Valentinians? The coming of the final day and the redemption of God depended on it.[1]

Still, the Gospel of Philip affirms that undefiled marriage is not a matter of flesh and desire but of the will, and the union achieved in such a sacramental bridal chamber restores the oneness of humankind. Ultimately, that union is a matter of union with the divine, whereby humans are joined to angels in the fullness of divinity. As Gospel of Philip 58 states, in a prayer,

> *You who have united perfect light with holy spirit,*
> *unite the angels also with us, as images.*

Such unity and completeness of humankind was lost, the Gospel of Philip declares, in the separation of Adam and Eve. Originally Adam was androgynous, but the fall from primordial oneness allowed humankind to slip into mortality and death. The Gospel of Philip states, "If the female had not separated from the male, the female and the male would not have died. The separation of male and female was the beginning of death." The role of Christ, then, is to bring wholeness and unity back to fragmented humankind: "Christ came to heal the separation that was from the beginning and reunite the two, in order to give life to those who died through separation and unite them." This happens in the bridal chamber: "A woman is united with her husband in the bridal chamber, and those united in the bridal chamber will not be separated again. That is why Eve became separated from Adam, because she had not united with him in the bridal chamber" (70).

Many of the meditations on salvation employed in the Gospel of Philip are memorable, but among the most remarkable are those with a mystical quality. Thus, the Gospel of Philip urges the reader not only to *follow* Christ but to *become* Christ. In the realm of truth, Gospel of Philip 61 states,

> *you have seen things there and have become those things,*
> *you have seen the spirit and have become spirit,*
> *you have seen Christ and have become Christ,*
> *you have seen the [father] and will become father.*

The vision of God leads to oneness with God. That final bliss, the Gospel of Philip concludes, is the realization of the divine fullness or *plērōma* of the eternal realm. That divine fullness is not simply a matter of heaven above; it is to be found within: "What is innermost is the fullness, and there is nothing further within" (68).

The Gospel of Philip is the third tractate in Codex II of the Nag Hammadi library, where it follows immediately after the Gospel of Thomas. Most likely it was originally written in Greek. Whether the text was composed in Syria during the second century, or a bit later, as has been proposed, remains somewhat uncertain, though the references to Syriac terms suggest an acquaintance with Syriac language and literature. Sometimes scholars have assigned numbers to this series of meditations, but the numbering systems have proved to be quite arbitrary. Hans-Martin Schenke follows the convention of numbering 127 meditations (with subdivisions), though he admits that in his analysis there may be 175 separate excerpts; Bentley Layton numbers 107 meditations. In the translation given here, no such numbering system is used.

For further reading: April D. DeConick, "The Great Mystery of Marriage"; Wesley W. Isenberg and Bentley Layton, "The Gospel According to Philip"; Bentley Layton, *The Gnostic Scriptures*, 325–53; Jacques-É. Ménard, *L'Évangile selon Philippe*; Hans-Martin Schenke, "Das Evangelium nach Philippus"; Hans-Martin Schenke, "The Gospel of Philip."

The Gospel of Philip[2]

(NHC II,3)

Converts

A Hebrew makes a Hebrew, and such a person is called a convert.[3] A convert does not make a convert. [Some people] are as they [are] and make others [like them], while others [52] simply are.

Inheriting the Living and the Dead

A slave seeks only to be free and does not seek the master's estate.

For a child it is not enough to be a child, but a child claims the father's inheritance.

Heirs to the dead are dead, and what they inherit is dead. Heirs to the living are alive, and they inherit both the living and the dead. The dead inherit nothing, for how could a dead person inherit? If a dead person inherits the living, the living will not die and the dead will come to life.[4]

Jesus, Gentiles, Christians

A gentile does not die, never having been alive so as to die. One who has believed in truth is alive, but this person is at risk of dying just by being alive.

Since Christ came, the world has been created, cities have been beautified, and the dead have been buried.

When we were Hebrews we were orphans, with only a mother, but when we became Christians we had a father and a mother.[5]

Sowing and Reaping

Whoever sows in winter reaps in summer. Winter is the world, summer is the other, eternal realm. Let us sow in the world to reap in summer. And for this reason we should not pray in winter.[6]

From winter comes summer. If someone reaps in winter, the person will not really reap but will pull out the young plants, and such do not produce a crop. [That person's field] is barren not only [now] but also on the sabbath.[7]

Christ Came

Christ came [53] to purchase some, to save some, to redeem some. He purchased strangers and made them his own, and he brought back his own whom he had laid down of his own will as a deposit. Not only when he appeared did he lay the soul of his own will as a deposit, but from the beginning of the world he laid down the soul, for the proper moment, according to his will. Then he came forth to take it back, since it had been laid down as a deposit. It had fallen into the hands of robbers and had been stolen, but he saved it. And he redeemed the good in the world, and the bad.

Light and Darkness

Light and darkness, life and death, and right and left are siblings[8] of one another, and inseparable. For this reason the good are not good, the bad are not bad, life is not life, death is not death. Each will dissolve into its original nature, but what is superior to the world cannot be dissolved, for it is eternal.

Words and Names

The names of worldly things are utterly deceptive, for they turn the heart from what is real to what is unreal. Whoever hears the word *god* thinks not of what is real but rather of what is unreal. So also with the words *father, son, holy spirit, life, light, resurrection, church,* and all the rest, people do not think of what is real but of what is unreal, [though] the words refer to what is real. The words [that are] heard belong to this world. [Do not be] [54] deceived. If words belonged to the eternal realm, they would never be pronounced in this world, nor would they designate worldly things. They would refer to what is in the eternal realm.

The Name of the Father

Only one name is not pronounced in the world: the name the father gave the son. It is the name above all; it is the father's name. For the son would not have become father if he had not put on the father's name. Those who have this name understand it but do not speak it. Those who do not have it cannot even understand it.

Truth

Truth brought forth names[9] in the world for us, and no one can refer to truth without names. Truth is one and many, for our sakes, to teach us about the one, in love, through the many.

The Rulers

The rulers wanted to fool people, since they saw that people have a kinship with what is truly good. They took the names of the good and assigned them to what is not good, to fool people with names and link the names to what is not good. So, as if they were doing people a favor, they took names from what is not good and transferred them to the good, in their own way of thinking. For they wished to take free people and enslave them forever.

The Forces

There are forces[10] that do [favors] for people. They do not want people to come to [salvation], but they want their own existence to continue. For if people come to salvation, sacrifice will [stop] . . . and animals will not be offered up [55] to the forces. In fact, those to whom sacrifices were made were animals.[11] The animals were offered up alive, and after being offered they died. But a human being[12] was offered up to God dead, and the human being came alive.

Christ Brought Bread

Before Christ came there was no bread in the world, just as paradise, where Adam lived, had many trees for animal food but no wheat for human food, and people ate like animals. But when Christ, the perfect human, came, he brought bread from heaven,[13] that humans might be fed with human food.

The Rulers and the Holy Spirit

The rulers thought they did all they did by their own power and will, but the holy spirit was secretly accomplishing all[14] through them by the spirit's will.[15]

Sowing and Reaping Truth

Truth, which has existed from the beginning, is sown everywhere, and many see it being sown but few see it being reaped.

Mary Conceiving

Some said Mary became pregnant by the holy spirit.[16] They are wrong and do not know what they are saying. When did a woman ever get pregnant by a woman?[17]

Mary is the virgin whom none of the powers defiled. This is greatly repugnant to the Hebrews, who are the apostles and apostolic persons. This virgin whom none of the powers defiled [wishes that][18] the powers would defile themselves.

My Father

The master[19] [would] not have said, "My [father who is] in heaven,"[20] if [he] did not also have another father. He would simply have said, "[My father]."

Take from Every House

The master said to the disciples, "[Take something] [56] from every house and bring it to the father's house, but do not steal while in the father's house and take something away."

Jesus Is a Hidden Name

Jesus is a hidden name,[21] Christ is a revealed name.[22] The name Jesus does not exist in any other language, but he is called by the name Jesus. The word for Christ in Syriac is *messias* and in Greek is *christos*, and likewise all other people have a word for it in their own language. *Nazarene* is the revealed form of the hidden name.

Christ Has Everything

Christ has everything within himself, whether human or angel or mystery, and the father.

Christ Arose, Then Died

Those who say that the master first died and then arose are wrong, for he first arose and then died. If someone is not first resurrected, would that person not die? As God lives, that one would <die>.[23]

The Precious in the Worthless

No one would hide something valuable and precious in a valuable container, but countless sums are commonly kept in a container worth only a cent.[24] So it is with the soul. It is something precious, and it has come to be in a worthless body.

Naked and Not Naked

Some people are afraid that they may arise from the dead naked, and so they want to arise in flesh. They do not know that it is those who wear the [flesh] who are naked. Those who are [able] to take it off are not naked.

"Flesh [and blood will] not inherit God's kingdom."[25] What is this flesh that will not [57] inherit? It is what we are wearing. And what is this flesh that will inherit? It is the flesh and blood of Jesus.

For this reason he said, "One who does not eat my flesh and drink my blood does not have life within."[26] What does this mean? His flesh is the word and his blood is the holy spirit. Whoever has received these has food, drink, and clothing.

And I also disagree with others who say that the flesh will not arise. Both views are wrong. You say that the flesh will not arise? Then tell me what will arise, so we may salute you. You say it is the spirit in the flesh, and also the light in the flesh? But what is in the flesh is the word, and what you are talking about is nothing other than flesh.[27] It is necessary to arise in this sort of flesh, since everything exists in it.

In this world those who wear clothes are superior to the clothes. In heaven's kingdom the clothes are superior to those who wear them.

Baptism and Anointing

By water and fire this whole realm is purified, the visible by the visible, the hidden by the hidden. Some things are hidden by the visible. There is water within water,[28] there is fire within the oil of anointing.

Jesus Tricked Everyone

Jesus tricked everyone, for he did not appear as he was, but he appeared so that he could be seen. He appeared to everyone. He [appeared] to the great as great, he [appeared] to the small as small, he [appeared [58] to the] angels as an angel and to humans as a human. For this reason his word was hidden from everyone. Some looked at him and thought they saw themselves. But when he appeared to his disciples in glory upon the mountain, he was not small. He became great. Or rather, he made the disciples great, so they could see him in his greatness.

Prayer of Thanksgiving

He[29] said on that day in the prayer of thanksgiving,[30]
You who have united perfect light with holy spirit,
unite the angels also with us, as images.[31]

The Lamb

Do not despise the lamb, for without it no one could see the king.[32]

Meeting the King

No one can meet the king while naked.

Children of the Perfect Human

The heavenly person has more children than the earthly person. If the children of Adam are numerous but die, how much more numerous are the children of the perfect human, who do not die but are continually being born.

A father produces children but a child cannot produce children. One who has just been born cannot be a parent. Rather, a child gets brothers and sisters,[33] not children.

All who are born in the world are born of nature, and the others [are nourished] from where they are born. People [are] nourished from the promise of the heavenly place. [If they would be] . . . from the mouth, from which the word comes, [59] they would be nourished from the mouth and would be perfect.

The perfect conceive and give birth through a kiss. That is why we also kiss each other. We conceive from the grace within each other.

Three Women Named Mary

Three women always walked with the master: Mary his mother, <his> sister,[34] and Mary of Magdala, who is called his companion. For "Mary" is the name of his sister, his mother, and his companion.

Father, Son, Holy Spirit

Father and *son* are simple names, *holy spirit* is a double name. They[35] are everywhere, above and below, in the hidden and in the visible. The holy spirit is in the visible, and then it is below, and the holy spirit is in the hidden, and then it is above.

The Holy Spirit and Evil Forces

Evil forces serve the saints, for they have been blinded by the holy spirit into thinking they are helping their own people when they really are helping the saints.

So a disciple once asked the master for something from the world, and he said, "Ask your mother, and she will give you something from another realm."

Wisdom and Salt

The apostles said to the disciples, "May our entire offering be provided with salt." For they called [wisdom][36] salt. Without it an offering is unacceptable.[37] Wisdom is barren, [with no] children, and so she is called [the pillar] of salt.[38] Whenever . . . the holy spirit . . . , [60] and she has many children.

Father and Child

A father's possessions belong to his child. As long as the child is young, the child will not have what belongs to it. When the child grows up, the father will turn over all the possessions.

The Lost

Those who have gone astray, who are offspring of the spirit, go astray also because of the spirit. Thus from one spirit the fire blazes and the fire is extinguished.

Wisdom and Wisdom of Death

There is Echamoth and there is Echmoth. Echamoth is simply wisdom, but Echmoth is the wisdom of death—that is, the wisdom that knows death, that is called little wisdom.[39]

Tame and Wild Animals

Some animals are tame, such as the bull, the donkey, and the like, while others are wild and live off in the wild. People plow fields with tame animals, and as a result people are nourished, together with animals, whether tame or wild.

So also the perfect human plows with powers that are tame and prepares everything to come into being. Thus the whole place has stability, good and evil, right and left. The holy spirit tends everything and rules over [all] the powers, whether tame or wild and running loose. For the spirit is [resolved] to corral them, so that they cannot escape even if [they] wish.

Adam and Cain

[The one] created[40] was [noble, and you would] expect his children to be [61] noble. If he had not been created but rather had been conceived, you would expect his offspring to be noble. But in fact he was created, and then he produced offspring.

And what nobility this is! First came adultery, then murder. One[41] was born of adultery, for he was the son of the serpent.[42] He became a murderer, like his father, and he killed his brother.[43] Every act of sexual intercourse between those unlike each other is adultery.

God the Dyer

God is a dyer. Just as the good dyes, said to be genuine dyes, dissolve into what is dyed in them, so also those whom God dyes become immortal through his colors, for his dyes are immortal. And God dips[44] those to be dipped[45] in water.[46]

Seeing

People cannot see anything that really is without becoming like it. It is not so with people in the world, who see the sun without becoming the sun and see the sky and earth and everything else without becoming them.

> Rather, in the realm of truth,
> you have seen things there and have become those things,
> you have seen the spirit and have become spirit,
> you have seen Christ and have become Christ,
> you have seen the [father] and will become father.[47]

[Here] in the world you see everything but do not [see] yourself, but there in that realm you see yourself, and you will [become] what you see.

Faith and Love

Faith receives, love gives. [No one can [62] receive] without faith, and no one can give without love. So to receive we have faith and to love we give. If someone gives without love, that person gets no benefit from what was given.[48]

Anyone who receives something but does not receive the lord is still a Hebrew.

Jesus's Names

The apostles who came before us used the names *Iēsous nazōraios messias,* which means "Jesus the Nazorean, the Christ."[49] The last name is "Christ," the first name is "Jesus," the middle name is "the Nazarene."[50] *Messias* has two meanings, "Christ"[51] and "measured."[52] In Hebrew "Jesus" means "redemption."[53] *Nazara* means "truth," and so "the Nazarene" means "truth."[54] "Christ" has been "measured," thus "the Nazarene" and "Jesus"[55] have been measured out.

A Pearl in Mud

If a pearl is thrown into mud, it will not lose its value, and if it is anointed with balsam, it will not increase its value. It is always precious in its owner's eyes. Likewise, the children of God are precious in the eyes of the father, whatever their circumstances of life.

The Name "Christian"

If you say, "I am a Jew," no one will be moved. If you say, "I am a Roman," no one will be disturbed. If you say, "I am a Greek, barbarian, slave, free," no one will be troubled. If you say, "I am a Christian," the [world] will be shaken. May I [receive the one] whose name the [world] cannot bear to hear.

God Is a Man-Eater

God[56] is a man-eater, [63] and so humans are [sacrificed] to him. Before humans were sacrificed, animals were sacrificed, because those to whom they were sacrificed were not gods.

Glass and Ceramic Vessels

Glass and ceramic vessels are both made with fire. If glass vessels break, they are redone, since they have been made through breath.[57] But if ceramic vessels break, they are destroyed, since they have been made without breath.

A Donkey Turning a Millstone

A donkey turning a millstone walked a hundred miles. When it was set loose, it found itself in the same place. Some people travel long distances but get nowhere. By nightfall they have seen no cities or villages, nothing man-made or natural, no powers or angels. These miserable people have labored in vain.

The Eucharist and Jesus

The eucharist is Jesus. In Syriac it is called *pharisatha*, which means, "that which is spread out." For Jesus came to crucify[58] the world.

The Dye Works of Levi

The master went into the dye works of Levi, took seventy-two colored cloths,[59] and threw them into a vat. He drew them out and they all were white. He said, "So the child of humankind[60] has come as a dyer."[61]

Wisdom and Mary of Magdala

Wisdom,[62] who is called barren, is the mother of the angels.

The companion of the [savior] is Mary of Magdala. The [savior loved] her[63] more than [all] the disciples, [and he] kissed her often on her [mouth].

The other [disciples] [64] . . . said to him, "Why do you love her more than all of us?"

The savior answered and said to them, "Why do I not love you like her? If a blind person and one who can see are both in darkness, they are the same. When the light comes, one who can see will see the light, and the blind person will stay in darkness."[64]

One Who Is

The master said, "Blessings on one who is before coming into being. For whoever is, was and will be."[65]

Human Beings and Animals

The superiority of human beings is not apparent to the eye but lies in what is hidden. Consequently, they are dominant over animals that are stronger than they are and greater in ways apparent and hidden. So animals survive. But when human beings leave them, animals kill and devour each other. Animals have eaten each other because they have found no other food. Now, however, they have food, because humans till the ground.

Going Down into the Water

Anyone who goes down into the water[66] and comes up without receiving anything and says, "I am a Christian," has borrowed the name. But one who receives the holy spirit has the name as a gift. A gift does not have to be paid back, but what is borrowed must be paid. This is how it is with us, when one of us experiences a mystery.

Marriage

The mystery of marriage is great. [Without] it, the world would [not] exist. The existence of [the world depends on] people, and the existence [of people depends on] marriage. Then think of the power of [pure] intercourse, though its image [65] is defiled.

Unclean Spirits

Unclean spirits are male and female in form. Males have sex with souls that are female in form, and females cavort promiscuously with souls that are male in form. Souls cannot escape them if the spirits seize them, unless they receive the male or female power of the bridegroom and the bride. These are received from the mirrored bridal chamber.

When foolish females see a man by himself, they jump on him, fondle him, and pollute him. Likewise, when foolish males see a beautiful woman by herself, they seduce and violate her in order to pollute her. But when they see a husband and wife together, the females cannot make advances on the man and the males cannot make advances on the woman. So also if the image and the angel are joined, none can dare to make advances on the male or the female.[67]

Whoever Leaves the World

Whoever leaves the world can no longer be held back as if still in the world. Such a person clearly is beyond desire . . . and fear, is dominant . . . , and is above envy.

If . . . ,[68] that person is grasped and choked. How can that person escape the [great grasping powers]? How can that person [hide from them]?

Some [say], "We are faithful," in order that they [may escape [66] unclean] spirits and demons. For if they had the holy spirit, no unclean spirit could grab them.

Do not fear the flesh and do not love it. If you fear the flesh, it will dominate you. If you love the flesh, it will swallow you up and strangle you.

This World, the Resurrection, and the Middle

A person is either in this world or in the resurrection—or in the middle place.[69] May I not be found there! In this world there is good and evil, but the good of the world is not really good and the evil of the world is not really evil. After this world there is evil that is really evil: this is called the middle. The middle is death. As long as we are in this world, we should acquire resurrection, so that when we take off the flesh[70] we may be found in rest and not wander in the middle. For many go astray on the way.

Will and Action

It is good to leave the world before one sins. Some have neither the will nor the strength to act. Others, even if they have the will, do themselves no good, for they have not acted. And if they do not have the will . . . . Righteousness is beyond their grasp, in either case. It always comes down to the will, not the action.[71]

Vision of Hell

In a vision an apostolic person saw people who were locked up in a house of fire, bound with [chains] of fire, and thrown [into] . . . fire [on account of . . . false] faith. It was said, "[They might have] saved [their souls], but they did not want to, so they got [this place of] punishment called [67] the [outer] darkness . . . ."[72]

Water and Fire

Soul and spirit have come into being from water[73] and fire. The attendant of the bridal chamber has come into being from water, fire, and light. Fire is chrism. Light is fire. I do not mean ordinary fire, which has no form, but other fire, which is pure white in appearance, beautifully bright and imparting beauty.

Truth and Nakedness

Truth did not come into the world naked but in symbols and images. The world cannot receive truth in any other way. There is rebirth and an image of rebirth, and it is by means of this image that one must be reborn. What image is this? It is resurrection. Image must arise through image. By means of this image the bridal chamber and the image must approach the truth. This is restoration.

Those who receive the name of the father, son, and holy spirit and have accepted them must do this. If someone does not accept them, the name[74] will also be taken from that person. A person receives them in the chrism with the oil of the power of the cross. The apostles called this power the right and the left. This person is no longer a Christian but is Christ.

Sacraments

The master [did] everything in a mystery: baptism, chrism, eucharist, redemption, and bridal chamber.

The Inner and the Outer

[For this reason] he[75] said, "I have come to make [the lower] like the [upper and the] outer like the [inner, and to unite] them in that place."[76] [He spoke] here in symbols [and images].

Those who say [there is a heavenly person and] one that is higher are wrong,[77] for they call the visible heavenly person [68] "lower" and the one to whom the hidden realm belongs "higher." It would be better for them to speak of the inner, the outer, and

the outermost.[78] For the master called corruption "the outermost darkness,"[79] and there is nothing outside it. He said, "My
father who is in secret." He said, "Go into your room, shut the
door behind you, and pray to your father who is in secret"[80]—that
is, the one who is innermost. What is innermost is the fullness,
and there is nothing further within. And this is what they call
uppermost.

Fall and Return to Fullness

Before Christ some came from a realm they could not reenter, and
they went to a place they could not yet leave. Then Christ came.
Those who went in he brought out, and those who went out he
brought in.[81]

When Eve Was in Adam

When Eve was in Adam, there was no death. When she was separated from him, death came. If <she> enters into him again and
he embraces <her>, death will cease to be.[82]

Why Have You Forsaken Me?

"My God, my God, why, lord, have you forsaken me?"[83] He spoke
these words on the cross, for he had left that place.

True Flesh

[The master] was conceived from what [is imperishable], through
God. The [master rose] from the dead, but [he did not come into
being as he] was. Rather, his [body] was [completely] perfect. [It

was] of flesh, and this [flesh] was true flesh. [Our flesh] is not true flesh but only an image of the true. [69]

The Wedding Chamber

Animals do not have a wedding chamber,[84] nor do slaves or defiled women. The wedding chamber is for free men and virgins.

Baptism

We are born again through the holy spirit, and we are conceived through Christ in baptism with two elements. We are anointed through the spirit, and when we were conceived, we were united.

No one can see oneself in the water or in a mirror without light, nor can you see yourself in the light without water or a mirror. So it is necessary to baptize with two elements, light and water, and light is chrism.

The Temple in Jerusalem

There were three structures for sacrifice in Jerusalem. One opened to the west and was called the holy place; a second opened to the south and was called the holy of the holy; the third opened to the east and was called the holy of holies, where only the high priest could enter. The holy place is baptism; the holy of the holy is redemption; the holy of holies is the bridal chamber. Baptism entails resurrection and redemption, and redemption is in the bridal chamber. The bridal chamber is within a realm superior to [what we belong to], and you cannot find anything [like it . . . . These] are the ones who worship [in spirit and in truth,[85] for they do not worship] in Jerusalem. There are people in Jerusalem who [do worship] in Jerusalem, and they await [the mysteries] called [the holy] of holies, the curtain [of which] was torn. [Our] bridal chamber is the image [of the bridal chamber] [70] above. That is why its curtain was torn from top to bottom, for some people from below had to go up.[86]

Wearing the Light

The powers cannot see those who have put on the perfect light, and they cannot seize them. One puts on the light in the mystery of union.

Union in the Bridal Chamber

If the female had not separated from the male, the female and the male would not have died. The separation of male and female was the beginning of death. Christ came to heal the separation that was from the beginning and reunite the two, in order to give life to those who died through separation and unite them.

A woman is united with her husband in the bridal chamber, and those united in the bridal chamber will not be separated again. That is why Eve became separated from Adam, because she had not united with him in the bridal chamber.

Adam's Soul

Adam's soul came from a breath.[87] The soul's companion is spirit, and the spirit given to him is his mother. His soul was [taken] from him and replaced with [spirit]. When he was united with spirit,

[he] uttered words superior to the powers, and the powers envied him.[88] They [separated him from his] spiritual companion . . . hidden . . . bridal chamber . . . .

Jesus at the Jordan

Jesus revealed himself [at the] Jordan River as the fullness of heaven's kingdom. The one [conceived] before all [71] was conceived again; the one anointed before was anointed again; the one redeemed redeemed others.

The Mystery of the Virgin Birth

It is necessary to utter a mystery. The father of all united with the virgin who came down, and fire shone on him.

On that day that one revealed the great bridal chamber, and in this way his body came into being.

On that day he came forth from the bridal chamber as one born of a bridegroom and a bride.

So Jesus established all within it, and it is fitting for each of the disciples to enter into his rest.

The Births of Adam and Christ

Adam came from two virgins, the spirit and the virgin earth.[89] Christ was born of a virgin to correct the fall that occurred in the beginning.

Two Trees in Paradise

There are two trees growing in paradise. One produces [animals] and the other produces people. Adam [ate] of the tree that produces animals, and [he] became an animal and brought forth animals. As a result Adam's children worship animals.[90] The tree [whose] fruit [he ate] is the [tree of knowledge, and because of this, sins] increased. [If he had] eaten the [fruit of the other tree], the fruit of [the tree of life, which] produces people, [gods would] worship people. As [in paradise] God created people [that people] [72] might create God,[91] so also in this world people make gods and worship what they have created. It would be more fitting for gods to worship people.

Accomplishments

The truth is, a person's accomplishments depend on that person's abilities, and for this reason we refer to accomplishments as abilities. Among such accomplishments are a person's children, and they come into being from a time of rest.[92] Now, one's abilities come to expression in what one accomplishes, and rest is clearly found in children. You will find this also applies to the image. These are the people made after the image,[93] who accomplish things through their strength and bring forth children through rest.

Slaves and the Free

In this world slaves serve the free. In heaven's kingdom the free will serve the slaves and the attendants of the bridal chamber will serve the wedding guests.

The attendants of the bridal chamber have only one name, and that is rest. When they are together, they need no other form, [for they are in] contemplation . . . perception. They are superior . . . among those in . . . the glories of glories . . . .

Jesus Going Down into the Water

[It] was [necessary for Jesus] to go down into the water [in order to perfect] and purify it. [So also] those who are [baptized] in his name [are perfected]. For he said, "[Thus] shall we perfect [73] all righteousness."[94]

Resurrection and Baptism

People who say they will first die and then arise are wrong. If they do not receive the resurrection first, while they are alive, they will receive nothing when they die. So it is said of baptism, "Great is baptism," for if people receive it, they will live.

Joseph the Carpenter

Philip the apostle said, "Joseph the carpenter planted a garden,[95] for he needed wood for his trade. He is the one who made the cross from the trees he planted, and his own offspring hung on what he planted. His offspring was Jesus and what he planted was the cross."

The tree of life, however, is in the middle of the garden.[96] It is an olive tree, and from it comes chrism, and from chrism comes resurrection.

This World Eats Corpses

This world eats corpses, and everything eaten in this world also dies. Truth eats life, and no one nourished by [truth] will die.[97] Jesus came from that realm and brought food from there, and he gave [life] to all who wanted it, that they might not die.

God Plants Paradise

[God planted] a garden,[98] and humans [lived in the] garden. There are some [who dwell] with . . . God . . . .

This garden [is where] it will be said to me, ". . . [eat] this and do not eat that, [as you] [74] wish." This is where I shall eat everything, where the tree of knowledge is.[99]

That tree killed Adam, but here the tree of knowledge has brought people back to life. That tree was the law. It can give knowledge of good and evil, but it neither freed Adam from evil nor made him good, and it brought death to those who ate of it. For when it was said, "Eat this and do not eat that," death began.

Chrism Is Superior to Baptism

Chrism is superior to baptism. We are called Christians from the word "chrism," not from the word "baptism." Christ[100] also has his name from chrism, for the father anointed the son, the son anointed the apostles, and the apostles anointed us. Whoever is anointed has everything: resurrection, light, cross, holy spirit. The father gave all this to the person in the bridal chamber, and the person accepted it. The father was in the son and the son was in the father. This is heaven's kingdom.

Laughing

The master put it very well: "Some have gone into heaven's kingdom laughing, and they have come out [laughing]."

Someone said, "[That is] a Christian."

The person said [again, "That is the one who went] down into the water and came [up as master][101] of all. [Redemption is no] laughing matter, but [a person goes laughing into] heaven's kingdom out of contempt for these rags.[102] If the person despises [the body] and considers it a laughing matter, [the person will come out] laughing."

So it is also [75] with bread, the cup, and oil,[103] though there are mysteries higher than these.

Creation through a Mistake

The world came into being through a mistake. The creator wanted to make it incorruptible and immortal, but he failed and did not get what he hoped for. For the world is not incorruptible and the creator of the world is not incorruptible. Things are not incorruptible, but offspring[104] are. Nothing can receive incorruptibility unless it is an offspring.[105] And whatever cannot receive certainly cannot give.

Eucharist and Baptism

The cup of prayer[106] contains wine and water, for it represents the blood for which thanksgiving is offered. It is full of the holy spirit, and it belongs to the completely perfect human. When we drink it, we take to ourselves the perfect human.

The living water is a body, and we must put on the living human. Thus, when one is about to go down into the water, one strips in order to put on the living human.[107]

Like Brings Forth Like

A horse brings forth a horse, a human brings forth humans, a deity brings forth deities. So also bridegrooms and brides come from the [bridegroom and bride].

No Jews ... from Greeks ... from Jews ... to Christians. [There was another generation of people], and these [blessed people] were called the chosen spiritual ones, [76] true humankind, the child of humankind, and the offspring of the child of humankind. This true generation is renowned in the world, and this is where the attendants of the bridal chamber are.

Strength and Weakness

In this world, where strength and weakness are to be found, there is union of male and female, but in the eternal realm there is a different kind of union.

Although we refer to these things with the same words, there are also other words that are superior to every word that is pronounced.

These are above strength. For there is strength and there are those superior to strength, and they are not different but the same. This is incomprehensible to hearts of flesh.

Know Yourself

All those who have everything should know themselves,[108] should they not? If some do not know themselves, they will not enjoy what they have, but those who know themselves will enjoy their possessions.

Putting on Light

The perfect human can be neither grasped nor seen. What is seen can be grasped. No one can obtain this grace without putting on perfect light and becoming perfect light. Whoever puts on light will enter [the place of rest]. This is perfect [light, and] we [must] become [perfect humans] before we leave [the world]. Whoever obtains everything [but does not separate] from this world will [not] be able [to attain] that realm but will [go to the] middle place,[109] for that one is not perfect. [77] Only Jesus knows the fate of that person.[110]

The Holy Person

The holy person[111] is completely holy, including the person's body. The holy person who takes up bread consecrates it, and does the same with the cup or anything else the person takes up and consecrates.[112] So how would the person not consecrate the body also?

The Water of Baptism and Death

As Jesus perfected[113] the water of baptism, he poured death out. For this reason we go down into the water but not into death, that we may not be poured out into the spirit[114] of the world. When it blows, winter comes. When the holy spirit blows, summer comes.

Knowledge and Love

Whoever knows[115] the truth is free,[116] and a free person does not sin, for "one who sins is a slave of sin."[117] Truth is the mother, knowledge is the father. Those who do not allow themselves to sin the world calls free. They do not allow themselves to sin, and knowledge of the truth lifts them up[118]—that is, it makes them free and superior to all. But "love builds up."[119] Whoever is free through knowledge is a slave because of love for those who do not yet have freedom of knowledge. Knowledge enables them to be free.

Love [never says] it owns something, [though] it owns [everything]. Love does not [say, "This is mine]" or "That is mine," but rather, "[All that is mine] is yours."

Spiritual Love

Spiritual love is wine and perfume. [78] People who anoint themselves with it enjoy it, and while these people are present, others who are around also enjoy it. If the people who are anointed leave them and go away, the others who are not anointed but are only standing around are stuck with their own bad odor.

The Samaritan gave nothing to the wounded person except wine and oil—that is, only ointment.[120] The ointment healed the wound, for "love covers a multitude of sins."[121]

Children and Love

The children a woman brings forth resembles the man she loves. If it is her husband, they resemble her husband. If it is a lover, they resemble the lover. Often, if a woman must sleep with her husband but her heart is with the lover with whom she usually has sex, the child she bears will resemble the lover.

So, you who live with the son of God, do not love the world but love the master,[122] that what you bring forth may not resemble the world but may resemble the master.

Sex and Spirit

Humans have sex with humans, horses have sex with horses, donkeys have sex with donkeys. Members of a species have sex with members of the same species. So also spirit has intercourse with spirit, word[123] mingles with word, light mingles [with light].

> *If [you] become human,*
> *[a human] will love you.*
> *If you become [spirit],*
> *spirit will unite with you.*
> *If you become word,*
> *word [79] will have intercourse with you.*
> *If you become light,*
> *light will mingle with you.*
> *If you become one of those above,*
> *those above will rest on you.*
> *If you become a horse or donkey or bull*
> *or dog or sheep or some other animal,*

wild or tame,
then neither human nor spirit
nor word nor light can love you.
Those above and those within cannot rest in you,
and you have no part in them.

Slave and Free

People who are slaves against their will can be free. People who are freed by favor of their master and then sell themselves back into slavery cannot be free again.

Farming

Farming in this world depends on four things, and a harvest is gathered and taken into the barn as a result of water, earth, air,[124] and light.

God's farming also depends on four things: faith, hope, love, and knowledge.[125] Faith is the earth in which we take root. Hope is the water with which we are nourished. Love is the air through which we grow. Knowledge is the light by which we [ripen].[126]

Grace exists [in four ways. It is] earthly; it is [heavenly] . . . the highest heaven . . . .

Blessings on One Who Never Grieves Anyone

[Blessings] on one who has never grieved [80] a soul. This is Jesus Christ. He came to the whole earth and never laid a burden upon anyone. Blessings on one like this, for this is a perfect human.

The word[127] tells us how difficult it is to bring this about. How can we accomplish such a feat? How can we give help[128] to everyone?

To begin with, one must not cause grief to anyone, whether great or small, unbeliever or believer, and one must not give help to those who are well off. There are some who profit by helping the rich. The person who does good deeds will not help the rich, for this person will not take just anything that may be desirable. Nor can such a person cause them grief, since this person does not give them trouble. The new rich sometimes cause others grief, but the person who does good deeds does not do this. It is the wickedness of these people that causes their grief. The person with the nature of a perfect human gives joy to the good, but some people are deeply distressed by all this.

A Householder and Food

There was a householder who had everything: children, slaves, cattle, dogs, pigs, wheat, barley, chaff, fodder, [oil], meat, and acorns. The householder was wise and knew the food of each. He fed the children [baked] bread [and meat]. He fed the slaves [oil and] grain. [He fed] the cattle barley, chaff, and fodder. He threw the dogs some bones. He fed the pigs acorns [81] and gruel.

So it is with the disciples of God. If they are wise, they understand discipleship. Bodily forms will not deceive them, but they will examine the condition of each person's soul and speak appropriately with the person. In the world many animals have human form. If the disciples of God identify them as pigs, they feed them acorns. If cattle, they feed them barley, chaff, and fodder. If dogs,

they throw them some bones. If slaves, they feed them what is pre-
liminary. If children, they feed them what is complete.[129]

Creating and Procreating

There is the child of humankind, and there is the child of the
child of humankind. The child of humankind is the master, and
the child of the child of humankind is the one who creates through
the child of humankind. The child of humankind received from
God the ability to create. He can also procreate. One who has received the ability to create is a creature, and one who has received
the ability to procreate is an offspring. One who creates cannot
procreate, but one who procreates can create. One who creates is
said to procreate, but the "offspring" are really creatures, because
these "offspring" are not children of procreation but [works of
creation].

One who creates works openly, and is visible. One who procreates does so [secretly], and is hidden, for one who procreates [is
beyond every] image. So then, one who creates does so openly, and
one who procreates [produces] offspring secretly.

Pure Marriage

No [one can] know when [a husband] [82] and wife have sex except
those two, for marriage in this world is a mystery for those married. If defiled marriage is hidden, how much more is undefiled
marriage a true mystery! It is not fleshly but pure. It belongs not
to desire but to will. It belongs not to darkness or night but to the
day and the light.

If marriage is exposed, it has become prostitution, and the bride plays the harlot not only if she is impregnated by another man but even if she slips out of her bedchamber and is seen. Let her show herself only to her father and her mother, the friend of the bridegroom, and the attendants of the bridegroom. They are allowed to enter the bridal chamber every day. But let the others yearn just to hear her voice and enjoy the fragrance of her ointment, and let them feed on the crumbs that fall from the table, like dogs.[130]

Bridegrooms and brides belong to the bridal chamber. No one can see a bridegroom or a bride except by becoming one.

Abraham's Circumcision

When Abraham [was able][131] to see what he was to see, [he] circumcised the flesh of the foreskin, thus teaching us that it is necessary to destroy the flesh.

Hidden Parts

As long as their [insides] are hidden, [most] beings in the world are alive and well. [If their insides] are exposed, they die, as is clear by the example of the visible part of a person. [As long as] a person's intestines are hidden, the person is alive. [83] If the intestines are exposed and come out, the person dies. Likewise, while its root is hidden, a tree sprouts and grows. If its root is exposed, the tree withers.

So it is with all things produced in the world, not only the visible but also the hidden. As long as the root of evil is hidden, it is strong. When it is recognized, it is undone, and if it is brought to light, it dies. For this reason the word[132] says, "Already the ax is laid at the root of the trees."[133] It will not merely cut them down, for what is cut down sprouts up again. Rather, the ax will dig down until it cuts out the root. Jesus pulled out the root of the whole place, but others did so only in part.

The Root of Evil

Let each of us also dig down after the root of evil within us and pull it out of our hearts from the root. It will be uprooted if we recognize it. But if we are ignorant of it, it takes root in us and produces fruit in our hearts. It dominates us. We are its slaves, and it takes us captive so that we do what we do [not] want and do [not] do what we want. It is powerful because we do not recognize it. As long as [it] exists, it stays active.

Ignorance Is the Mother of Evil

Ignorance is the mother of [all evil]. Ignorance leads to [death, because] those who come from [ignorance] neither were nor [are] nor will be. [But those in the truth] [84] will be perfect when all truth is revealed. For truth is like ignorance. While hidden, truth rests in itself, but when revealed and recognized, truth is praised in that it is stronger than ignorance and error. It gives freedom.

The word[134] says, "If you know the truth, the truth will make you free."[135] Ignorance is a slave, knowledge[136] is freedom. If we know the truth, we shall find the fruit of truth within us. If we join with it, it will bring us fulfillment.

Things Visible and Hidden

At present we encounter the visible things of creation, and we say that they are mighty and worthy and the hidden things are weak and insignificant. It is <not>[137] so with the visible things of truth. They are weak and insignificant, but the hidden things are mighty and worthy.

Temple, Cross, Ark

The mysteries of truth are made known in symbols and images. The bedchamber is hidden, and it is the holy of the holy. At first the curtain[138] concealed how God manages creation, but when the curtain is torn[139] and what is inside appears, this building will be left deserted, or rather will be destroyed. And the whole godhead[140] will flee from here but not into the holy of holies, for it cannot mingle with pure [light] and [perfect] fullness. Instead it will remain under the wings of the cross [and under] its arms.[141] This ark will be salvation [for people] when floodwaters [85] surge over them.[142]

Whoever belongs to the priestly order can go inside the curtain along with the high priest. For this reason the curtain was not torn only at the top, for then only the upper realm would have been opened. It was not torn only at the bottom, for then it would have revealed only the lower realm. No, it was torn from top to bottom. The upper realm was opened for us in the lower realm,[143] that we might enter the hidden realm of truth. This is what is truly worthy and mighty, and we shall enter through symbols that are weak and insignificant. They are weak compared to perfect glory.

There is glory that surpasses glory, there is power that surpasses power. Perfect things have opened to us, and hidden things of truth. The holy of holies was revealed, and the bedchamber invited us in.

Revelation of the Seed

As long as the seed[144] of the holy spirit is hidden, wickedness is ineffective, though it is not yet removed from the midst of the seed, and they are still enslaved to evil. But when the seed is revealed, then perfect light will shine on everyone, and all who are in the light will [receive the] chrism.[145] Then slaves will be freed [and] captives ransomed. "Every plant that my father in heaven has not planted [will be] pulled out."[146] What is separated will be united, [what is empty] will be filled.

Eternal Light

Everyone who [enters] the bedchamber will kindle the [light. This is] like marriages that occur [in secret and] take place at night. The light of the fire [shines] [86] during the night and then goes out. The mysteries of that marriage, however, are performed in the day and the light, and neither that day nor its light ever sets.

If someone becomes an attendant of the bridal chamber, that person will receive the light. If one does not receive it while here in this place, one cannot receive it in the other place.

Those who receive the light cannot be seen or grasped. Nothing can trouble such people even while they are living in this world. And when they leave this world, they have already received truth through images, and the world has become the eternal realm. To these people the eternal realm is fullness.

This is the way it is. It is revealed to such a person alone, hidden not in darkness and night but hidden in perfect day and holy light.

The Gospel According to Philip

PART FOUR

The Gospel of Truth by Valentinus

THE GOSPEL OF TRUTH is a Valentinian sermon on the saving knowledge of God. The text is named the Gospel of Truth in its incipit, and the title is also mentioned by Irenaeus of Lyon, who claims that Valentinian Christians read a Gospel of Truth. The Gospel of Truth is sometimes attributed to the great teacher and preacher Valentinus. Bentley Layton considers such attribution to be plausible, and he mentions three good reasons the Gospel of Truth may be thought to have come from Valentinus: 1) the style of the Gospel of Truth resembles the style of the fragments of Valentinus found mainly in Clement of Alexandria and Hippolytus of Rome; 2) Valentinus was thought to be eloquent, and he would be a good candidate to be author of such an eloquent gospel; and 3) prominent features of the Gospel of Truth suggest an early date of composition, prior to the development of more complex Valentinian systems of thought.[1]

The sermon opens with the memorable line, "The gospel of truth is joy . . . ." It is joy, the sermon continues, for those who come to know God through the word, which is said to originate, in a manner recalling the opening of the Gospel of John, from God, here specifically "from the fullness (*plērōma*) in the father's thought and mind." The word is the savior Jesus Christ. The

problem the savior has come to address is forgetfulness and ignorance of God: because of forgetfulness and ignorance, people are
haunted by terror and fear. The savior has brought people out of
their forgetfulness and ignorance by giving light to those who
were in darkness: "He enlightened them and showed the way, and
that way is the truth he taught them" (18). Anger, personified and
apparently also a psychological reality within people, persecutes
Jesus by having him hanged on a tree. In his crucifixion, the text
proclaims, Jesus is nailed to the tree, but anger proves to be impo-
tent, and Jesus becomes "fruit of the knowledge of the father."
When this fruit, which is Jesus, is eaten, it brings life to those who
have eaten of it. In the words of the gospel, "They were joyful in
this discovery, and he found them within himself and they found
him within themselves" (18).

The balance of the Gospel of Truth explains this vision of salvation through metaphor, parable, interpretation, and elaboration.
Jesus is a guide, at rest yet busy in places of learning (19). He reveals the living book, which reflects God's thought and mind, in
the crucifixion, through which the knowledge of God is published
(20). Those lost in ignorance are called by name, and thus they
come to themselves and to knowledge of themselves (21–22). They
are brought from deficiency to fullness and completeness (24–25).
All of this is like having jars that are empty or full (25–26), or living in a nightmare and then awakening (28–30), or losing and
finding sheep (31–32), or feeling cold water become warm (34).
Those who come to knowledge come to the father:

> They are truth. The father is in them and they are in the father, perfect,
> inseparable from him who is truly good. They lack nothing at all but
> are at rest, fresh in spirit. They will hearken to their root and be involved

with concerns in which they may find their root and do no harm to their souls. (42)

The gospel concludes, "Children like this the father loves" (43).

The Gospel of Truth is preserved as the third tractate in Codex I of the Nag Hammadi library. A few fragments from Codex XII, tractate 2, also come from an edition of the Gospel of Truth. The sermon was composed in Greek but survives only in Coptic translation. The date of composition is most likely sometime in the second century, during the lifetime of Valentinus, who died around 175 CE. Where it was written is unknown, but Valentinus spent much of his life in Alexandria and Rome.

For further reading: Harold W. Attridge and George W. MacRae, "The Gospel of Truth"; Kendrick Grobel, *The Gospel of Truth*; Bentley Layton, *The Gnostic Scriptures*, 250–64; Jacques-É. Ménard, *L'Évangile de Vérité*; Hans-Martin Schenke, "Evangelium Veritatis"; Hans-Martin Schenke, *Die Herkunft des sogennanten Evangelium Veritatis*.

The Gospel of Truth[2]

(NHC I,3; XII,2)

The gospel of truth is joy for people who have received grace from the father of truth, that they might know him through the power of the word.[3] The word has come from the fullness[4] in the father's thought and mind. The word is called "savior," a term that refers to the work he is to do to redeem those who had not known [17] the father. And the term "gospel" refers to the revelation of hope, since it is the means of discovery for those who seek him.

Ignorance Brings Error

All have sought for the one from whom they have come forth. All have been within him, the illimitable, the inconceivable, who is beyond all thought. But ignorance of the father brought terror and fear, and terror grew dense like a fog, so that no one could see. Thus error grew powerful. She worked on her material substance in vain.[5] Since she did not know the truth, she assumed a fashioned figure and prepared, with power and in beauty, a substitute for truth.

This was not humiliating for the illimitable, inconceivable one. For this terror and forgetfulness and this deceptive figure were as

95

nothing, whereas established truth is unchanging, unperturbed, and beyond beauty.

For this reason despise error.

Error had no root; she was in a fog regarding the father. She was there preparing works and deeds of forgetfulness and fear in order, by them, to attract those of the middle and take them captive.[6]

The forgetfulness of error was not apparent. It is not [18] . . . from the father. Forgetfulness did not come into being from the father, but if it did come into being, it is because of the father.[7] What comes into being within him is knowledge, which appeared so that forgetfulness might be destroyed and the father might be known. Forgetfulness came into being because the father was not known, so as soon as the father comes to be known, forgetfulness will cease to be.

Jesus as Fruit of Knowledge

This is the gospel of him whom they seek, revealed to the perfect through the father's mercy. Through the hidden mystery Jesus Christ enlightened those who were in darkness because of forgetfulness. He enlightened them and showed the way, and that way is the truth he taught them.[8]

For this reason error was angry with him and persecuted him, but she was restrained by him and made powerless. He was nailed to a tree, and he became fruit of the knowledge of the father. This fruit of the tree, however, did not bring destruction when it was eaten, but rather it caused those who ate of it to come into being. They were joyful in this discovery, and he found them within himself and they found him within themselves.[9]

And as for the illimitable, inconceivable perfect father who made all, the realm of all is within him and needs him. Although the father kept within himself their perfection, which he had not given to all, he was not jealous. What jealousy could there be between the father and his own members? For even if [19] the members of the eternal realm had [received] their [perfection], they could not have approached . . . the father. He kept their perfection within himself, giving it to them as a means to return to him with complete, single-minded knowledge. He is the one who set the realm of all in order, and the realm of all is within him and needs him.

Just as a person who is not known to other people wants them to know him and love him, so also with the father. For what did the realm of all need if not the knowledge of the father?

Jesus as Guide and Teacher

Jesus became a guide, a person of rest who was busy in places of instruction. He came forward and spoke the word as a teacher. Those wise in their own eyes came to test him, but he refuted them, for they were foolish, and they hated him because they were not really wise.

After them came the little children, who have knowledge of the father. When they gained strength and learned about the expressions of the father, they knew, they were known, they were glorified, they gave glory.

The Living Book Is Revealed

In their hearts the living book of the living was revealed, the book that was written in the father's thought and mind and was, [20] since the foundation of all, in his incomprehensible nature. No one had been able to take up this book, since it was ordained that the one who would take it up would be slain. And nothing could appear among those who believed in salvation unless that book had come out.

For this reason the merciful, faithful Jesus was patient and accepted his sufferings to the point of taking up that book, since he knew that his death would be life for many.[10]

As in the case of a will that has not been opened, the fortune of the deceased owner of the house is hidden, so also in the case of all that had been hidden while the father of all was invisible but that issues from him from whom every realm comes.

> Jesus appeared,
> put on that book,
> was nailed to a tree,
> and published the father's edict on the cross.
> Oh, what a great teaching!
> He humbled himself even unto death,
> though clothed in eternal life.
> He stripped off the perishable rags
> and clothed himself in incorruptibility,
> which no one can take from him.[11]

When he entered the empty ways of fear, he passed by those stripped by forgetfulness. For he encompasses knowledge and perfection, and he proclaims what is in the heart [21] . . . . [He] teaches those who will learn. And those who will learn are the living who are inscribed in the book of the living. They learn about themselves, receiving instruction from the father, returning to him.

Since the perfection of all is in the father, all must go up to him. When all have received knowledge, they receive what is theirs and draw it to themselves. For those who are ignorant are in need, and their need is great, because they need what would make them perfect. Since the perfection of all is in the father, all must go up to him and receive what is theirs. The father inscribed these things first, having prepared them to be given to those who came from him.

The Father Utters the Names of People Who Know

Those whose names the father knew at the beginning were called at the end, as it is with every person who has knowledge. Such names the father has uttered. One whose name has not been spoken is ignorant, for how could a person hear if that person's name had not been pronounced? Whoever remains ignorant until the end is a creature of forgetfulness and will perish with it. Otherwise why do these wretches have no [22] name, why no voice?

So whoever has knowledge is from above. If called, that person hears, replies, turns to the one who is calling, and goes up to him. He knows how he is called. That person has knowledge and does the will of him who called. That person wishes to please him, finds rest, and has the appropriate name. Those who have knowledge in this way know where they come from and where they are going. They know as one who, having become intoxicated, has turned from his drunkenness, and having come to his senses, has gotten control of himself.

The savior[12] has brought many back from error. He went before them to the places from which they had turned when they followed error, because of the depth of him who surrounds every place, though nothing surrounds him. Indeed, it is amazing that they were in the father without knowing him and that they could leave on their own, since they were not able to contemplate or know the one in whom they were.

For if his will had not come from him . . . he revealed it as knowledge that is in harmony with the expressions of his will—that is, knowledge of the living book, which he revealed to the eternal realms at the end [23] as his [letters]. He showed that they are not merely vowels or consonants, so that one may read them and think them devoid of meaning. Rather, they are letters of truth; they speak and know themselves. Each letter is a perfect truth[13] like a perfect book, for they are letters written in unity, written by the father for the eternal realms, so that by means of his letters they might come to know the father.

The Word of the Father Appears

As for the word,
his wisdom meditates on it,
his teaching utters it,
his knowledge has revealed it,
his patience is a crown upon it,
his joy is in harmony with it,
his glory has exalted it,
his character has revealed it,
his rest has received it,
his love has incarnated it,
his faith has embraced it.

Thus the father's word goes out in the realm of all as the fruition [24] of his heart and expression of his will. It supports all and chooses all. It also takes the expression of all and purifies it, bringing it back to the father, to the mother. This is Jesus of infinite sweetness.[14]

The father opens his bosom, and his bosom is the holy spirit. He reveals his hidden self, and his hidden self is his son, so that through the father's mercy the eternal realms may know him, end their wearying search for the father, and rest in him, knowing that he is rest. For he has filled what was deficient and has done away with its appearance. The mere appearance of what was deficient is the world, and mere appearance serves in the world.

For where there is envy and strife there is deficiency, but where there is unity there is completeness. Since deficiency came about because the father was not known, from the moment that the father is known, deficiency will cease to be. As one's ignorance about another vanishes when one gains knowledge, and as darkness departs when light comes, [25] so also deficiency disappears in completeness. From then on the world of appearance will no longer be evident, but rather it will disappear in the harmony of unity.

Now the works of all lie scattered. In time unity will make the heavenly places complete, and in unity all individually will come to themselves. By means of knowledge they will purify themselves from multiplicity into unity, devouring matter within themselves like fire, darkness by light, death by life.

Since these things have happened to each of us, it is right for us to see to it above all that this house be holy and silent for the sake of unity.

Parable of the Broken Jars

This is like people who moved from one house to another. They had jars around that were not good, and they broke, but the owner suffered no loss. Rather, the owner was glad because instead of these defective jars there were full jars that were perfect.

This is the judgment that has come [26] from above and has judged every person, a drawn two-edged sword cutting on this side and that, since the word that is in the heart of those who speak the word appeared.[15] It is not merely a sound but it was embodied.

A great disturbance occurred among the jars, for some were empty and others were filled, some were ample and others were depleted, some were purified and others were broken.

All the realms were shaken and disturbed, for they had no order or stability. Error was agitated, and she did not know what to do. She was troubled, she lamented, she attacked herself, because she knew nothing.[16] For knowledge, which leads to the destruction of error and all her expressions, approached. Error is empty; there is nothing within her.

The Appearance of Truth and the Emanations of the Father

Truth appeared, and all its expressions recognized it. They greeted the father in truth and power that is complete and joins them with the father.

Whoever loves truth, whoever touches [27] truth, touches the father's mouth, because truth is the father's mouth. His tongue is the holy spirit, and from his tongue one will receive the holy spirit. This is the manifestation of the father and his revelation to his eternal realms. He revealed his hidden self and explained it. For who has anything within if not[17] the father alone?

All the realms are from the father. They know that they have come from him as children who were within a mature person but who knew that they had not yet received form or been given a name. The father brings forth each of them when they receive the essence of his knowledge. Otherwise, though they were in him, they could not know him. The father is perfect, and he knows every realm within himself. If he wishes, what he wishes appears when he gives it form and a name—and he does give it a name. He brings into being those who before coming into being were ignorant of the one who made them.

I am not saying that those who have not yet come to be are nothing.[18] They are [28] within one who may wish that they come into being if at some future point he so wishes. On the one hand, he knows, before anything appears, what he will produce. On the other hand, the fruit that has not yet appeared knows nothing and does nothing. Thus each realm in the father comes from what is, but what has set itself up is from what is not. For whatever has no root has no fruit, and although thinking, "I have come into being," it will perish by itself. So whatever does not exist will never exist.

What then does he want such a one to think? It is this: "I have come into being like shadows and phantoms of the night." When the light shines, the person knows the terror that had been experienced was nothing.

Ignorance Is a Nightmare

Thus they were ignorant of the father, for they did not see him. [29] Since there had been terror and confusion and uncertainty and doubt and division, there were many illusions among them, and inane ignorance—as if they were fast asleep and found themselves a prey to nightmares.[19] In these dreams they are fleeing somewhere, or they cannot get away when chased, or they are in a fight, or they themselves are beaten, or they are falling from on high, or they fly through the air with no wings. Or, it seems people are trying to kill them, though there is no one chasing them, or they are killing their neighbors and are covered with their blood. This continues until those experiencing all these dreams wake up. Those caught in the middle of all these confusing things see nothing because the dreams are nothing.

So it is with those who cast off ignorance from themselves like sleep. They do not consider it to be anything, nor do they regard its [30] features as real, but they put them aside like a dream in the night and understand the father's knowledge to be the dawn. This is how each person acts while in ignorance, as if asleep, and this is how a person comes to knowledge, as if awakened. Good for one who comes to himself and awakens. And blessings on one who has opened the eyes of the blind.[20]

The spirit came to this person in haste when the person awakened. Having given its hand to the one lying prone on the ground, the spirit placed him firmly on his feet, for he had not yet risen.

The Beloved Son Reveals What Is New

Knowledge of the father and the revelation of his son gave them the means of knowing. For when they saw and heard him, he let them taste him and smell him and touch the beloved son. He appeared, informing them of the father, the illimitable, and he inspired them with what is in the father's thought, doing his will. Many received the light and turned [31] to him. But material people were strangers to him and did not discern his appearance or recognize him. For he came in the likeness of flesh, and nothing blocked his way, for incorruptibility cannot be grasped. Moreover, while saying new things and speaking about what is in the father's heart, he produced the faultless word. Light spoke through his mouth and his voice brought forth life. He gave them thought and understanding and mercy and salvation and the spirit of strength from the father's infinity and sweetness. He made punishments and afflictions cease, for they caused those in need of mercy to stray from him in error and bondage. He destroyed them with might and confounded them with knowledge.

> *He became a way for those who strayed,*
> *knowledge for those who were ignorant,*
> *discovery for those who sought,*
> *support for those who tremble,*
> *purity for those who were defiled.*[21]

Parables of Sheep

He is the shepherd who left behind the ninety-nine [32] sheep that had not strayed and went in search of the one that was lost.[22] He rejoiced when he found it. For ninety-nine is a number expressed with the left hand, but when another one is found, the numerical sum is transferred to the right hand. In this way what needs one more—that is, the whole right hand—attracts what it needs, takes it from the left and brings it to the right, and so the number becomes one hundred.[23] This is the meaning of the pronunciation of these numbers.

The father is like that. He labored even on the sabbath for the sheep that he found fallen into the pit. He saved the life of the sheep and brought it up from the pit.[24]

Understand the inner meaning, for you are children of inner meaning. What is the sabbath? It is a day on which salvation should not be idle. Speak of the heavenly day that has no night and of the light[25] that does not set because it is perfect. Speak from the heart, for you are the perfect day and within you dwells the light that does not fail. Speak of truth with those who seek it and of knowledge with those who have sinned in their error. [33]

Do the Father's Will

Steady the feet of those who stumble and extend your hands to the sick. Feed the hungry and give rest to the weary. Awaken those who wish to arise and rouse those who sleep, for you embody vigorous understanding. If what is strong acts like this, it becomes even stronger.

Focus your attention upon yourselves. Do not focus your attention upon other things—that is, what you have cast away from yourselves. Do not return to eat what you have vomited. Do not be moth-eaten, do not be worm-eaten, for you have already gotten rid of that. Do not be a place for the devil, for you have already destroyed him. Do not strengthen what stands in your way, what is collapsing, to support it. One who is lawless is nothing. Treat the lawless one more harshly than the just one, for the lawless does what he does because he is lawless, but the just does what he does with people because he is righteous. Do the father's will, then, for you are from him.

The Sweetness of the Father

For the father is sweet, and goodness is in his will. He knows what is yours, in which you find rest. By the fruit one knows what is yours.[26] For the father's children [34] are his fragrance; they are from the beauty of his face. The father loves his fragrance and disperses it everywhere, and when it mixes with matter, it gives his fragrance to the light. Through his quietness he makes his fragrance superior in every way to every sound. For it is not ears that smell the fragrance, but it is the spirit[27] that possesses the sense of smell, draws the fragrance to itself, and immerses itself in the father's fragrance. Thus the spirit cares for it and takes it to where it came from, the original fragrance, which has grown cold in psychical form.[28] It is like cold water that has sunk into soft soil, and those who see it think there is only soil. Later the water evaporates when the wind draws it up, and it becomes warm. So cold fragrances are from division.

For this reason faith came, did away with division, and brought the warm fullness of love, so that what is cold may not return, but the unity of perfect thought may prevail.

The Father Restores Fullness

This <is> the word of the gospel about the discovery of fullness, for those who await [35] salvation coming from above. Their hope, for which they are waiting, is in waiting, and this is their image, the light in which there is no shadow. At this time the fullness is about to come. Deficiency of matter is not from the infinity of the father, who came to give time to deficiency. In fact, it is not right to say that the incorruptible would actually come in this manner. The father's depth is profound, and the thought of error is not with him. It is something that has fallen, and something that can readily be set upright through the discovery of the one who has come to what he would restore.

This restoration is called repentance. The reason that the incorruptible breathed out and followed after the one who sinned was so that the sinner might find rest. Forgiveness is what remains for the light in deficiency, the word of fullness. For a doctor rushes to where there is sickness, since that is the doctor's wish. The person in need does not hide it, because the doctor has what the patient needs. Thus fullness, which has no deficiency but fills up deficiency, [36] is provided to fill a person's need, so that the person may receive grace. While deficient, the person had no grace, and because of this a diminishing took place where there was no grace. When the diminished part was restored, the person in need was revealed as fullness. This is what it means to discover the light of truth that has shone toward a person: it is unchangeable.

Because of the coming of Christ[29] it was said openly, "Seek, and the troubled will be restored, and he will anoint them with ointment." The ointment is the mercy of the father, who will have mercy on them, and those anointed are the perfect. For filled jars are usually sealed with wax. But when the seal of a jar is broken, it may leak, and the cause of its defect is the lack of a seal. For then a breath of wind and the power that it has can make it evaporate. But on the jar that is without defect the seal is not broken, nor does it leak, and the perfect father fills again what it lacks.

The Father Knows His Plants in Paradise

The father is good. He knows his plants because he planted them in his paradise. And his paradise is his place of rest. Paradise [37] is the perfection within the father's thought, and the plants are the words of his meditation. Each of his words is the product of his will and the revelation of his speech. Since they were the depth of his thought, the word that came forth caused them to appear, along with mind that speaks the word, and silent grace. It[30] was called thought, because they dwelled in silent grace[31] before being revealed. So it happened that the word came forth when it was pleasing to the will of him who willed it.

The father is at rest in will. Nothing happens without the father's pleasure, nothing happens without the father's will. And his will is incomprehensible. His will is his footprint, but none can understand him, nor does he exist so that they might study him[32] in order to grasp him. Rather, when he wills, what he wills is this, even if the view does not please people before God: it is the father's will. For the father knows the beginning and the end of all, and at their end he will greet them. The end is the recognition of him who is hidden, and he is the father, [38] from whom the beginning has come and to whom all will return who have come from him. They have appeared for the glory and joy of his name.

The Father's Name Is Revealed

The name of the father is the son. In the beginning he gave a name to the one who came from him, while he remained the same, and he conceived him as a son. He gave him his name, which belonged to him. All that exists with the father belongs to him. He has the name; he has the son. The son can be seen, but the name is invisible, for it alone is the mystery of the invisible, which comes to ears completely filled with it, through the father's agency. Yet the father's name is not pronounced; it is revealed through a son, and the name is great.

Who then can utter his name, the great name, except him alone to whom the name belongs, and the children of the name, on whom the father's name rests, and who themselves rest on his name? Since the father has no beginning, he alone conceived it for himself as a name before he created the eternal realms, that the father's name might be supreme over them. This is the [39] true name, which is confirmed by his authority in perfect power. This name does not derive from ordinary words or name-giving, for it is invisible.

The father alone gave the son a name, because he alone saw him and he alone could name him. One who does not exist has no name, for what name would someone give to one who does not exist? One who exists exists with his name. He alone knows it, and to him alone the father has given a name.[33] This is the father, and his name is the son. He did not hide it within, but it was in existence, and the son himself disclosed the name. The name, then, belongs to the father, just as the father's name is the beloved son. Otherwise where would he find a name except from the father?

But someone may say to an acquaintance, "Who could give a name to someone who existed before himself? Do not children receive their names [40] from their parents?" First, we should consider this point: what is a name? This is the true name, the name from the father, and this is the proper name. The father[34] did not receive the name on loan, as is the case with others, who receive names that are made up. This is the proper name, and there is no one else who gave it to him. He is unnameable, indescribable, until the time when the perfect one[35] spoke of him, for the perfect one alone is able to pronounce his name and see him.

When it was pleasing to the father that his son should be his pronounced name, and when he who came from the depth[36] disclosed this name, he divulged what was hidden, for he knew that the father is free of evil. That is why the father brought him forth, so that he might speak about the place from which he had come and his place of rest, [41] and that he might glorify the fullness, the majesty of his name, and the father's sweetness.

The Place of Rest

All will speak individually about where they have come from and how they were established in the place of rest. They will hasten to return and receive from that place, the place where they stood once before, and they will taste of that place, be nourished, and grow.

Their own place of rest is their fullness. All the emanations from the father are fullnesses, and all his emanations find their root in the one who caused them all to grow from himself. He assigned their destinies. They all appear so that through their own thought [they might be perfected].[37] For the place to which they extend their thought is their root, which lifts them up through all the heights to the father.

They embrace his head, which is rest for them, and they hold him close so that, in a manner of speaking, they have caressed his face with kisses. But they do not make [42] this obvious. For they neither exalt themselves nor diminish the father's glory. And they do not think of the father as insignificant or bitter or angry, but as free of evil, unperturbed, sweet, knowing all the heavenly places before they came into being, and having no need of instruction.

Such are those who possess something of this immeasurable majesty from above, as they await that unique and perfect One who is a mother to them.[38] And they do not go down to the underworld, nor do they have envy or groaning, nor is death with them. They rest in one who rests, and they are not weary or confused about truth.

They are truth. The father is in them and they are in the father, perfect, inseparable from him who is truly good. They lack nothing at all but are at rest, fresh in spirit. They will hearken to their root and be involved with concerns in which they may find their root and do no harm to their souls.

Such is the place of the blessed, such is their place. As for the others, let them know, in their own places, that I should not [43] say more, for I have been in the place of rest. There I shall dwell, to devote myself, constantly, to the father of all and the true brothers and sisters,[39] upon whom the father's love is lavished, and in whose midst nothing of him is lacking. They appear in truth, dwelling in true and eternal life, and they speak of the perfect light filled with the father's seed, which is in his heart and in the fullness. His spirit rejoices in this and glorifies him in whom it was. For the father is good, and his children are perfect and worthy of his name. Children like this the father loves.

PART FIVE

The Holy Book
of the Great
Invisible Spirit

or

The Egyptian Gospel

THE HOLY BOOK of the Great Invisible Spirit, or the Egyptian Gospel, is a Sethian baptismal handbook that features a baptismal ceremony introduced by an account of the origin of the universe, in Sethian cosmological terms. According to the conclusion to the Holy Book of the Great Invisible Spirit, the handbook was composed by great Seth—that is, heavenly Seth—and deposited high in the mountains. It may be that the text means to imply that the Holy Book was left in the mountains inscribed on steles, as is also suggested in two other Nag Hammadi texts, the Three Steles of Seth and the Discourse on the Eighth and Ninth. These accounts in turn are reminiscent of the story of the Jewish historian Josephus, who tells how the descendants of Seth preserved the wisdom of Adam, Eve, and Seth on two steles of brick and stone, so that their insights would be preserved in all circumstances, through fire or flood. In a copyist's note at the very end of the Holy Book of the Great Invisible Spirit, the name of the scribe is also given: Gongessos, in Latin Concessus, with the spiritual nickname Eugnostos, meaning "well versed in knowledge." The same spiritual name is given as the title of another Nag Hammadi text, Eugnostos, in this case Eugnostos the Blessed (NHC III,3 and V,1).

The cosmological introduction to the Holy Book of the Great Invisible Spirit opens with an affirmation of the transcendent one, the great invisible spirit, parent and father of all. The account describing the great invisible spirit is replete with glorious names and descriptions, and terms are used, especially terms of negation, to magnify the ineffability of the great invisible spirit. From the great invisible spirit come three powers—father, mother, and child—and from these three come more beings of light. The realm of Doxomedon, or Domedon Doxomedon, appears, "the eternal realm of eternal realms, with thrones in it, powers around it, and glories and incorruptions" (III, 43), and in rapid succession Yoel, Christ the anointed, Esephech, and the human Adamas and great Seth come forth, along with a bewildering array of luminaries and glorious entities. When the word is expressed, so says the text, "humankind came into being through the word" (III, 49). Eventually the whole world is made, through Sophia, the great demon Nebrouel, and Sakla the fool, the arrogant world ruler. The world is not a congenial place for the descendants of Seth, but in spite of the hostility of the authority figures of this world, the seed of Seth survives the vicissitudes of history—flood, conflagration, judgment—and great Seth acts to save the holy people. The whole career of Seth is narrated in the text, so that the Holy Book of the Great Invisible Spirit could be considered the good news of Seth.

Against this cosmological background, the Holy Book of the Great Invisible Spirit describes a baptismal ceremony that includes an ecstatic baptismal hymn. It is claimed that Seth himself has instituted baptism and the baptismal ceremony, and that Seth has become clothed with or incarnate in "the living Jesus." Jesus is the manifestation of Seth. The baptismal ceremony is celebrated in the company of a multitude of heavenly glories, and the hymn itself incorporates exalted names, chanted vowels, exquisite epithets, glossolalia, and words of praise and power. The Sethian baptismal ceremony is also mentioned at the conclusion of the Secret Book of John, where the text portrays Jesus raising and sealing a person "in luminous water with five seals" (II, 310). Here, in the Holy Book of the Great Invisible Spirit, the one who is undergoing baptism and is singing the hymn states that he or she is assuming the name of Jesus and is uniting with Jesus:

> *This great name of yours is upon me,*
> *you who lack nothing,*
> *you self-conceived one,*
> *who are close to me.*
> *I see you,*
> *you who are invisible to all.*
> *Who can comprehend you?*

In another voice:

> *Having known you,*
> *I have now mingled with your constancy.*
> *I have armed myself with the armor of light.*
> *I have become bright.*
> *The mother was there for the lovely beauty of grace.*
> *So I have stretched out my two hands.*
> *I have been formed in the circle of the riches of light in my breast,*
> *giving form to the many beings*
> *produced in light beyond reproach.*
> *In truth I shall declare your glory,*
> *I have comprehended you:*
> *yours, Jesus;*
> *look,*
> *forever $\bar{O}$*

forever E
O Jesus
O eternal realm, eternal realm,
God of silence,
I honor you completely. (III, 66–67)

Questions remain about the Sethian baptismal ceremony. How was it performed? How often? To what extent was it spiritualized? Whatever it might have been, such baptism was a transforming experience.

The Holy Book of the Great Invisible Spirit is found in two Coptic versions in the Nag Hammadi library, as tractate 2 in Codex III and tractate 2 in Codex IV. Like other texts in the Nag Hammadi library, the Holy Book of the Great Invisible Spirit was composed in Greek. The circumstances of composition are unknown.

For further reading: Alexander Böhlig and Frederik Wisse, eds., *Nag Hammadi Codices III,2 and IV,2;* Bentley Layton, *The Gnostic Scriptures,* 101–20; Uwe-Karsten Plisch, "Das heilige Buch des großen unsichtbaren Geistes"; John D. Turner, *Sethian Gnosticism and the Platonic Tradition.*

The Holy Book of
the Great Invisible Spirit

or

The Egyptian Gospel[1]

(NHC III,2; IV,2)

The holy book of the . . . great invisible [spirit],[2]
the parent, the father[3] whose name cannot be named,
who came from the heights of fullness,
light of light of the realms of light,
light of the silence[4] of forethought
and the father of silence,
light of word and truth,
light of the [41] incorruptions,
infinite light,
radiance from the realms of light
of the unrevealed, undisclosed,
unaging, unannounced father,
eternal realm of eternal realms,
self-conceived,[5] self-conceiving,
self-producing, foreign,
truly true eternal realm.

Three Heavenly Powers Come from
the Great Invisible Spirit

Three powers came forth from the great invisible spirit: the father, the mother, and the child.[6] They came from the living silence of the incorruptible father, from the silence of the unknown father.

The realm of Domedon Doxomedon[7] came from it, the eternal realm of eternal realms and the light of each of their powers.

The child appeared fourth, the mother [fifth], the father sixth.[8] The great invisible spirit was . . . unrecognized, undisclosed among all the powers, glories, and incorruptions.

So from the great invisible spirit came three powers, [42] three realms of eight that the father conceives from within,[9] in silence, with forethought: the father, the mother, and the child.

THE FATHER

The first realm of eight,[10] for whose sake the child that is three times male came forth:

    thought
    word
    incorruptibility
    [life] eternal
    will
    mind
    foreknowledge
    the androgynous father

THE MOTHER

The second power or realm of eight:

> the mother
>
> the virgin Barbelo[11]
>
> Epititioch . . . ai
>
> Memeneaimen . . . , who is over heaven
>
> Karb . . . [12]
>
> Adonai[13]
>
> . . . , the inexplicable power
>
> the ineffable mother[14]

She shone and appeared, and she took pleasure in the father of the silent silence.

THE CHILD

The third power or realm of eight:

> the child
>
> of the silent silence,
>
> the crown
>
> of the silent silence,
>
> the glory
>
> of the father,
>
> the virtue
>
> of the [43] mother.

From within, the child produces seven powers of great light, which are the seven vowels,[15] and the word completes them.

These are the three powers or three realms of eight that the father conceived from within through forethought. The father conceived them there.

The Realm of Doxomedon

Domedon Doxomedon appeared, the eternal realm of eternal realms, with thrones in it, powers around it, and glories and incorruptions. The father of the great light [who came] forth in silence is [the great] realm of Doxomedon, in which [the triple] male[16] child rests. The throne of its glory was established in it, and the undisclosed name [is inscribed] on it, on the tablet, . . . the word, the father of the light of all, who came from silence and rests in silence, whose [44] name is in an invisible symbol. A hidden, [invisible] mystery came forth:

IIIIIIIIIIIIIIIIIIIII

EEEEEEEEEEEEEEEEEEEEEEE

OOOOOOOOOOOOOOOOOOOOOOO

YYYYYYYYYYYYYYYYYYYYYYY

EEEEEEEEEEEEEEEEEEEEEEE

AAAAAAAAAAAAAAAAAAAAAAA

ŌŌŌŌŌŌŌŌŌŌŌŌŌŌŌŌŌŌŌŌŌŌŌ [17]

And so the three powers offered praise to the great invisible unnameable ineffable virgin spirit, and the male virgin.

Yoel, Christ, Esephech

They asked for power.[18] A silence of living silence appeared, glories and incorruptions in the eternal realms, . . . realms, myriads in addition, . . . triple male beings, [triple] male offspring, [male] generations, [glories of the father], glories of the great [Christ and the] male offspring. The [generations][19] filled the great realm of Doxomedon with the power of the word of all the [fullness].

The triple male [child, the great] Christ, whom the [great] invisible spirit had anointed and whose power [is called] Ainon,[20] offered praise to the great invisible spirit and the male virgin Yoel, [and] the silence of silent silence, and the majesty [55][21] . . . , ineffable . . . , unspeakable . . . , unanswered, uninterpreted, the first to [appear], unannounced, . . . , [56] wonderful . . . , unspeakable . . . , who has all the majesties of majesty of the silence of silence there. The triple [male child] offered praise and asked for power from the [great invisible virgin] spirit.

There appeared in that place . . . [who] beholds [glories] . . . treasures . . . [invisible] mysteries . . . of silence . . . [the male] virgin [Youel].

[The child of the] child Esephech [appeared].

[So] it was completed:

    the [father]

    the mother

    the child

    the five seals[22]

    the invincible power

who is the great [Christ] of all those who are incorruptible . . . .
[57] holy . . . the end . . . incorruptible . . . are powers, [glories],
and incorruptions . . . came forth . . . . This one offered [praise]
to the undisclosed hidden [mystery] . . . hidden . . . in . . . the eternal realms . . . thrones, . . . and each one . . . myriads of [powers]
without number around [them, [58] glories] and incorruptions . . .
and they . . . the father, the mother, and the child, and all [the full-
ness], already [mentioned, and the] five seals, [and the mystery] of
[mysteries]. They [appeared . . . who] is [over] . . . and the eternal
realms, in truth, truly, . . . eternal . . . and the [eternal] realms, forever in truth, truly.

Divine Emanation

[An emanation[23] appeared in silence], with the [living] silence of
the spirit, the father's word, and light. [She . . . the five] [59] seals,
which the [father conceived] from within, and she passed [through]
all the eternal realms, already mentioned. She established glorious
thrones [and myriads] of angels [without] number around them,
[powers and incorruptible] glories, and they all [sang songs], gave
glory, and offered praise with [one voice], with one accord, [with a
sound] that is never silent . . . to

the father,
the [mother],
the child . . . ,
[all the] fullnesses, [already] mentioned,
that is, [the great] Christ,
who came from [silence],
who is the [incorruptible] child,

Telmael Telmachael [Eli Eli] Machar Machar [Seth],
the power that truly lives,
[and the] male [virgin] with [him], Youel,
and Esephech, master of glory and [child] of the child,
and the [crown of] its glory,
. . . of the five seals,
the fullness, [already mentioned]. [60]

The Word

The great living self-conceived [word appeared, the] true [God],
the unborn nature, whose name I utter by saying,

> . . . *AIA . . . THAŌTHŌSTH . . . ,*
> *child of the [great] Christ,*
> *child of ineffable silence,*
> *[who] came from the great [invisible] incorruptible [spirit].*

The [child] of silence appeared with [silence . . . invisible . . . hidden . . . and the] treasures of its glory. It appeared in the visible . . . and [established] four [eternal realms]. Through the word it established them.

The word offered [praise] to the great invisible virgin spirit, [the silence] of the [father], in silence of the living silence of [silence], where humankind rests . . . .

Mirothea and Adamas

Then there came forth from [49][24] that place the cloud of great light, living power, the mother of the holy incorruptible ones, the

great power Mirothea.[25] She gave birth to the being whose name I
utter by saying,

> [You are one],
> you are one,
> you are one,
> EA EA EA.[26]

This is Adamas, light that has radiated [from light], the eye of
the [light], the first human being,[27] through whom and to whom
is everything, without whom is nothing.[28] The unknowable, incomprehensible father came forth and descended from above to
undo the deficiency.

The great divine self-conceived word and the incorruptible
human Adamas joined with each other, and a human power of the
word was produced. So humankind came into being through the
word.

This human power of the word offered praise to

the great invisible incomprehensible virgin spirit

the male virgin [Barbelo][29]

the triple male child [50]

the male [virgin] Youel

Esephech, master of glory and child of the child

the crown of its glory

the great realm of Doxomedon

the thrones in it

the powers around it

glories, incorruptions, and all their fullness, already
  mentioned

the ethereal earth, receiving God

where holy people of the great light take shape

people of the father of the silent living silence

the father and all their fullness, already mentioned

Four Eternal Realms, Seth, Four Luminaries

The great divine self-conceived word and the incorruptible human Adamas offered praise. They requested power and eternal strength for the one self-conceived, so that four eternal realms may be fully completed and through them there may appear [51] the glory and power of the invisible father of the holy people of the great light coming into the world. The world resembles the night.

Then the incorruptible human Adamas requested that a child come from himself, so that the child may be father of the immovable incorruptible generation, and through this generation silence and speech may appear and through it the dead realm may rise and then fade away.

So the power of the great light came from above. She was revelation,[30] and she gave birth to four great luminaries,[31]

Harmozel

Oroiael

Daveithe

Eleleth

along with great incorruptible Seth, son of the incorruptible human Adamas.

And so was completed the perfect realm of seven, which exists in hidden mysteries. [52] When it receives [glory], it becomes eleven realms of eight.

Partners and Attendants for the Luminaries

The father nodded approval, and the whole fullness of the luminaries agreed. Partners for the luminaries appeared to complete the realm of eight of the self-conceived God:

> grace, for the first luminary Harmozel
>
> perception, for the second luminary Oroiael
>
> intelligence, for the third luminary Daveithe
>
> understanding, for the fourth luminary Eleleth

This is the first realm of eight of the self-conceived God.

The father nodded approval, and the whole fullness of the luminaries agreed. The attendants appeared:

> first, great Gamaliel, for the first great luminary Harmozel
>
> great Gabriel, for the second great luminary Oroiael
>
> great Samblo,[32] for the great luminary Daveithe
>
> great Abrasax,[33] for [53] [the great luminary] Eleleth

Partners for the attendants appeared by the will and good pleasure of the father:

> memory, for the first, great Gamaliel
>
> love, for the second, great Gabriel

peace, for the third, great Samblo

life eternal, for the fourth, great Abrasax

Thus were the five realms of eight completed, forty in all, as inexplicable power.

The great self-conceived word and the expression of the fullness of the four luminaries offered praise to

the great invisible unnameable virgin spirit

the male virgin

the great realm of Doxomedon

the thrones in them

the powers around them

glories, authorities, and powers

the triple male child

the male virgin Youel

Esephech, [54] master of glory and [child] of the child

the crown of its glory

all the fullness

all the glories that are there

the infinite fullnesses and the unnameable realms

that they may call upon the father as the fourth,[34] along with the incorruptible generation, and call the seed[35] of the father the seed of great Seth.

The Luminaries Are Enthroned

Then everything shook, and the incorruptible ones trembled. The triple male child[36] came down from above to those unborn and self-conceived, and to those conceived in the realm of birth. The majesty appeared, all the majesty of the great Christ, and established thrones of glory, myriads without number, in the four realms around them, myriads without number, powers, glories, [55] and incorruptions. They came forth in this way.

The incorruptible spiritual assembly[37] expanded within the four luminaries of the great living self-conceived God of truth. They praised, sang, and gave glory with one voice, with one accord, with a mouth that is not silent, to

> the father,
> the mother,
> the child,
> and all their fullness, already mentioned.
> The five seals of the myriads,
> the rulers over the realms,
> and the couriers of the glory of the governors
> were ordered to appear to those who are worthy.
> Amen.

The Seed of Great Seth

Great Seth, son of the incorruptible human Adamas, offered praise to

> the great invisible unnameable unspeakable virgin spirit
> the male virgin

the triple male child

the male[38] virgin Youel

Esephech, master of glory

the crown of its glory and child of the child [56]

the great realms of Doxomedon

and the fullness, already mentioned

Seth asked for his seed.
Then Plesithea[39] came from that place,

the great power of great light

mother of the angels

mother of the luminaries

glorious mother

virgin with four breasts

bearing fruit from the wellspring of Gomorrah and Sodom

fruit of the wellspring of Gomorrah within her[40]

Plesithea came forth through great Seth.

Great Seth rejoiced over the gift given him by the incorruptible child. He took his seed from the virgin Plesithea with the four breasts and established it with him[41] in the four realms,[42] in the third great luminary Daveithe.

Sophia of Matter, Sakla, Nebrouel, and Angels

Five thousand years later the great luminary Eleleth said, "Let someone reign over chaos and Hades."

A cloud [57] [named] Sophia of matter appeared . . . . [She] surveyed the regions [of chaos], and her face looked like . . . in her appearance . . . blood.

[The great] angel Gamaliel spoke [to great Gabriel], the attendant of [the great luminary] Oroiael, and [said, "Let an] angel appear to reign over chaos [and Hades]."

The cloud of wisdom [agreed and produced] two individuals[43] . . . a little light . . . [the angel] she had established in the cloud [above].

Sakla[44] the great [angel observed] Nebrouel the great demon[45] who is with him. [Together] they brought a spirit of reproduction to the earth, and [they produced] angelic assistants.

Sakla [said] to Nebrouel the great [demon], "Let twelve realms come into being in [the] . . . realm, worlds . . . ."

Through the will of the one self-conceived, [Sakla] the great angel said, [58] "There shall be . . . seven in number . . . ."

He said to the [great angels], "Go, [each] of you reign over your own [world]." And each [of these] twelve [angels] left.

> [The first] angel is Athoth, whom [the great] generations of people call . . .
>
> the second is Harmas, [the eye of fire]
>
> the third [is Galila]
>
> the fourth is Yobel
>
> [the fifth is] Adonaios, who is [called] Sabaoth[46]
>
> the sixth [is Cain, whom] the [great generations of] people call the sun
>
> the [seventh is Abel]
>
> the eighth, Akiressina

the [ninth, Youbel]

the tenth is Harmoupiael

the eleventh is Archir-Adonin

the twelfth [is Belias][47]

These are set over Hades [and chaos].

The Arrogance of Sakla, the Coming of Repentance

After [the world] was founded, Sakla said to his [angels], "I am a [jealous] god, and nothing has [come into being] apart from me."[48] [He] [59] felt certain of his nature.

A voice called from on high and said, "Humankind[49] exists, and the child of humankind."[50]

The first modeled creature was formed from the descent of the image above. The image resembles its voice on high, the voice of the image. The image gazed out, and from the gaze of the image above, the first creature was formed. And for the sake of this creature repentance[51] came to be.

Repentance was completed and empowered through the will and good pleasure of the father. The father approved of the great incorruptible immovable generation of great mighty people of great Seth, so that he might sow repentance in the realms that had been produced, and through repentance the deficiency might become full. For repentance came down from above to the world, which resembles the night. When she came, she prayed for the seed of the ruler of this realm and the authorities derived from him, which is the defiled seed from the god who produces demons and who is destined to be destroyed, and she prayed for the seed [60] of Adam and great Seth, which is like the sun.

Hormos and the Seed of Seth

Then the great angel Hormos[52] came to prepare the seed of great Seth, through the holy spirit, in a holy body[53] conceived by the word, by means of virgins of the defiled sowing of seed in this realm.[54]

Great Seth came with his seed, and he sowed it in the realms brought into being here below, whose number is the number of Sodom. Some say Sodom is the pastureland of great Seth—that is, Gomorrah. But others say great Seth took his crop from Gomorrah and planted it in a second location, which he named Sodom.

This is the generation that appeared through Edokla. For by the word she gave birth to truth and justice. This is the source of the seed of life eternal, which belongs to those who endure through knowledge[55] of where they came from. This is the great incorruptible generation that has come through three [61] worlds into this world.

Flood, Fire, Plagues, Famines, Temptations

The flood has come to indicate the end of the age, and it will be sent into the world. Because of this generation a conflagration will come upon the earth, but to those who belong to this generation grace will be granted through prophets and guardians who protect the life of this generation. Because of this generation there will be famines and plagues, which will take place because of this great incorruptible generation. Because of this generation there will be temptations, and deception by false prophets.

Great Seth saw what the devil[56] was doing, his many guises, his schemes against the incorruptible immovable generation, the persecutions by his powers and angels, their deception. They acted rashly against themselves.

Great Seth offered praise to

the great unnameable virgin spirit

the male [62] virgin Barbelo[57]

the triple male child Telmael Telmael Heli Heli Machar Machar Seth

the power that truly lives in truth

the male virgin Youel

Esephech, master of glory

the crown of its glory

the great realm of Doxomedon

the thrones in it

the powers around them

all the fullness, already mentioned

Guardian Angels and Incarnations of Seth

Seth requested guardians for his seed. Four hundred ethereal angels came from the great realms, accompanied by great Aerosiel and great Selmechel,[58] to protect the great incorruptible generation, its fruitfulness, and the great people of great Seth, from the time and era of truth and justice until the end of the age and its rulers, whom the great judges condemned to death.

Great Seth was sent by the four luminaries, according to the will of the one self-conceived [63] and all the fullness, through the gift and good pleasure of the great invisible spirit, the five seals, and all the fullness.

Seth went through three advents, already mentioned: flood, conflagration, and judgment of the rulers, powers, and authorities. He did this to save the generation that went astray,

> by means of the destruction[59] of the world,
> and baptism through a body conceived by the word,
> which great Seth prepared for himself,
> mystically, through the virgin,
> that the holy people may be conceived by the holy spirit,
> through invisible secret symbols,
> through the destruction of world against world,[60]
> through the renunciation of the world
> and the god of the thirteen realms,[61]
> and the appeals of the holy ineffable incorruptible ones,
> in the heart and great light of the father,
> which preexists in his forethought.

Seth Establishes Baptism through Jesus

Through forethought Seth has instituted the holy baptism that surpasses heaven, by means of the incorruptible one, [64] conceived by the word, the living Jesus,[62] with whom great Seth has been clothed. He has nailed down the powers of the thirteen realms.[63] Through this means[64] he has established those who are brought in and go out,[65] and he has equipped them with armor of the knowledge of truth, with incorruptible, invincible power.

There appeared to them

the great attendant Yesseus Mazareus Yessedekeus,[66] the
    living water

the great commanders, Jacob the great, Theopemptos,
    Isaouel

one stationed over grace, Mep . . . el[67]

those stationed over the wellspring of truth, Micheus,
    Michar, Mnesinous

one stationed over the baptism of the living, and the
    purifiers, Sesengenbarpharanges[68]

those stationed over the gates of the waters, Micheus and
    Michar

those stationed over the height, Seldao and Elainos

those receiving the great generation

the incorruptible mighty people of great Seth

the attendants of the four luminaries

great Gamaliel, great Gabriel, great Samblo, great [65]
    Abrasax

those stationed over sunrise, Olses, Hypneus,[69]
    Heurumaious

those stationed over the entrance into the state of rest of
    life eternal

the governors[70] Mixanther and Michanor

the guardians of chosen souls,[71] Akramas and
    Strempouchos

the great power Heli Heli Machar Machar Seth[72]

the great invisible unnameable unspeakable virgin spirit, and
silence

the great luminary Harmozel, where the living self-
conceived God of truth is

with whom is the incorruptible human Adamas

the second luminary Oroiael, where great Seth and Jesus are

Jesus who has life

and who has come and crucified what is under the law[73]

the third luminary Daveithe, where the children of great
Seth are

the fourth luminary Eleleth, where the souls of the children
are at rest

fifth, Yoel, stationed over the name of the one who will be
ordained to baptize

with the holy incorruptible baptism that surpasses heaven

From now on, [66] through the incorruptible human Poimael,[74]
with regard to those worthy of the invocation and words of re-
nunciation of the five seals in the baptism of running water,[75] they
will know those who receive them, as they are instructed, and they
will be known by them, and they shall not taste death.[76]

Baptismal Hymn

Yesseus[77]
ĒŌ OU ĒŌ ŌUA
in truth truly

Yesseus Mazareus Yessedekeus
living water
child of the child
glorious name
in truth truly
eternal being
IIII
ĒĒĒĒ
EEEE
OOOO
YYYY
ŌŌŌŌ
AAAA
in truth truly
ĒI AAAA ŌŌŌŌ [78]
being who sees the eternal realms
in truth truly
A
EE
ĒĒĒ
IIII
YYYYYY
ŌŌŌŌŌŌŌŌ [79]
being who exists forever
in truth truly
IĒA AIŌ [80]
in the heart
being who exists
U [81]

forever and ever
you are what you are
you are who you are.[82]

This great name of yours is upon me,
you who lack nothing
you self-conceived one,
who are close to me.
I see you,
you who are invisible to all.
Who can comprehend you?

In another voice:[83] [67]

Having known you,
I have now mingled with your constancy.
I have armed myself with the armor of light.
I have become bright.
The mother was there for the lovely beauty of grace.
So I have stretched out my two hands.
I have been formed in the circle of the riches of light in my breast,
giving form to the many beings
produced in light beyond reproach.
In truth I shall declare your glory,
I have comprehended you:
yours,[84] *Jesus;*
look,
forever $\bar{O}$
forever E[85]
O Jesus
O eternal realm, eternal realm,

God of silence,
I honor you completely.
You are my place of rest,
child,
Ē͞S Ē͞S [86]
the E
formless one existing among formless ones,
raising the person by whom you will purify me into your life,
according to your imperishable name.
So the sweet smell of life is within me.
I have mixed it with water as a model for all the rulers,
that I may live with you in the peace of the saints,
you who exist forever,
in truth truly. [68]

Conclusion

This is the book great Seth composed and placed high in mountains on which the sun has not risen and cannot rise. Since the days of the prophets, apostles, and preachers, the name has never risen in their hearts and cannot rise in their hearts, and their ears have not heard it.

Great Seth wrote this book letter by letter in a period of 130 years. He placed it on the mountain called Charaxio, so that, at the end of the times and ages, according to the wish of the self-conceived God and the entire fullness, through the gift of the unsearchable inconceivable fatherly will, he[87] may come forth and appear to this holy incorruptible generation of the great savior and those dwelling with them in love, and the great invisible eternal spirit and its only child, and eternal light, [69] and its great incorruptible partner, and incorruptible Sophia, and Barbelo, and all the fullness, in eternity. Amen.

Copyist's Note

The Egyptian Gospel, a holy secret book, written by God. Grace, intelligence, perception, and understanding be with the copyist, Eugnostos the beloved in the spirit—my worldly name is Gongessos[88]—and my fellow luminaries in incorruptibility. Jesus Christ, son of God, savior, ICHTHYS![89] The Holy Book of the Great Invisible Spirit is written by God. Amen.

The Holy Book of the Great Invisible Spirit.
Amen.

PART SIX

The Secret Book
of John

THE SECRET BOOK OF JOHN, or the Apocryphon of John, is a classic Sethian gnostic account of the origin, fall, and salvation of the world and the people in the world. Four copies of the text have survived, three in the Nag Hammadi library and one in Berlin Gnostic Codex 8502, and the account of Irenaeus of Lyon on the Barbelognostics closely resembles passages in the early part of the Secret Book of John.

In its present form the Secret Book of John is a Christian document with Jesus as the revealer of cosmological and soteriological knowledge, but the Secret Book of John seems to be based on an earlier Jewish text that addressed the problem of evil and vindicated the goodness of God by interpreting the opening chapters of Genesis and other passages in the Jewish scriptures in an innovative manner and with a Greek philosophical and mythological flair. The recipient of the revelation of Jesus is John the son of Zebedee, and thus the Secret Book of John stands in the Johannine tradition. Karen King has proposed that the Sethian gnostics may have considered the Secret Book of John to be the second part of the Gospel of John.

The account of the Secret Book of John is the story of the unfolding of the divine mind and the implications for human life. In the beginning, Jesus says in the text, there is the One, the invisible virgin spirit, the parent and father of all. The transcendent nature of the One is depicted in a carefully articulated statement of negative theology:

> *The One is not corporeal and it is not incorporeal.*
> *The One is not large and it is not small.*
> *It is impossible to say,*
> *How much is it?*
> *What [kind is it]?*
> *For no one can understand it. (II, 3)*

The invisible spirit is the divine mind, and, with an apparent mythological allusion to Narcissus, Jesus describes the divine mind falling in love with its own image in the spiritual water and producing a thought, forethought, called Barbelo. From the parent of all and forethought come a host of spiritual beings and mental attributes that constitute the fullness (*plērōma*) of divinity, but through a lapse in wisdom, Sophia, some of the brilliance of the divine realm is lost. The child of Sophia, the creator or demiurge, who is named Yaldabaoth, or Sakla, or Samael, fashions a world of mortality that snares human beings, and the seed of Seth, who have some of the light and life of the divine within, are victimized by the ignorance and megalomania of Yaldabaoth and his partners in crime.

The story of the Secret Book of John has a happy ending, however. The divine attends to the human situation, and forethought, insight (*epinoia*), and even Jesus (probably as a manifestation of Seth or of forethought) come to the aid of humankind. Human beings, who have become forgetful of divinity and have fallen under the shadow of death, are called to remember where they came from and who they are. Insight returns to people. As the Secret Book of John puts it, all this takes place "so that when the spirit descends from the holy realms, it may raise up the seed and heal what it lacks, that the entire realm of fullness may be holy and lack nothing" (II, 25). In this way God saves and is saved, when the light and life of God in people is saved, and with God all those called the seed of Seth, who participate in the light and life of God, are saved. Divine wisdom, Sophia, is restored, and the glorious fullness of the divine is realized.

The hymn of the savior—of Jesus in the Christianized Secret Book of John, of forethought in the earlier Jewish version—is presented near the end of the longer version of the Secret Book of John. In the hymn the savior uses aretalogical self-predications ("I am" statements) to describe his—or her—multiple appearances in the world. Three appearances are highlighted, and in the account of the third appearance the savior says, "I brightened my face with light from the consummation of their realm and entered the midst of their prison, which is the prison of the body" (II, 31). Christian Sethian gnostics would most likely interpret this to be a reference to the incarnation of Jesus. The savior calls to those languishing in deep sleep, and a person hears the call and responds to it. In the hymn the savior calls upon the person to arise, remember, and trace the person's root, the root that goes back to the divine. That person who is called and remembers is every person, every gnostic who comes to knowledge and understands the divine that is within. In a way that recalls the Holy Book of the Great Invisible Spirit, Jesus in the Secret Book of John concludes with an affirmation of baptism "in luminous water with five seals" as the passage from death to the life of *gnōsis*.

The Secret Book of John is preserved in Coptic translation in the Nag Hammadi library (NHC II,*1;* III,*1;* IV,*1*) and Berlin Gnostic Codex 8502 (BG 8502,2), and Irenaeus of Lyon provides a summary of some of the ideas of the text in Against Heresies 1.29.1–4. The text was most likely composed in Greek, in the second century, though an earlier version may have appeared prior to that. The text is known in a shorter version and a longer version; the longer version is translated here, and a few notes offer comments on variations in the texts.

For further reading: Karen L. King, "The Apocryphon of John: Part II of the Gospel of John?"; Karen L. King, "Sophia and Christ in the Apocryphon of John"; Bentley Layton, *The Gnostic Scriptures,* 23–51; Elaine H. Pagels, *Beyond Belief,* 114–85; Michel Tardieu, *Écrits gnostiques;* Michael Waldstein, "Das Apokryphon des Johannes"; Michael Waldstein and Frederik Wisse, eds., *The Apocryphon of John.*

The Secret Book of John

or

The Apocryphon of John[1]

(NHC II,1; III,1; IV,1; BG 8502,2)

The teaching of the savior, and [the revelation] of the mysteries [and the things][2] hidden in silence, things he taught his disciple John.

The Revealer Appears to John

One day when John the brother of James, who are the sons of Zebedee, went up to the temple, it happened that a Pharisee named Arimanios[3] came up to him and said to him, "Where is your teacher, whom you followed?"

I[4] said to him, "He has returned to the place from which he came."

The Pharisee said to me, "This Nazarene really has deceived you, filled your ears with lies, closed [your minds], and turned you from the traditions of your ancestors."

When I, John, heard this, I turned away from the temple and went to a mountainous and barren place. I was distressed within, and I asked how the savior was chosen:

Why was he sent into the world by his father?
Who is his father who sent him?
To what kind of eternal realm shall we go?
And why did he tell us, when he spoke,
that this eternal realm [to which we shall go]
is modeled after the incorruptible realm,
but he did not teach us what kind of realm that one is?

At the moment I was thinking about this, look, the heavens opened, all creation under heaven lit up, and the world shook. [2] I was afraid, and look, I saw within the light [someone[5] standing] by me. As I was looking, it seemed to be an elderly person. Again it changed its appearance to be a youth.[6] Not that there were several figures before me. Rather, there was a figure with several forms within the light. These forms were visible through each other, and the figure had three forms.

The figure said to me, "John, John, why are you doubting? Why are you afraid? Are you not familiar with this figure? Then do not be faint-hearted. I am with you always. I am [the father], I am the mother, I am the child. I am the incorruptible and the undefiled one. [Now I have come] to teach you what is, what [was], and what is going to come, that you may [understand] what is invisible and what is visible; and to teach you about the [unshakable generation of] the perfect [human]. So now, lift up your [head] that you may [hear] the things I shall tell you today, and that you may relate them to your spiritual friends who are from the unshakable generation of the perfect human."

The One

I asked if I might understand this, and it said to me:

The One[7] is a sovereign that has nothing over it. It is God and parent, father[8] of all, the invisible one that is over all, that is incorruptible, that is pure light at which no eye can gaze.

The One is the invisible spirit. We should not think of it as a god or like a god. For it is greater than a god, because it has nothing over it and no [3] lord above it. It does not [exist] within anything inferior [to it, since everything] exists within it, [for it established] itself.[9] It is eternal, since it does not need anything. For it is absolutely complete. It has never lacked anything in order to be completed by it. Rather, it is always absolutely complete in light.

The One is

> illimitable, since there is nothing before it to limit it
>
> unfathomable, since there is nothing before it to fathom it
>
> immeasurable, since there was nothing before it to measure it
>
> invisible, since nothing has seen it
>
> eternal, since it exists eternally
>
> unutterable, since nothing could comprehend it to utter it
>
> unnameable, since there is nothing before it to give it a name

The One is the immeasurable light, pure, holy, immaculate. It is unutterable, and is perfect in incorruptibility. Not that it is just perfection, or blessedness, or divinity: it is much greater.

The One is not corporeal and it is not incorporeal.

The One is not large and it is not small.

It is impossible to say,

How much is it?

What [kind is it]?[10]

For no one can understand it.

The One is not among the things that exist, but it is much greater. Not that it is greater. Rather, as it is in itself, it is not a part of the eternal realms or time. For whatever is part of a realm was once prepared by another. Time was not allotted to it, since it receives nothing from anyone: what would be received would be on loan. The one who is first does not need to receive anything from another. It beholds itself in [4] its light.

The One is majestic and has an immeasurable purity.

The One is a realm that gives a realm,
life that gives life,
a blessed one that gives blessedness,
knowledge that gives knowledge,[11]
a good one that gives goodness,
mercy that gives mercy and redemption,
grace that gives grace.

Not that the One possesses this. Rather, the One gives immeasurable and incomprehensible light.

What shall I tell you about it? Its eternal realm is incorruptible, at peace, dwelling in silence, at rest, before everything.

It is the head of all realms, and it is the one who sustains them through its goodness.

We would not know [what is ineffable], we would not understand what is immeasurable, were it not for the one who has come from the father. This is the one who has told these things to us [alone].

Barbelo Appears

This father[12] is the one who beholds itself in the light surrounding it, which is the spring of living water, and provides all the realms. It reflects on its image everywhere, sees it in the spring of the spirit, and becomes enamored of its luminous water, [for its image is in] the spring of pure luminous water surrounding it.[13]

The father's thought became a reality, and she who appeared in the presence of the father in shining light came forth. She is the first power who preceded everything and came forth from the father's mind as the forethought of all. Her light shines like the father's light; she, the perfect power, is the image of the perfect and invisible virgin spirit.[14]

She, [the first] power, the glory of Barbelo,[15] the perfect [5] glory among the realms, the glory of revelation, she glorified and praised the virgin spirit, for because of the spirit she had come forth.

She is the first thought, the image of the spirit. She became the universal womb, for she precedes everything,

the mother-father[16]

the first human

the holy spirit

the triple male[17]

the triple power

the androgynous one with three names

the eternal realm among the invisible beings

the first to come forth

Barbelo asked the invisible virgin spirit to give her foreknowledge, and the spirit consented.[18] When the spirit consented, foreknowledge appeared and stood by forethought. This is the one who came from the thought of the invisible virgin spirit.[19] Foreknowledge glorified the spirit and the spirit's perfect power, Barbelo, for because of her, foreknowledge had come into being.

She asked again to be given incorruptibility, and the spirit consented. When the spirit consented, incorruptibility appeared and stood by thought and foreknowledge. Incorruptibility glorified the invisible one and Barbelo. Because of her they had come into being.

Barbelo asked to be given life eternal, and the invisible spirit consented. When the spirit consented, life eternal appeared, and they stood together and glorified the invisible spirit and Barbelo. Because of her they had come into being.

She asked again to be given truth, and the invisible spirit consented. Truth appeared, and they stood together and glorified the good invisible [6] spirit and its Barbelo. Because of her they had come into being.

These are the five realms of the father. They are

the first human, the image of the invisible spirit—that is, forethought, which is Barbelo, and thought[20]

along with foreknowledge

incorruptibility

life eternal

and truth

These are the five androgynous realms, which are the ten realms, which is the father.[21]

Barbelo Conceives

The father gazed into Barbelo, with the pure light surrounding the invisible spirit, and its radiance. Barbelo conceived from it, and it produced a spark of light similar to the blessed light but not as great. This was the only child of the mother-father that had come forth, the only offspring, the only child of the father, the pure light.[22] The invisible virgin spirit rejoiced over the light that was produced, that came forth from the first power of the spirit's forethought, who is Barbelo. The spirit anointed it with its own goodness[23] until it was perfect, with no lack of goodness, since it was anointed with the goodness of the invisible spirit. The child stood in the presence of the spirit as the spirit anointed the child. As soon as the child received this from the spirit, it glorified the holy spirit and perfect forethought. Because of her it had come forth.

The child asked to be given mind[24] as a companion to work with, and the spirit consented. When the invisible spirit consented, [7] mind appeared and stood by the anointed,[25] and glorified the spirit[26] and Barbelo.

All these beings came into existence in silence.

Mind wished to create something by means of the word of the invisible spirit.[27] Its will became a reality and appeared, with mind and the light, glorifying it. Word followed will. For the anointed, the self-conceived God,[28] created everything by the word. Life eternal, will, mind, and foreknowledge stood together and glorified the invisible spirit and Barbelo, for because of her they had come into being.

The holy spirit brought the self-conceived divine child of itself and Barbelo to perfection, so that the child might stand before the great invisible virgin spirit as the self-conceived God, the anointed, who honored the spirit[29] with loud acclaim. The child came forth through forethought. The invisible virgin spirit set the true, self-conceived God over everything, and caused all authority and the truth within to be subject to it, so that the child might understand everything, the one called by a name greater than every name, for that name will be told to those who are worthy of it.

The Four Luminaries

Now from the light, which is the anointed, and from incorruptibility, by the grace of the spirit, the four luminaries that derive from the self-conceived God gazed out[30] in order to stand [8] before it. The three beings are

> will
>
> thought
>
> life

The four powers are

> understanding
>
> grace

perception

thoughtfulness

Grace dwells in the eternal realm of the luminary Harmozel, who is the first angel.[31] There are three other realms with this eternal realm:

grace

truth

form

The second luminary is Oroiael, who has been appointed over the second eternal realm. There are three other realms with it:

insight[32]

perception

memory

The third luminary is Daveithai, who has been appointed over the third eternal realm. There are three other realms with it:

understanding

love

idea

The fourth eternal realm has been set up for the fourth luminary, Eleleth. There are three other realms with it:

perfection

peace

Sophia

These are the four luminaries that stand before the self-conceived God; these are the twelve eternal realms that stand before the child of the great self-conceived one, the anointed,[33] by the will and grace of the invisible spirit. The twelve realms belong to the child of the self-conceived one, and everything was established by the will of the holy spirit through the self-conceived one.

Pigeradamas and Seth

From the foreknowledge of the perfect mind, through the expressed will of the invisible spirit and the will of the self-conceived, came the perfect human, the first revelation, the truth. The virgin spirit named the human Pigeradamas,[34] and appointed Pigeradamas to [9] the first eternal realm with the great self-conceived, the anointed, by the first luminary, Harmozel. Its powers dwell with it. The invisible one gave Pigeradamas an invincible power of mind.

Pigeradamas spoke and glorified and praised the invisible spirit by saying,

> Because of you everything has come into being,
> and to you everything will return.
> I shall praise and glorify you,
> the self-conceived,
> the eternal realms,
> the three, father, mother, child,
> perfect power.

Pigeradamas appointed his son Seth to the second eternal realm, before the second luminary, Oroiael.

In the third eternal realm were stationed the offspring of Seth, with the third luminary, Daveithai. The souls of the saints were stationed there.

In the fourth eternal realm were stationed the souls of those who were ignorant of the fullness. They did not repent immediately, but held out for a while and repented later. They came to be with the fourth luminary, Eleleth.

These are creatures that glorify the invisible spirit.

The Fall of Sophia

Now Sophia, who is the wisdom of insight and who constitutes an eternal realm, conceived of a thought from herself, with the conception of the invisible spirit and foreknowledge. She wanted to bring forth something like herself, without the consent of the spirit, who had not given approval, without her partner and without his consideration.[35] The male did not give approval. She did not find her partner, and she considered this without the spirit's consent and without the knowledge of her partner. Nonetheless, she gave birth. [10] And because of the invincible power within her, her thought was not an idle thought. Something came out of her that was imperfect and different in appearance from her, for she had produced it without her partner. It did not resemble its mother, and was misshapen.

When Sophia saw what her desire had produced, it changed into the figure of a snake with the face of a lion. Its eyes were like flashing bolts of lightning. She cast it away from her, outside that realm, so that none of the immortals would see it. She had produced it ignorantly.

She surrounded it with a bright cloud and put a throne in the middle of the cloud so that no one would see it except the holy spirit, who is called the mother of the living. She named her off-spring Yaldabaoth.

Yaldabaoth's World Order

Yaldabaoth is the first ruler, who took great power from his mother. Then he left her and moved away from the place where he was born. He took control and created for himself other realms with luminous fire, which still exists. He mated with the mindlessness[36] in him, and produced authorities for himself:

The name of the first is Athoth, whom generations call the [reaper].[37]

The second is Harmas, who is the jealous eye.[38]

The third is Kalila-Oumbri.

The fourth is Yabel.

The fifth is Adonaios, who is called Sabaoth.[39]

The sixth is Cain, whom generations of people call the sun.

The seventh is Abel.

The eighth is Abrisene.

The ninth is Yobel. [11]

The tenth is Armoupieel.

The eleventh is Melcheir-Adonein.

The twelfth is Belias, who is over the depth of the underworld.[40]

Yaldabaoth stationed seven kings, one for each sphere of heaven, to reign over the seven heavens, and five to reign over the depth of the abyss.[41] He shared his fire with them, but he did not give away any of the power of the light he had taken from his mother. For he is ignorant darkness.

When light mixed with darkness, it made the darkness shine. When darkness mixed with light, it dimmed the light, and it became neither light nor darkness, but rather gloom.

This gloomy ruler has three names: the first name is Yaldabaoth, the second is Sakla, the third is Samael.[42]

He is wicked in the mindlessness within him. He said, "I am God and there is no other god beside me,"[43] since he did not know from where his own strength had come.

The rulers each created seven powers for themselves, and the powers each created six angels, until there were 365 angels.[44] These are the names and the corresponding physiques:

> The first is Athoth, and has the face of sheep.
>
> The second is Eloaios, and has the face of a donkey.
>
> The third is Astaphaios, and has the face of a hyena.
>
> The fourth is Yao,[45] and has the face of a snake with seven heads.
>
> The fifth is Sabaoth, and has the face of a snake.
>
> The sixth is Adonin, and has the face of an ape.
>
> The seventh is Sabbataios,[46] and has a face of flaming fire.

This is the sevenfold nature of the week.[47]

Yaldabaoth has many [12] faces, more than all of these, so that he could show whatever face he wanted when he was among the seraphim.[48] He shared his fire with them, and lorded it over them because of the glorious power he had from his mother's light.

That is why he called himself God, and defied the place from which he came.

In his thought he united the seven powers with the authorities that were with him. When he spoke, it was done. He named each of the powers, beginning with the highest:

> First is goodness, with the first power, Athoth.
>
> Second is forethought, with the second power, Eloaios.[49]
>
> Third is divinity, with the third power, Astaphaios.[50]
>
> Fourth is lordship, with the fourth power, Yao.
>
> Fifth is kingdom, with the fifth power, Sabaoth.[51]
>
> Sixth is jealousy, with the sixth power, Adonin.
>
> Seventh is understanding, with the seventh power, Sabbataios.[52]

Each has a sphere in its own realm.

They were named after the glory above for the destruction of the powers. While the names given them by their maker were powerful, the names given them after the glory above would bring about their destruction and loss of power. That is why they have two names.

Yaldabaoth organized everything after the pattern of the first realms that had come into being, so that he might [13] create everything in an incorruptible form. Not that he had seen the incorruptible ones. Rather, the power that is in him, that he had taken from his mother, produced in him the pattern for the world order.

When he saw creation surrounding him, and the throng of angels around him that had come forth from him, he said to them, "I am a jealous god and there is no other god beside me."[53]

But by announcing this, he suggested to the angels with him that there is another god. For if there were no other god, of whom would he be jealous?

Sophia Repents

Then the mother began to move around. She realized that she was lacking something when the brightness of her light diminished. She grew dim because her partner had not collaborated with her.

I[54] said, "Master,[55] what does it mean that she moved around?"

The master laughed and said, Do not suppose that it is as Moses said, above the waters.[56] No, when she recognized the wickedness that had taken place, and the robbery her son had committed, she repented. When she became forgetful in the darkness of ignorance, she began to be ashamed. She did not dare to return, but she was agitated.[57] This agitation is the moving around.

The arrogant one took power from his mother. He was ignorant, for he thought no one existed except his mother alone. When he saw the throng of angels he had created, he exalted himself over them.

When the mother realized that the trappings[58] of darkness had come into being imperfectly, she understood that her partner had not collaborated with her. She repented [14] with many tears. The whole realm of fullness heard her prayer of repentance and offered praise on her behalf to the invisible virgin spirit, and the spirit consented. When the invisible spirit consented,[59] the holy spirit poured upon her some of the fullness of all. For her partner did not come to her on his own, but he came to her through the realm of fullness, so that he might restore what she lacked. She was taken up not to her own eternal realm, but instead to a position above her son. She was to remain in the ninth heaven until she restored what was lacking in herself.[60]

The Human Appears

A voice called from the exalted heavenly realm,

> Humankind[61] exists
> and the child of humankind.[62]

The first ruler, Yaldabaoth, heard the voice and thought it had come from his mother. He did not realize its source.

> The holy perfect mother-father,
> the complete forethought,
> the image of the invisible one,
> being the father of all,
> through whom everything came into being,
> the first human—

this is the one who showed them and appeared in human shape.[63]

The entire realm of the first ruler quaked, and the foundations of the abyss shook. The bottomside of the waters above the material world was lit up by this image that had appeared. When all the authorities and the first ruler stared at this appearance, they saw the whole bottomside as it was lit up. And through the light they saw the shape of the image in the water.[64] [15]

The Creation of Adam

Yaldabaoth said to the authorities with him, "Come, let us create a human being after the image of God and with a likeness to ourselves, so that this human image may give us light."[65]

They created through their respective powers, according to the features that were given. Each of the authorities contributed a psychical feature corresponding to the figure of the image they had seen. They created a being like the perfect first human, and said, "Let us call it Adam, that its name may give us power of light."[66]

The powers began to create:

The first one, goodness, created a soul of bone.

The second, forethought, created a soul of sinew.

The third, divinity, created a soul of flesh.

The fourth, lordship, created a soul of marrow.

The fifth, kingdom, created a soul of blood.

The sixth, jealousy, created a soul of skin.

The seventh, understanding, created a soul of hair.

The throng of angels stood by and received these seven psychical substances from the authorities,[67] in order to create a network of limbs and trunk, with all the parts properly arranged.

The first one, who is Raphao, began by creating the head

Abron created the skull[68]

Meniggesstroeth created the brain

Asterechme the right eye

Thaspomocha the left eye

Yeronumos the right ear

Bissoum the left ear

Akioreim the nose [16]

Banen-Ephroum the lips

Amen the teeth

Ibikan the molars

Basiliademe the tonsils

Achcha the uvula

Adaban the neck

Chaaman the vertebrae

Dearcho the throat

Tebar the right shoulder

N . . . the left shoulder

Mniarchon the right elbow

. . . e the left elbow[69]

Abitrion the right underarm

Euanthen the left underarm

Krus the right hand

Beluai the left hand

Treneu the fingers of the right hand

Balbel the fingers of the left hand

Krima the fingernails

Astrops the right breast

Barroph the left breast

Baoum the right shoulder joint

Ararim the left shoulder joint

Areche the belly

Phthaue the navel

Senaphim the abdomen

Arachethopi the right ribs

Zabedo the left ribs

Barias the right hip

Phnouth the left hip[70]

Abenlenarchei the marrow

Chnoumeninorin the bones

Gesole the stomach

Agromauma the heart

Bano the lungs

Sostrapal the liver

Anesimalar the spleen

Thopithro the intestines

Biblo the kidneys

Roeror the sinews

Taphreo the backbone

Ipouspoboba the veins

Bineborin the arteries

Aatoimenpsephei the breaths in all the limbs

Entholleia all the flesh

Bedouk the right buttock

Arabeei the left [buttock][71]

. . . the penis

Eilo the testicles

Sorma the genitals

Gormakaiochlabar the right thigh

Nebrith the left thigh

Pserem the muscles of the right leg

Asaklas the muscle of the left

Ormaoth the right leg

Emenun the left leg

Knux the [17] right shin

Tupelon the left shin

Achiel the right ankle

Phneme the left ankle

Phiouthrom the right foot

Boabel its toes

Trachoun the left foot

Phikna its toes

Miamai the toenails

Labernioum . . .

Those who are appointed over all these are seven in number:

Athoth

Armas

Kalila

Yabel

Sabaoth

Cain

Abel[72]

Those who activate the limbs are, part by part,

the head, Diolimodraza

the neck, Yammeax

the right shoulder, Yakouib

the left shoulder, Ouerton

the right hand, Oudidi

the left one, Arbao

the fingers of the right hand, Lampno

the fingers of the left hand, Leekaphar

the right breast, Barbar

the left breast, Imae

the chest, Pisandraptes

the right shoulder joint, Koade

the left shoulder joint, Odeor

the right ribs, Asphixix

the left ribs, Sunogchouta

the abdomen, Arouph

the womb, Sabalo

the right thigh, Charcharb

the left thigh, Chthaon

all the genitals, Bathinoth

the right leg, Choux

the left leg, Charcha

the right shin, Aroer

the left shin, Toechtha

the right ankle, Aol

the left ankle, Charaner

the right foot, Bastan

its toes, Archentechtha

the left foot, Marephnounth

its toes, Abrana

Seven have been empowered over all these:

Michael

Uriel

Asmenedas

Saphasatoel

Aarmouriam

Richram

Amiorps

Those who are over the senses are Archendekta.

The one who is over perception is Deitharbathas.

The one who is over imagination is Oummaa.

The one who is over arrangement [18] is Aachiaram.

The one who is over all impulse to action is
    Riaramnacho.

The source of the demons that are in the entire body is divided into four:

heat

cold

wetness

dryness

and the mother of them all is matter.

The one who is lord over heat is Phloxopha.

The one who is lord over cold is Oroorrothos.

The one who is lord over what is dry is Erimacho.

The one who is lord over wetness is Athuro.

The mother of all these, Onorthochras, stands in the midst of them, for she is unlimited and mingles with them all. She is matter, and by her they are nourished.

The four principal demons are

Ephememphi, the demon of pleasure

Yoko, the demon of desire

Nenentophni, the demon of grief

Blaomen, the demon of fear

The mother of them all is Esthesis-Ouch-Epi-Ptoe.[73]

From the four demons have come passions:

From grief come jealousy, envy, pain, trouble, distress, hard-heartedness, anxiety, sorrow, and others.

From pleasure come an abundance of evil, vain conceit, and the like.

From desire come anger, wrath, bitterness, intense lust, greed, and the like.

From fear come terror, servility, anguish, and shame.

All these are like virtues and vices. The reflection of their true nature is Anaro, who is head of the material soul, [19] and it dwells with Esthesis-Z-Ouch-Epi-Ptoe.[74]

This is the number of angels. In all they number 365.[75] They all worked together until, limb by limb, the psychical and material body was completed. Now, there are others over the remaining passions, and I have not told you about them. If you want to know about them, the information is recorded in the Book of Zoroaster.[76]

Adam Receives Spirit and Life

All the angels and demons worked together until they fashioned the psychical body. But for a long time their creation did not stir or move at all.

When the mother wanted to take back the power she had relinquished to the first ruler, she prayed to the most merciful mother-father of all. With a sacred command the mother-father sent five luminaries down upon the place of the angels of the first ruler. They advised him so that they might recover the mother's power.

They said to Yaldabaoth, "Breathe some of your spirit into the face of Adam, and the body will arise."

He breathed his spirit into Adam.[77] The spirit is the power of his mother, but he did not realize this, because he lives in ignorance. The mother's power went out of Yaldabaoth and into the psychical body that had been made to be like the one who is from the beginning.

The body moved, and became powerful. And it was enlightened.

At once the rest of [20] the powers became jealous. Although Adam came into being through all of them, and they gave their power to this human, Adam was more intelligent than the creators and the first ruler. When they realized that Adam was enlightened, and could think more clearly than they, and was stripped of evil,[78] they took and threw Adam into the lowest part of the whole material realm.

The blessed, benevolent, merciful mother-father had compassion for the mother's power that had been removed from the first ruler. The rulers might be able to overpower the psychical, perceptible body once again. So with its benevolent and most merciful spirit the mother-father sent a helper to Adam—enlightened insight, who is from the mother-father and who was called life.[79] She helped the whole creature, laboring with it, restoring it to its fullness, teaching it about the descent of the seed,[80] teaching it about the way of ascent, which is the way of descent.[81]

Enlightened insight was hidden within Adam so that the rulers might not recognize her but that insight might be able to restore what the mother lacked.

The Imprisonment of Humanity

The human being Adam was revealed through the bright shadow within. And Adam's ability to think was greater than that of all the creators. When they looked up, they saw that Adam's ability to think was greater, and they devised a plan with the whole throng of rulers and angels. They took fire, earth, [21] and water, and combined them with the four fiery winds.[82] They wrought them together and made a great commotion.[83]

The rulers brought Adam into the shadow of death so that they might produce a figure again, from earth, water, fire, and the spirit that comes from matter[84]—that is, from the ignorance of darkness, and desire, and their own phony spirit. This figure is the cave for remodeling the body that these criminals put on the human, the fetter of forgetfulness.[85] Adam became a mortal person, the first to descend and the first to become estranged.

Enlightened insight within Adam, however, was rejuvenating Adam's mind.

The rulers took Adam and put Adam in paradise. They said, "Eat," meaning, Do so in a leisurely manner.[86] But in fact their pleasure is bitter and their beauty is perverse. Their pleasure is a trap, their trees are a sacrilege, their fruit is deadly poison, and their promise is death.

They put their tree of life in the middle of paradise.[87]

I[88] shall teach you what the secret of their life is—the plan they devised together, the nature of their spirit. The root of their tree is bitter, its branches are death, its shadow is hatred, a trap is in its leaves, its blossom is bad ointment, its fruit is death, desire is its seed, and it blossoms in darkness. The dwelling place of those who taste [22] of it is the underworld, and darkness is their resting place.

But the rulers lingered in front of what they call the tree of the knowledge of good and evil, which is enlightened insight,[89] so that Adam might not behold its fullness[90] and recognize his shameful nakedness.

But I[91] was the one who induced them to eat.

I[92] said to the savior, "Master, was it not the snake that instructed Adam to eat?"

The savior laughed and said, The snake instructed them to eat of the wickedness of sexual desire and destruction so that Adam might be of use to the snake.

The first ruler[93] knew Adam was disobedient to him because of enlightened insight within Adam, which made Adam stronger of mind than he. He wanted to recover the power that he himself had passed on to Adam. So he brought deep sleep upon Adam.

I said to the savior, "What is this deep sleep?"

The savior said, It is not as Moses wrote and you heard. He said in his first book,[94] "He put Adam to sleep."[95] Rather, this deep sleep was a loss of sense. Thus the first ruler said through the prophet, "I shall make their minds sluggish, that they may neither understand nor discern."[96]

The Creation of Eve

Enlightened insight hid herself within Adam. The first ruler wanted to take her from Adam's side, but enlightened insight cannot be apprehended. While darkness pursued her, it did not apprehend her. The first ruler removed part of Adam's power and created another figure in the form of a female, like the image of insight that had appeared to him. He put [23] the part he had taken from the power of the human being into the female creature. It did not happen, however, the way Moses said: "Adam's rib."[97]

Adam saw the woman beside him. At once enlightened insight appeared and removed the veil that covered his mind. He sobered up from the drunkenness of darkness. He recognized his counterpart and said, "This is now bone from my bones and flesh from my flesh."[98]

For this reason a man will leave his father and his mother and will join himself to his wife, and the two of them will become one flesh. For his partner will be sent to him, and he will leave his father and his mother.[99]

Our sister Sophia is the one who descended in an innocent manner to restore what she lacked. For this reason she was called life[100]—that is, the mother of the living—by the forethought of the sovereignty of heaven and by [the insight that appeared] to Adam.[101] Through her have the living tasted perfect knowledge.[102]

As for me, I appeared in the form of an eagle[103] upon the tree of knowledge, which is the insight of pure enlightened forethought, that I might teach the human beings and awaken them from the depth of sleep. For the two of them were fallen and realized that they were naked.[104] Insight appeared to them as light and awakened their minds.

Yaldabaoth Defiles Eve

When Yaldabaoth realized that the humans had withdrawn from him, he cursed his earth. He found the woman as she was [24] preparing herself for her husband. He was master over her. And he did not know the mystery that had come into being through the sacred plan. The two of them were afraid to denounce Yaldabaoth. He displayed to his angels the ignorance within him, and he threw the humans out of paradise and cloaked them in thick darkness.[105]

The first ruler saw the young woman standing next to Adam and noticed that enlightened insight of life had appeared in her.

Yet Yaldabaoth was full of ignorance. So when the forethought of all realized this, she dispatched emissaries, and they stole life[106] out of Eve.

The first ruler defiled Eve, and produced in her two sons, a first and a second: Elohim and Yahweh.[107]

> *Elohim has the face of a bear,*
> *Yahweh has the face of a cat.*
> *One is just, the other is unjust.*
> *He placed Yahweh over fire and wind,*
> *he placed Elohim over water and earth.*
> *He called them by the names Cain and Abel,*
> *with a view to deceive.*[108]

To this day sexual intercourse has persisted because of the first ruler. He planted sexual desire within the woman who belongs to Adam. Through intercourse the first ruler produced duplicate bodies, and he blew some of his false spirit into them.

He placed these two rulers[109] over the elements so that they might rule over the cave.[110]

When Adam came to know the counterpart of his own fore-knowledge, he produced a son like [25] the child of humankind. He called him Seth, after the manner of the generation in the eternal realms.[111] Similarly, the mother sent down her spirit, which is like her and is a copy of what is in the realm of fullness, for she was going to prepare a dwelling place for the eternal realms that would come down.

The human beings were made to drink water of forgetfulness[112] by the first ruler, so that they might not know where they had come from. For a time the seed remained and helped so that when the spirit descends from the holy realms, it may raise up the seed and heal what it lacks, that the entire realm of fullness may be holy and lack nothing.

On Human Destiny

I said to the savior, "Master, will all the souls then be led safely into pure light?"

He answered and said to me, These are great matters that have arisen in your mind, and it is difficult to explain them to anyone except those of the unshakable generation.

Those upon whom the spirit of life will descend and whom the spirit will empower will be saved, and will become perfect and worthy of greatness, and will be cleansed there of all evil and the anxieties of wickedness, since they are no longer anxious for anything except the incorruptible alone, and concerned with that from this moment on, without anger, jealousy, envy, desire, or greed for anything.

They are affected by nothing but being in the flesh alone, and they wear the flesh as they look forward to a time when they will be met [26] by those who receive them. Such people are worthy of the incorruptible, eternal life and calling. They endure everything and bear everything so as to finish the contest[113] and receive eternal life.

I said to him, "Master, will the souls of people be [rejected][114] who have not done these things, but upon whom the power and the spirit of life have descended?"

He answered and said to me, If the spirit descends upon them,[115] by all means they will be saved and transformed. Power will descend upon every person, for without it no one could stand.[116] After birth, if the spirit of life grows, and power comes and strengthens that soul, no one will be able to lead it astray with evil actions. But people upon whom the false spirit descends are misled by it and go astray.

I said, "Master, where will their souls go when they leave their flesh?"

He laughed and said to me, The soul in which there is more power than the contemptible spirit is strong. She escapes from evil, and through the intervention of the incorruptible one, she is saved and is taken up to eternal rest.[117]

I said, "Master, where will the souls go of people who have not known to whom they belong?"

He said to me, The contemptible spirit has [27] grown stronger in such people while they were going astray. This spirit lays a heavy burden on the soul, leads her into evil deeds, and hurls her down into forgetfulness. After the soul leaves the body, she is handed over to the authorities who have come into being through the ruler. They bind her with chains and throw her into prison.[118] They go around with her until she awakens from forgetfulness and acquires knowledge. This is how she attains perfection and is saved.

I said, "Master, how can the soul become younger and return into its mother's womb,[119] or into the human?"

He was glad when I asked him about this, and he said to me, You are truly blessed, for you have understood. This soul will be made to follow another soul in whom the spirit of life dwells, and she is saved through that one. Then she will not be thrust into flesh again.

I said, "Master, where will the souls go of people who had knowledge but turned away?"

He said to me, They will be taken to the place where the angels of misery go, where there is no repentance. They will be kept there until the day when those who have blasphemed against the spirit will be tortured and punished eternally.

I said, "Master, where did the contemptible spirit come from?"

He said to me, The mother-father is great in mercy, the holy spirit, who in every way is compassionate, [28] who sympathizes with you, the insight of enlightened forethought. This one raised up the offspring of the perfect generation and their thought and the eternal light of the human. When the first ruler realized that these people were exalted above him and could think better than he, he wanted to grasp their thought. He did not know that they surpassed him in thought and that he would be unable to grasp them.

He devised a plan with his authorities, who are his powers. Together they fornicated with Sophia, and through them was produced bitter fate,[120] the final, fickle bondage. Fate is like this because the powers are fickle. To the present day fate is tougher and stronger than what gods, angels, demons, and all the generations have encountered. For from fate have come all iniquity and injustice and blasphemy, the bondage of forgetfulness, and ignorance, and all burdensome orders, weighty sins, and great fears.

Thus all of creation has been blinded so that none might know the God that is over them all. Because of the bondage of forgetfulness, their sins have been hidden. They have been bound with dimensions, times, and seasons, and fate is master of all.

The first ruler regretted everything that had happened through him. Once again he made a plan, to bring a flood [29] upon the human creation.[121] The enlightened majesty of forethought, however, warned Noah. Noah announced this to all the offspring, the human children, but those who were strangers to him did not listen to him. It did not happen the way Moses said: "They hid in an ark."[122] Rather, they hid in a particular place, not only Noah, but also many other people from the unshakable generation. They entered that place and hid in a bright cloud. Noah knew about his supremacy. With him was the enlightened one who had enlightened them, since the first ruler had brought darkness upon the whole earth.

The first ruler plotted with his powers. He sent his angels to the human daughters so they might take some of them and raise offspring for their pleasure.[123] At first they were unsuccessful. When they had proven unsuccessful, they met again and devised another plan. They created a contemptible spirit similar to the spirit that had descended, in order to adulterate souls through this spirit. The angels changed their appearance to look like the partners of these women, and filled the women with the spirit of darkness that they had concocted, and with evil.

They brought gold, silver, gifts, copper, iron, metal, and all sorts of things. They brought great anxieties to the people who followed them, [30] leading them astray with many deceptions. These people grew old without experiencing pleasure and died without finding truth or knowing the God of truth. In this way all creation was forever enslaved, from the beginning of the world until the present day.

The angels took women, and from the darkness they produced children similar to their spirit. They closed their minds and became stubborn through the stubbornness of the contemptible spirit until the present day.

Hymn of the Savior[124]

Now I, the perfect forethought of all, transformed myself into my offspring. I existed first and went down every path.

I am the abundance of light,
I am the remembrance of fullness.

I traveled in the realm of great darkness, and continued until I entered the midst of the prison. The foundations of chaos shook, and I hid from them because of their evil, and they did not recognize me.

Again I returned, a second time, and went on. I had come from the inhabitants of light—I, the remembrance of forethought.

I entered the midst of darkness and the bowels of the underworld, turning to my task. The foundations of chaos shook as though to fall upon those who dwell in chaos and destroy them. Again I hurried back to the root of my light so they might not be destroyed before their time.

Again, a third time, I went forth—

I am the light dwelling in light,
I am the remembrance of forethought—

so that I might enter the midst of darkness and the bowels [31] of the underworld. I brightened my face with light from the consummation of their realm and entered the midst of their prison, which is the prison of the body.

I said, Let whoever hears arise from deep sleep.[125]

A person wept and shed tears. Bitter tears the person wiped away, and said, "Who is calling my name? From where has my hope come as I dwell in the bondage of prison?"

I said,

I am the forethought of pure light,
I am the thought of the virgin spirit,
who raises you to a place of honor.

Arise, remember that you have heard
and trace your root,
which is I, the compassionate.
Guard yourself against the angels of misery,
the demons of chaos, and all who entrap you,
and beware of deep sleep
and the trap[126] *in the bowels of the underworld.*

I raised and sealed the person in luminous water with five seals, that death might not prevail over the person from that moment on.

Conclusion

Look, now I shall ascend to the perfect realm. I have finished everything for you in your hearing. I have told you everything for you to record and communicate secretly to your spiritual friends. This is the mystery of the unshakable generation.

The savior communicated this to John for him to record and safeguard. He said to him, "Cursed be anyone who will trade these things for a gift, for food, drink, clothes, or anything [32] like this."

These things were communicated to John in a mystery, and at once the savior disappeared. Then John went to the other disciples and reported what the savior had told him.

Jesus Christ
Amen[127]
The Secret Book According to John

PART SEVEN

The Secret Book
of James

THE SECRET BOOK OF JAMES, or the Apocryphon of James, is a letter said to be sent by James, most likely James the righteous, the brother of Jesus and the leader of the Jerusalem church, to a certain recipient, perhaps Cerinthos, who was a second-century Christian leader and, according to the heresiologists, one of the early gnostics. The title of the text is suggested by the reference to a secret book (*apokryphon*) within the document, but because the text is in the form of a letter, it sometimes is described as the Letter of James (or Secret Letter of James) in the scholarly literature. The Secret Book of James contains themes that are typical of gnostic literature (knowledge, fullness, deficiency). More specifically, the text may be considered a Valentinian document. It takes its place within Codex I of the Nag Hammadi library, and that codex includes other texts that are Valentinian (for example, the Gospel of Truth). Further, some of the material in the Secret Book of James may reflect Valentinian interests (for instance, the threefold division of people into body, soul, and spirit).

Near the opening of the Secret Book of James, James describes a scene in which he, with the twelve disciples, are all busy at work writing their books, perhaps gospels and other texts: "The twelve disciples were all sitting together, recalling what the savior had said to each of them, whether in a hidden or an open manner, and organizing it in books. I was writing what is in [my book]" (2). Then Jesus appears to the disciples to provide more insight into what is of concern to them.

The body of the Secret Book of James consists of a dialogue between Jesus and his disciples, particularly James and Peter, and sayings of Jesus are presented and expanded in the context of questions and comments from the disciples. The words of Jesus take the form of statements of blessing and shame, parables and stories, and discourses on such topics as being filled and lacking, on suffering, and on knowing oneself. Many of the sayings of Jesus in the Secret Book of James are previously unknown, and some of the sayings may reflect aspects of the teaching of the historical Jesus. Some of the sayings are enigmatic and paradoxical. Peter claims that the disciples already are characterized by fullness, and Jesus responds with an obscure but thought-provoking statement on how one may be filled and how one may lack (4). Jesus discusses his crucifixion as the undeserved death of a righteous person, and he uses the discussion as the occasion to encourage the disciples to face their own suffering with courage and understanding:

> Do you dare to spare the flesh, you for whom the spirit is a wall surrounding you? If you consider how long the world has existed before you and how long it will exist after you, you will see that your life is but a day and your sufferings but an hour. The good will not enter the world. Disdain death, then, and care about life. Remember my cross and my death, and you will live. (5)

Jesus in the Secret Book of James tells the disciples to know themselves, for salvation does not come simply through the generosity of God or through prayer. A comment of Jesus assumes that such blind confidence in God's graciousness and in the power of prayer is mistaken: "Or maybe you think that the father is a lover of humankind, or that he is won over by prayers, or that he is gracious to one because of another, or that he tolerates whoever is seeking?" (11). Rather, salvation comes through knowledge, and the way to knowledge requires dedication and commitment. People need to save themselves. Jesus pronounces a blessing on "those who have spoken out and acquired grace for themselves" (11). If people follow the way to knowledge, they may even surpass Jesus. Jesus says, "Become better than I. Be like the child of the holy spirit" (6).

The Secret Book of James is the second tractate in Codex I of the Nag Hammadi library. It is preserved in Coptic, but it was most likely composed in Greek, although the text itself claims to have been written in Hebrew. At the beginning of the Secret Book of James the author alludes to another secret book, but nothing is known of such a book. The Secret Book of James was probably composed in the first half of the second century, though portions of the text may be older. The place of composition is unknown. The reference to Jesus "being buried in the sand" (5) may suggest that the author was from Egypt, where burial took place in the dry sand (but see possible emended wording in the note to that passage).

For further reading: Ron Cameron, *Sayings Traditions in the Apocryphon of James*; Judith Hartenstein and Uwe-Karsten Plisch, "Der Brief des Jakobus"; Dankwart Kirchner and Einar Thomassen, "The Apocryphon of James"; Donald Rouleau, *L'Épître apocryphe de Jacques*; Francis E. Williams, "The Apocryphon of James."

The Secret Book of James,
The Apocryphon of James,

or

The Letter of James[1]

(NHC I,2)

[James][2] writes to [the student Cerinthos]:[3]

Peace be [with you from] peace,
[love] from love,
[grace] from grace,
[faith] from faith,
life from holy life.

Secret Books

You have asked me to send you a secret book revealed to me and Peter by the master,[4] and I could not turn you down, nor could I speak to you, so [I have written] it in Hebrew[5] and have sent it to you, and to you alone. But since you are a minister of the salvation of the saints, do your best to be careful not to communicate to many people this book that the savior did not want to communicate even to all of us, his twelve disciples. Nonetheless, blessings will be on those who will be saved through the faith of this treatise.

Ten months ago I sent you another secret book[6] that the savior revealed to me. Think of that book as revealed to me, James. But as for this book, [2] I [have not yet fully understood it, and it was also] revealed [for you and] those who are yours, so [try] to comprehend [its meaning]. This is how [you can be] saved, and [then] you should [also make it known].[7]

Jesus Appears to Peter and James

The twelve disciples were all sitting together, recalling what the savior had said to each of them, whether in a hidden or an open manner, and organizing it in books.[8] I was writing what is in [my book]. Look, the savior appeared, after he had left [us, while we] were watching for him.

Five hundred fifty days[9] after he rose from the dead, we said to him, "Did you depart and leave us?"

Jesus said, "No, but I shall return to the place from which I came. If you want to come with me, come."

They all answered and said, "If you order us, we shall come."

He said, "I tell you the truth, no one will ever enter heaven's kingdom because I ordered it, but rather because you yourselves are filled. Leave James and Peter to me that I may fill them."

When he called the two of them, he took them aside and commanded the rest to keep doing what they were doing.

The savior said, "You have been favored [3] [through the father to receive my sayings. The other disciples also] have written [my sayings in their] books as if [they have understood, but be careful.

They have done their] work without [really understanding]. They have listened like [foolish people], and . . .[10] they have not understood.[11]

> *Do you not want to be filled?*
> *Your hearts are drunk.*
> *Do you not want to be sober?*
> *You ought to be ashamed.*

"From now on, awake or asleep, remember that you have seen the child of humankind[12] and have spoken with him and have listened to him.

"Shame on those who have seen the child of humankind.

"Blessings will be on you who have not seen the human, or associated with him, or spoken with him, or listened to anything from him. Yours is life.[13]

"Understand that he healed you when you were sick, that you might reign.

"Shame on those who have found relief from their sickness, for they will relapse into sickness.

"Blessings on you who have not been sick, and have known relief before getting sick. God's kingdom is yours.

"So I tell you, be filled and leave no space within you empty, or he who is coming will mock you."

Being Filled and Lacking

Then Peter answered, "Look, three times you have told us, [4] 'Be [filled,' but] we are filled."

The [savior answered] and said, "For [this reason I have told] you, '[Be filled],' that you may not [lack. Those who lack] will not [be saved]. To be filled is good and to lack is bad. Yet since it is also good for you to lack but bad for you to be filled, whoever is filled also lacks. One who lacks is not filled in the way another who lacks is filled, but whoever is filled is brought to an appropriate end. So you should lack when you can fill yourselves and be filled when you lack that you may be able to [fill] yourselves more. Be filled with spirit but lack in reason, for reason is of the soul. It is soul."[14]

Believe in My Cross

I answered and said to him, "Master, we can obey you if you wish, for we have forsaken our fathers and our mothers and our villages and have followed you. Give us the means not to be tempted by the evil devil."

The master answered and said, "What good is it to you if you do the father's will but you are not given your part of his bounty when you are tempted by Satan? But if you are oppressed by Satan and persecuted and do the father's [5] will, I [say] he will love you, make you my equal, and consider you beloved through his forethought,[15] and by your own choice. Will you not stop loving the flesh and fearing suffering? Do you not know that you have not yet been abused, unjustly accused, locked up in prison, unlawfully condemned, crucified <without> reason,[16] or buried in the sand[17] as I myself was by the evil one? Do you dare to spare the flesh, you for whom the spirit is a wall surrounding you? If you consider how long the world has existed before you and how long it will exist after you, you will see that your life is but a day and your sufferings but an hour. The good will not enter the world. Disdain death, then, and care about life. Remember my cross and my death, and you will live."

I answered and said to him, "Master, do not mention to us the cross and death, for they are far [6] from you."

The master answered and said, "I tell you the truth, none will be saved unless they believe in my cross, for God's kingdom belongs to those who have believed in my cross. Be seekers of death, then, like the dead who seek life, for what they seek becomes apparent to them. And what is there to cause them concern? As for you, when you search out death, it will teach you about being chosen. I tell you the truth, no one afraid of death will be saved, for the kingdom of death[18] belongs to those who are put to death.[19] Become better than I. Be like the child of the holy spirit."[20]

The Head of Prophecy

Then I asked him, "Master, how can we prophesy to those who ask us to prophesy to them? There are many who bring a request to us and look to us to hear our pronouncement."

The master answered and said, "Do you not know that the head of prophecy was cut off with John?"[21]

I said, "Master, it is impossible to remove the head of prophecy, is it not?"

The master said to me, "When you realize what 'head' means, and that prophecy comes from the head, then understand the meaning of 'its head was [7] removed.'

"First I spoke with you in parables, and you did not understand. Now I am speaking with you openly, and you do not grasp it. Nevertheless, you were for me a parable among parables and a disclosure among things revealed.

"Be eager to be saved without being urged. Rather, be fervent on your own and, if possible, outdo even me, for this is how the father will love you.

"Come to hate hypocrisy and evil intention. Intention produces hypocrisy, and hypocrisy is far from truth.

"Do not let heaven's kingdom wither away. It is like a palm shoot whose dates dropped around it. It produced buds, and after they grew, its productivity dried up. This is also what happened with fruit that came from this single root. After it was harvested, fruit was obtained by many. It certainly would be good if you could produce new growth now. You would find it.[22]

"Since I was glorified like this once before, why do you hold me back when I am eager to go? [8] After my labor[23] you have made me stay with you another eighteen days[24] because of the parables. For some people it was enough to listen to the teaching and understand 'The Shepherds,' 'The Seed,' 'The Building,' 'The Lamps of the Young Women,' 'The Wage of the Workers,' and 'The Silver Coins and the Woman.'[25]

"Be eager for the word. The first aspect of the word is faith, the second is love, the third is works, and from these comes life.

"The word is like a grain of wheat. When someone sowed it, he had faith in it, and when it sprouted, he loved it, because he saw many grains instead of just one. And after he worked, he was saved because he prepared it as food and he still kept some out to sow.

"This is also how you can acquire heaven's kingdom for yourselves. Unless you acquire it through knowledge,[26] you will not be able to find it."

Be Sober, Be Saved

"So I say to you, be sober. Do not go astray. And often have I said to you all together, and also to you alone, James, be saved. I have commanded you to follow me, and I have taught you how to speak before the rulers.

"See that I have come down and have spoken and have exerted myself and have won my crown [9] when I saved you. I came down to live with you that you might also live with me. And when I found that your houses had no roofs, I lived in houses that could receive me when I came down.

"Trust in me, my brothers. Understand what the great light is. The father does not need me. A father does not need a son, but it is the son who needs the father. To him I am going, for the father of the son is not in need of you.

"Listen to the word, understand knowledge,[27] love life, and no one will persecute you and no one will oppress you other than you yourselves."

Shame on You, Blessings on You

"You wretches! You poor devils! You pretenders to truth! You falsifiers of knowledge! You sinners against the spirit! Do you still dare to listen when from the beginning you should have been speaking? Do you still dare to sleep when from the beginning you should have been awake so that heaven's kingdom might receive you? [10] I tell you the truth, it is easier for a holy person to sink into defilement and for an enlightened person to sink into darkness, than for you to reign—or not to reign.[28]

"I have remembered your tears, your mourning, and your grief. They are far from us. You who are outside the father's inheritance, weep when you should, mourn, and preach what is good. The son is ascending, as is proper.

"I tell you the truth, if I had been sent to those who would listen to me and had spoken with them, I would never have come down to earth.[29] Now be ashamed.

"Look, I shall be leaving you and go away, and I do not want to stay with you any longer, just as you yourselves have not wanted this. Follow me quickly. This is why I tell you, for you I came down. You are loved ones. You are the ones who will bring life to many. Invoke the father, pray to God frequently, and he will be generous with you.

"Blessings on one who has seen you with him when he is proclaimed among the angels and glorified among the saints. Yours is life. Rejoice and be glad as [11] children of God. Observe his will that you may be saved. Accept correction from me and save yourselves. I am mediating for you with the father, and he will forgive you many things."

Few Find Heaven's Kingdom

When we heard this, we were delighted. We had become gloomy because of what we[30] said earlier. But when he saw us happy, he said,

"Shame on you who are in need of an advocate.

"Shame on you who stand in need of grace.

"Blessings will be on those who have spoken out and acquired grace for themselves.

"Compare yourselves to foreigners. How are they viewed in your city? Why are you anxious to banish yourselves on your own and distance yourselves from your city? Why abandon your dwelling on your own and make it available for those who want to live in it? You exiles and runaways, shame on you, for you will be captured.

"Or maybe you think that the father is a lover of humankind, or that he is won over by prayers, or that he is gracious to one because of another, or that he tolerates whoever is seeking?

"He[31] knows about desire and what the flesh needs. Does it not desire the soul? The body does not sin apart from the soul just as [12] the soul is not saved apart from the spirit. But if the soul is saved from evil and the spirit too is saved, the body becomes sinless. The spirit animates the soul but the body kills it. The soul kills itself.[32]

"I tell you the truth, he certainly will not forgive the sin of the soul or the guilt of the flesh, for none of those who have worn the flesh will be saved. Do you think that many have found heaven's kingdom?

"Blessings on one who has seen oneself as a fourth one in heaven."[33]

Know Yourselves

When we heard this, we became sad. But when he saw that we were sad, he said, "I say this to you that you may know yourselves.[34]

"Heaven's kingdom is like a head of grain that sprouted in a field. And when it was ripe, it scattered its seed, and again it filled the field with heads of grain for another year. So with you, be eager to harvest for yourselves a head of the grain of life that you may be filled with the kingdom.

"And as long as I am with you, pay attention to me and trust in me, but when I am far from you, remember me. And remember me because I was with you and you did not know me.

"Blessings will be on those who have known me.

"Shame on those who have heard and have not believed.

"Blessings will be on those who [13] have not seen but yet have [believed].[35]

"Once again I appeal to you. I am disclosed to you as I am building a house useful to you when you find shelter in it, and it will support[36] your neighbors' house when theirs threatens to collapse.

"I tell you the truth, shame on those for whom I was sent down here.

"Blessings will be on those who are going up to the father.

"Again I warn you, you who exist. Be like those who do not exist that you may dwell with those who do not exist.[37]

"Do not let heaven's kingdom become a desert within you. Do not be proud because of the light that enlightens. Rather, act toward yourselves as I myself have toward you. I have put myself under a curse for you, that you might be saved."

The Last Word

Peter responded to these comments and said, "Sometimes you urge us on toward heaven's kingdom, but at other times you turn us away, master. Sometimes you encourage us, draw us toward faith, and promise us life, but at other times you drive us away from heaven's kingdom."

The master answered and said to us, "I have offered you faith many times—and have revealed myself to you, [14] James—and you have not known me. Now I see you often rejoicing. And although you are delighted about the promise of life, you are sad and gloomy when you are taught about the kingdom.

"Nevertheless, you, through faith and knowledge, have received life. So disregard rejection when you hear it, but when you hear about the promise, be joyful all the more.

"I tell you the truth, whoever will receive life and believe in the kingdom will never leave it, not even if the father wants to banish him.

"This is all I shall tell you at this time. Now I shall ascend to the place from which I have come. When I was eager to go, you have driven me off, and instead of accompanying me, you have chased me away.

"Be attentive to the glory that awaits me, and when you have opened your hearts, listen to the hymns that await me up in heaven. Today I must take my place at the right hand of my father.

"I have spoken my last word to you; I shall depart from you, for a chariot of spirit[38] has carried me up, and from now on I shall strip myself that I may clothe myself.[39]

"So pay attention: blessings on those who have proclaimed the son before he came down, so that, when I did come, I might ascend.

"Blessings three times over [15] on those who were proclaimed by the son before they came into being, so that you might share with them."

Apocalyptic Ascent

When he said this, he left. Peter and I knelt down, gave thanks, and sent our hearts up to heaven. We heard with our ears and saw with our eyes the noise of wars, a trumpet blast, and great turmoil.[40]

When we passed beyond that place, we sent our minds up further. We saw with our eyes and heard with our ears hymns, angelic praises, and angelic rejoicing. Heavenly majesties were singing hymns, and we rejoiced too.

Again after this we wished to send our spirits up to the majesty. When we ascended, we were not allowed to see or hear anything. For the other disciples called to us and asked us, "What did you hear from the teacher? What did he tell you? Where did he go?"

We answered them, "He ascended. He gave us his right hand, and promised all of us life. He showed us children coming after us and commanded [16] [us] to love them, since we are to be [saved] for their sakes."

When they heard this, they believed the revelation, but they were angry about those who would be born. Not wishing to give them reason to take offense, I sent each of them to a different location. I myself went up to Jerusalem, praying that I might acquire a share with the loved ones who are to appear.[41]

Final Advice

I pray that the beginning may come from you. This is how I can be saved. They will be enlightened through me, by my faith, and through another's that is better than mine. I wish mine to be the lesser.

Do your best to be like them, and pray that you may acquire a share with them. Beyond what I have said, the savior did not disclose any revelation to us on their behalf. We proclaim a share with those for whom the message was proclaimed, those whom the lord has made his children.

PART EIGHT

The Book
of Thomas

THE BOOK OF THOMAS is a dialogue between Jesus and Judas Thomas on issues involved in ethical living. To put it more precisely, the Book of Thomas is in the form of a dialogue at the beginning of the text (138–42) and a monologue of Jesus at the end (142–45). The title, given at the end, is also of two parts: "The Book of Thomas—The Contender Writing to the Perfect." The title has led some scholars to refer to the text as the Book of Thomas the Contender. These features of the text have prompted John D. Turner to conclude that the Book of Thomas is based on two sources, a dialogue between Jesus and Judas Thomas and a collection of sayings of Jesus. According to Turner, the collection of sayings may account for the description in the incipit: "The hidden sayings that the savior spoke to Judas Thomas, which I, Mathaias, in turn recorded." The incipit of the Book of Thomas, in turn, parallels the incipit of the Gospel of Thomas.

Hans-Martin Schenke suggests a different theory for the origin of the Book of Thomas. He proposes that the document is based on a Hellenistic Jewish text that has been Christianized in the Book of Thomas as a dialogue between Jesus and Judas Thomas. The earlier Hellenistic Jewish text is indicated, according to Schenke, by the second part of the title of the present text: "The

Contender Writing to the Perfect." In Schenke's view, the contender would have been the patriarch Jacob, who in the Hellenistic Jewish text would have been referred to as sending a letter on wisdom and virtue to those designated as "the perfect."

The message of the Book of Thomas builds upon the words of the savior that ignorance must be eradicated and knowledge embraced. Jesus says to Judas Thomas,

> Since it is said that you are my twin and true friend, examine yourself and understand who you are, how you exist, and how you will come to be. Since you are to be called my brother, it is not fitting for you to be ignorant of yourself. And I know that you have understood, for already you have understood that I am the knowledge of truth. So while you are walking with me, though you are ignorant, already you have obtained knowledge and you will be called one who knows oneself. For those who have not known themselves have known nothing, but those who have known themselves already have acquired knowledge about the depth of the universe. (138)

On the basis of this declaration concerning knowledge, Jesus utters strong words about how to avoid both the fire of passion and the fire of judgment. These words are shaped by the concerns of Jewish wisdom and Greek philosophy, especially Platonic philosophy. Jesus says that "everyone who seeks truth from true wisdom (sophia) will fashion wings to fly, fleeing from the passion that inflames human spirits" (140); and he adds, in terms that recall Plato's Phaedo, that the fire that drives people in their passion imprisons them and constrains them like a stake in the heart or a bit in the mouth. Jesus offers a vivid portrayal of the fire of hell worthy of the (Ethiopic) Revelation (or, Apocalypse) of Peter from early Christian literature, and Dante's Inferno, and he adds final words of shame and blessing.

The Book of Thomas is a part of the Thomas tradition, and "the hidden sayings" of Jesus in the Book of Thomas resemble sayings in the Gospel of Thomas. As in that earlier gospel, in the Book of Thomas Jesus is in the company of Judas Thomas the Twin, and he discusses knowledge of self, the hidden and the visible, the desires of the flesh, and wisdom and foolishness. When Jesus, in Book of Thomas 140–41 and 145, says that the wise person should seek (or pray) and find and reign and rest, he speaks in terms familiar from Gospel of Thomas 2. At the same time, the perspective of the Book of Thomas is more radically ascetic than the Gospel of Thomas, and the Book of Thomas uses harsh language in its condemnation of the fire of passion.

The Book of Thomas is preserved in Coptic translation as the seventh tractate in Codex II of the Nag Hammadi library. It was likely composed in Greek, perhaps in Syria, where Thomas was revered, though Hans-Martin Schenke also identifies Alexandrian traits in the text. The date of composition may be the early third century or even the second century—that is, after the Gospel of Thomas and before the Acts of Thomas.

For further reading: Raymond Kuntzmann, *Le Livre de Thomas*; Hans-Martin Schenke, "Das Buch des Thomas"; Hans-Martin Schenke, *Das Thomas-Buch*; Hans-Martin Schenke and Einar Thomassen, "The Book of Thomas"; John D. Turner, *The Book of Thomas the Contender*; John D. Turner and Bentley Layton, "The Book of Thomas the Contender Writing to the Perfect."

The Book of Thomas

or

The Contender Writing to the Perfect[1]

(NHC II,7)

The hidden sayings that the savior spoke to Judas Thomas, which I, Mathaias, in turn recorded.[2] I was walking, listening to them speak with each other.

Jesus Speaks with Brother Thomas

The savior said, "Brother Thomas, while you are still in the world, listen to me and I shall reveal to you what you have thought about in your heart.

"Since it is said that you are my twin and true friend, examine yourself and understand who you are, how you exist, and how you will come to be. Since you are to be called my brother, it is not fitting for you to be ignorant of yourself. And I know that you have understood, for already you have understood that I am the knowledge of truth. So while you are walking with me, though you do lack understanding, already you have obtained knowledge and you will be called one who knows oneself.³ For those who have not known themselves have known nothing, but those who have known themselves already have acquired knowledge about the depth of the universe. So then, my brother Thomas, you have seen what is hidden from people, what they stumble against in their ignorance."

The Hidden and the Visible

Thomas said to the master,⁴ "That is why I beg you to tell me what I ask before your ascension. When I hear from you about what is hidden, I can speak of it. And it is clear to me that the truth is difficult to accomplish before people."

The savior answered and said, "If what is visible to you is obscure to you, how can you comprehend what is invisible? If deeds of truth visible in the world are difficult for you to accomplish, how will you accomplish things of the exalted majesty and fullness, which are invisible?⁵ How will you be called workers? You are beginners and have not attained the greatness of perfection."

Thomas answered and said to the savior, "Tell us about these things that you say are invisible and hidden from us."

The savior said, "[All] bodies [have come into being in the same irrational way] that animals are produced, and so they are visible, as [creatures lusting after creatures]. Those that are above, however, [do not exist like] those that are visible.⁶ Rather, [they] live⁷ [139] from their own root, and their crops nourish them. But the visible bodies feed on creatures that are like them, and so the bodies are subject to change. Whatever is subject to change will perish and be lost, and henceforth has no hope of life, because this body is an animal body. Just as an animal body perishes, these modeled forms also will perish. Are they not from sexual intercourse like that of the animals? If the body too is from intercourse, how will it give birth to anything different from them? So then, you are children until you become perfect."

Thomas answered, "This is why I say to you, master, those who speak about what is invisible and difficult to explain are like people who shoot their arrows at a target during the night. Of course, they shoot their arrows as any people do, since they are shooting at the target, but it is not visible. When light comes, however, and banishes darkness, then the accomplishment of each person will be clear. And you, our light, bring enlightenment, master."

Jesus said, "It is through light that light exists."

Thomas spoke and said, "Master, why does this visible light that shines for people rise and set?"[8]

The savior said, "Blessed Thomas, surely this visible light has shone for you, not to keep you here, but that you might leave. And when all the chosen ones lay down their animal nature, this light will withdraw up to its being, and its being will welcome it to itself, because the light is a good helper."

Wisdom and Foolishness

The savior continued and said, "Oh, unsearchable love of light! Oh, bitterness of the fire! You blaze in the bodies of people, and in the marrow of their bones, blazing in them night and day, burning their limbs and [making] their minds drunk and their souls deranged. [You dominate] males and females day and night; you move [and arouse] them secretly and visibly. When the males are [aroused, they are attracted to the] females and the females to the males.[9] That is why it is said [140] that everyone who seeks truth from true wisdom[10] will fashion wings to fly, fleeing from the passion that burns human spirits. And one will fashion wings to flee from every visible spirit."

Thomas answered and said, "Master, this is precisely what I ask you, since I understand that you are beneficial to us through what you say."

Again the savior answered and said, "This is why we must speak to you, because this is the teaching for the perfect. If you wish to become perfect, keep these sayings. If not, the name for you is 'ignorant,' since an intelligent person cannot associate with a fool. The intelligent person is perfect in all wisdom, but to the fool good and evil are the same. The wise person will be nourished by truth, and will be like a tree growing by the stream of water.[11] Some people have wings but rush toward visible things that are far from truth. The fire that guides them gives them an illusion of truth. It will shine on them with a perishable beauty, and it will imprison them in dark delight and capture them in sweet-smelling pleasure. And it will make them blind with insatiable desire, inflame their souls, and be like a stake that is jammed into their heart and can never be removed. Like a bit in the mouth, it leads them according to its own wish.[12]

"It has bound them with its chains, and tied all their limbs with the bitterness of the bondage of desire for those visible things that perish and change and fluctuate impulsively. They have always been drawn downward. When they are slain, they are drawn to all the animals of corruption."

Thomas answered and said, "It is clear and has been said that [many are] . . . those who do not know . . . soul."

[The savior] answered and said, "[Blessings] on the wise person who has [sought truth, and] when it has been found, has rested [141] upon it forever, and has not been afraid of those who wish to trouble him."[13]

Our Own and the Others

Thomas answered and said, "Master, is it beneficial for us to rest among our own?"

The savior said, "Yes, it is useful, and it is good for you, since the things visible among people will pass away. For the vessel of their flesh will pass away, and when it disintegrates, it will come to be among visible things, among things that can be seen. The visible fire gives them pain, because of the love of faith they once had. They will be gathered back to the visible realm.[14] Moreover, among the invisible things, those who can see will perish, without the first love, in their concern for this life and the burning of the fire. There is only a little time before what is visible will pass away. Then shapeless phantoms will come and dwell forever in the midst of the tombs on corpses, in pain and destruction of soul."[15]

Thomas answered and said, "What can we say in the face of these things?[16] What shall we say to those who are blind? What teaching shall we give those miserable mortals who say, 'We have come to [do] good and not to curse,' and will [say] further, 'If we had not been born in the flesh, we would not have known iniquity'?"

The savior said, "To tell the truth, do not think of these as human beings, but regard them [as] animals. As animals devour each other, so people like this devour each other. They are deprived of the kingdom,[17] since they love the delight of fire and are slaves of death and rush to deeds of corruption. They fulfill the desire of their parents. They will be cast down into the abyss and

be afflicted by the compulsion of the bitterness of their evil nature. They will be whipped to drive them down to a place they do
not know, and they will leave their limbs behind, not with forti-
tude but with despair. And they rejoice in [the fire, they love]
madness and derangement, because they are [fools]. They pursue
derangement, not realizing their madness but thinking they are
wise. They . . . the love of their body . . . ,[18] [142] their hearts turning to themselves and their thoughts being on their affairs. But fire
will consume them."

Thomas answered and said, "Master, what can one cast down to
them do? I am very concerned about them, for many oppose them."

The savior answered and said, "What is evident to you?"

Judas, called Thomas, said, "Master, you should speak and I
should listen."

The savior answered, "Listen to what I tell you and believe the
truth. What sows and what is sown will pass away in their fire, in
fire and water, and will be hidden in tombs of darkness. And after
a long time the fruit of evil trees will appear and be punished and
slain in the mouths of animals and people through the agency of
the rains, the winds, the air, and the light shining above."[19]

Thomas answered, "You certainly have convinced us, master.
We realize in our hearts, it is clearly so, and your word is not mea-
ger. But these sayings that you tell us are laughable and ridiculous
to the world, since they are not understood. How can we go forth
and preach them when we are [not] respected in the world?"

Jesus Preaches about Judgment

The savior answered and said, "I tell you the truth, whoever listens to [your] word and turns away or sneers at it or smirks at

these things, I tell you the truth, that person will be handed over to the ruler who is on high, who rules as king over all the powers, and the ruler will turn him away and cast him down from on high into the abyss, and he will be imprisoned in a cramped, dark place. So he cannot turn or move because of the great depth of Tartaros[20] and the [burdensome bitterness] of Hades. Whoever relies on what [is brought] to him . . . will not be forgiven [his] madness, but will [be judged. Whoever has] persecuted you will be handed over to the angel Tartarouchos,[21] [who has flaming] fire that pursues them,[22] [143] and fiery whips that spew forth sparks into the face of one pursued. If he flees to the west, he finds fire. If he turns south, he finds it there as well. If he turns north, the threat of erupting fire meets him again. Nor can he find the way to the east, to flee there and be saved, for he did not find it while embodied so as to find it on the day of judgment."

Shame on You

Then the savior continued and said, "Shame on you, godless people, who have no hope, who are secure in things that do not last.

"Shame on you who hope in the flesh and in the prison that will perish.[23] How long will you sleep, and think that what is imperishable will also perish? Your hope is based upon the world, and your god is this present life. You are destroying your souls.

"Shame on you with the fire that burns within you. It is insatiable.

"Shame on you because of the wheel that turns in your minds.

"Shame on you because of the smoldering within you. It will devour your flesh visibly, tear your souls secretly, and prepare you for each other.

"Shame on you, prisoners, for you are bound in caves. You laugh, you rejoice in mad laughter. You do not perceive your destruction. Neither do you perceive your plight, nor have you understood that you dwell in darkness and death. Rather, you are drunk with fire and [full] of bitterness. Your hearts are deranged because of the smoldering within you, and the poison and blows of your enemies are a delight to you. Darkness has risen in you like the light, for you have surrendered your freedom to slavery. You have darkened your hearts and surrendered your minds to foolishness. You have filled your minds with the smoke of the fire within you, and your light has been hidden in the [dark] cloud. You [love] the garment[24] you wear, [although it is filthy], and you have been gripped [by] nonexistent hope. [You have] believed in what you do [not] know. You all live in [bondage] but pride yourselves [in your freedom].[25] [144] You have baptized your souls in the water of darkness. You have pursued your own wishes.

"Shame on you who dwell in error, not seeing that the light of the sun, which judges the universe and looks down on the universe, will encircle everything to make slaves of the enemies. Nor do you perceive how the moon looks down night and day, seeing the bodies of your slaughters.

"Shame on you who love intercourse and filthy association with the female.

"And shame on you because of the powers of your bodies, for they will mistreat you.

"Shame on you because of the actions of the evil demons.

"Shame on you who entice your limbs with fire. Who will sprinkle a restful dew on you, to extinguish the many fires within you, and your burning? Who will make the sun shine on you, to dispel the darkness within you, and hide the darkness and filthy water?

"The sun and the moon will give a fragrant aroma to you, as will the air, the spirit, the earth, and the water.[26] If the sun does not shine on these bodies, they will rot and perish just like weeds or grass. If the sun shines on them, they grow strong and choke the grapevine. But if the grapevine becomes strong and casts its shadow over the weeds and all the rest of the brush growing with it, and [spreads] and fills out, it alone inherits the land where it grows, and dominates wherever it has cast its shadow. So when it grows, it dominates the whole land, and it is productive for its master and pleases him greatly. He would have gone to great pains because of the weeds before pulling them out, but the grapevine by itself disposed of them and choked them, and they died and became like earth."

Then Jesus continued and said to them, "Shame on you, for you have not accepted the teaching, and those who [wish to accept it] will suffer when they preach. [You will persecute them], but you will rush into [your own traps]. You will cast them down [to the lions][27] and put them to death, daily,[28] [145] and they will rise from death.[29]

Blessings on You

"Blessings on you who understand beforehand the temptations and flee from things that are alien.

"Blessings on you who are mocked and are not respected because of the love your master has for you.

"Blessings on you who weep and are oppressed by those who have no hope, for you will be released from all bondage.

"Watch and pray that you may not remain in the flesh, but that you may leave the bondage of the bitterness of this life. And when

you pray, you will find rest, for you have left pain and reproach behind. When you leave the pains and the passions of the body, you
will receive rest from the good one. You will reign with the king,
you united with him and he with you, from now on and forever.
Amen."[30]

The Book of Thomas
The Contender Writing
to the Perfect

Scribal Note

Remember me also, my siblings,[31] in your prayers.
Peace be with the holy[32] and the spiritual.[33]

PART NINE

The Dialogue
of the Savior

A S THE TITLE INDICATES, the Dialogue of the Savior is a dialogue between Jesus and his disciples. In the case of this text, the disciples who are named as dialogue partners with Jesus are Judas, Matthew, and Mary—in all likelihood, Judas Thomas the Twin, Matthew the disciple or replacement apostle or scribe, and Mary of Magdala. The topics of conversation in the discussion are many, but the focus is upon the life of *gnōsis,* and the agenda for the discussion seems to be set by a comment of the master, Jesus, at Dialogue of the Savior 129: "Let one who [knows] seek and find and rejoice." This comment, which reverberates through the Dialogue of the Savior, represents the same understanding of seeking and finding as the saying of Jesus in Gospel of Thomas 2, and the Dialogue of the Savior may well have made use of this and other sayings that are found in the Gospel of Thomas.

According to Helmut Koester and Elaine Pagels, as many as five sources may be discernible behind the present version of the Dialogue of the Savior, and these five have shaped the character of the text. Koester and Pagels have identified the following sources: 1) a dialogue between "the master" Jesus and his disciples, with sayings of Jesus that are particularly reminiscent of the Gospel of Thomas (124ff.); 2) a fragment of a creation myth (127–31); 3) a cosmological wisdom list (133–34); 4) a fragment of an apocalyptic vision (134–37); and 5) an introduction about "the savior" Jesus, added by the final author (120–24).

The Dialogue of the Savior opens as the savior says to the disciples, "Now the time has come, brothers and sisters, for us to leave our labor behind and stand at rest, for whoever stands at rest will rest forever." After Jesus recites a prayer of praise, he teaches the disciples (as best we can tell) about the end of all things by offering an eschatological perspective that the end is "already but not yet" present. The dialogue commences, and in the course of the conversation Jesus and the disciples discuss the inner life, spirit, body, light, darkness, creation, the word, fire, water, the world, the rulers of the world, fullness, deficiency, life, death— themes well known from gnostic texts. There are also baptismal allusions within the text. Mary herself pronounces three wisdom sayings usually attributed to Jesus:

> The wickedness of each day < is sufficient >.
>
> Workers deserve their food.
>
> Disciples resemble their teachers.

Mary is praised for her insight, and the text observes, "She spoke this utterance as a woman who understood everything" (139). The goal of the inquiry into knowledge in the Dialogue of the Savior is salvation, and Jesus explains the nature of the seeking and finding. He says, "I tell you [the truth], look, what you seek and inquire about [is] within you, and it [has] the power and mystery [of the] spirit, for [it is] from [the spirit]" (128).

The Dialogue of the Savior is the fifth tractate in Codex III of the Nag Hammadi library. A fragment of the text, Yale inv. 1784, found its way to the Beinecke Library at Yale University, where it was identified by Stephen Emmel. The Dialogue of the Savior is preserved in Coptic translation but was most likely composed in Greek. The state of preservation of the Coptic text is not good, and the many lacunae make it difficult to understand the text fully. A second-century date of composition for the Dialogue of the Savior is a reasonable conjecture. Koester and Pagels argue that the Dialogue of the Savior may have been composed in the early second century, though the dialogue source incorporated into it may have been written in the last decades of the first century. Sometimes scholars add section numbers in the Dialogue of the Savior to facilitate ease of reference, but that convention is not followed here.

For further reading: Beate Blatz and Einar Thomassen, "The Dialogue of the Saviour"; Stephen Emmel, ed., *Nag Hammadi Codex III, 5;* Julian V. Hills, "The Dialogue of the Savior"; Helmut Koester and Elaine H. Pagels, "Introduction," in *Nag Hammadi Codex III, 5,* ed. Stephen Emmel; Pierre Létourneau, *Le Dialogue du Sauveur;* Silke Peterson and Hans-Gebhard Bethge, "Der Dialog des Erlösers."

The Dialogue of the Savior[1]

(NHC III,5; Yale inv. 1784)

The Savior Teaches about Rest

The savior said to his disciples, "Now the time has come, brothers and sisters,[2] for us to leave our labor[3] behind and stand at rest,[4] for whoever stands at rest will rest forever. I say to you, always rise above . . . time . . . . [I say] to you, . . . [do not] be afraid of [those] . . . you. I [say to you], anger is frightening, [and whoever] stirs up anger is a [frightening person]. But since you have [been able to endure], it may come from [you] . . . .

"People received these words about anger[5] with fear and trembling. Anger established rulers over them, for no one escapes anger. But when I came, I opened a path and taught people about the way of passage for those who are chosen and alone,[6] [121] who have known the father and have believed the truth. And you offered praise.

Giving Praise to the Father

"Now, when you offer praise, do so in this way:

> Hear us, father,
> as you have heard your only son
> and have received him to yourself.[7]

225

[You have] given him rest from many [labors].
Your power is [invincible],
[because] your armaments are [invincible],
. . . light . . . alive . . . inaccessible . . . [alive].
The [true] word[8] [has brought] repentance for life,
[and this has come] from you.
You are the thought and supreme serenity
of those who are alone.[9]
Again, hear us
as you have heard your chosen.
Through your sacrifice the chosen will enter.
Through their good works they have freed their souls
from blind bodily limbs,
so that they may come to be [122] forever.
Amen."

Overcoming the Power of Darkness

"I shall teach you. At the time of destruction the first power of darkness will come upon you. Do not be afraid and say, 'Look, the time has come.' But when you see a single staff . . . understand that . . . from some such thing . . . and the rulers . . . come upon you . . . . In truth, fear is the power [of darkness]. So if you are afraid of what is about to come upon you, it will overwhelm you, and not one among them will spare you or show you mercy. Rather, look at [what is] within, since you have mastered every word on earth. This [123] [will] take you up to a [place] where there is no dominion [and no] tyrant. When you . . . you will see those . . . and you will also [hear them. I] tell you, reflection . . . . Reflection is . . . [where] truth [is] . . . but they . . . and you . . . truth. This [is . . . in] living [mind]. Therefore . . . and your joy . . . in order that . . . your souls . . . lest the word . . . which they raised . . . and they could not [understand] it . . . . Make what is [inside] you and what is [outside you a single one].[10] To be sure, the place [124] of crossing is frightening in [your] sight, but without hesitation pass by.[11] Its depth is great, [its] height [is] staggering. [Be of a single mind] . . . and the fire . . . dew drops . . . all powers . . . you. They will . . . and [all] powers . . . they . . . in front. I tell [you], . . . the soul . . . becomes . . . in each one . . . you are . . . and that . . . sleep not . . . the children . . . and you . . . you . . . ."

The Savior and His Disciples
Discuss the Inner Life

Matthew[12] said, "How . . . ?" [125]

The savior said, "[If you do not keep] what is within you [in order, your work] will remain, but you [will not]."

Judas[13] [said], "Master,[14] [I want to understand all] the works of the souls [that are in] these little ones. When . . . , where will they be? . . . the spirit . . . ?"

The master [said, ". . . receive] them. They do not die and are not destroyed, because they have known [their] companions and the one who will receive them. For truth seeks the wise and the righteous."

The savior [said], "The lamp [of the] body is the mind. As long as [what is within] you is kept in order—that is, [the soul][15]—your bodies are [enlightened]. As long as your hearts are dark, your light, which you [126] expect, [is far from you].[16] I have called [you to myself], since I am about to depart, so that [you may receive] my word among [yourselves. Look], I am sending it to [you]."[17]

Who Seeks, Who Reveals?

His disciples [said, "Master], who seeks and [who] reveals?"

[The master] said [to them], "One who seeks [also] reveals."

Matthew [said to him again, "Master], when I [listen to you] and I speak, who is it who [speaks and] who listens?"

The [master] said, "One who speaks also [listens], and one who can see also reveals."

Mary[18] said, "Master, look, [while I] wear a body, where do my tears come from, where does my laughter come from?"

The master said, "[The body] weeps because of its works [and what] remains to be done. The mind laughs [because of [127] the fruits[19] of] the spirit. Whoever does not [stand] in darkness will [not] be able to see [the light].[20] I tell you, [what has no] light is darkness, [and whoever does not] stand in [darkness will] not [be able] to see the light. [The children of] falsehood, however, were taken out . . . . You will put on light, and [so you will live] forever . . . . [If] . . . ,[21] then [all] the powers above and below will treat you harshly. In that place [there will] be weeping and [gnashing] of teeth over the end of all."

The Creation of the World

Judas said, "Tell [us], master, what [existed] before [heaven and] earth came into being?"[22]

The master said, "There was darkness and water, and [128] spirit upon [water].²³ And I tell you [the truth], look, what you seek and inquire about [is] within you, and it [has] the power and mystery [of the] spirit, for [it is] from [the spirit].²⁴ Wickedness entered [in order to destroy] the mind, [forever]. Look . . . ."²⁵

[Matthew] said,²⁶ "Master, tell us, where is [the soul] established and where does the true [mind] dwell?"

The master [said], "The fire of the spirit came into existence [between] the two, and so there came to be [spirit]²⁷ and the true mind within them. [If] someone establishes the soul on high, then [the person will] be exalted."

Seek, Find, Rejoice

Matthew asked him [129], "[Is not . . .²⁸ necessary], when it is understood [in the true sense]?"²⁹

The master [said, ". . . is] more useful than your [work. Remove] from yourselves [what can] pursue you and everything [in] your hearts. For as your hearts . . . ,³⁰ so [will you find] a way to overcome the powers above and below. And I say to you, let one [who has] power renounce [it and] repent,³¹ and let one who [knows] seek and find and rejoice."³²

Judas said, "Look, [I] see that all things are [just] like signs over [the earth], and that is why they have come to be in this way."

The Emergence of the Word

The master [said], "When the father established the world, he [collected] some of its water, and the word³³ came from it. [130]

It[34] experienced many [troubles, but] it was more exalted than the path [of the stars] around the entire earth."[35]

[He continued],[36] "The water collected [above] is beyond the stars, and [beyond] the water <is> a great fire encircling them like a wall. Periods of time [began to be measured] once many of the beings [that] were within had separated from the rest.

"When the [word] was established, he looked [down]. The father said to him, 'Go, [send something] from yourself, so that [the earth] may not be in want from generation to [generation and] from age to age.'

"So [he] sent from himself fountains of milk, fountains of honey, oil, wine, and fine fruit and delicious flavors and sound roots, [so that] the earth might not be deficient from generation [to] generation and from age to age.

"The word is above . . . [131] stood [and showed] his beauty . . . . And outside [was a great light], brighter [than] the one like it,[37] for that one rules over [all] the realms above and below. [Light was] taken from the fire and dispersed in the [firmament][38] above and below. Those over the heaven above and the earth below depend upon them. Everything is dependent upon them."

When Judas heard this, he bowed down, fell on his knees,[39] and praised the master.

The Savior and His Disciples Discuss the Place of Life

Mary asked her brothers, "Where are you going to store [these] questions you ask of the child of [humankind]?"

The master [said] to her, "Sister, [no one] can ask about these things [except] someone who has a place [132] to store them in the heart. And such a person can leave [the world] and enter the place [of life], and will not be held back in this world of poverty."[40]

Matthew said, "Master, I want [to see] that place of life, [where] there is no wickedness but only pure light."

The master replied, "Brother Matthew, you will not be able to see it as [long as you] wear flesh."

Matthew said, "Master, [if I] cannot see it, at least let me understand it."

The master said, "Everyone who has known oneself[41] has seen oneself. Everything that person is given to do that person does. So such a person has come to [resemble] that place[42] in goodness."[43]

How Does an Earthquake Shake?

Judas answered and said, "Tell me, master, how does an [earthquake] shake when it shakes the earth?"

The master picked up a stone and held it in his hand. [He [133] said to him, "What] am I holding in my hand?"

He answered, "[It is] a stone."

He said to them, "What supports the [earth] is also what supports heaven. When a word comes from the majesty, it will go to what supports heaven and earth. The earth does not move. If it moved, it would collapse. But it does not, so that the first word might not fail. The word established the world and dwelled in it and smelled the fragrance from it.[44] I make known to you, all you children of humankind, all [the things] that do not move, for you are from that place. You live in the hearts of those who speak out in joy and truth. If the word comes from the father's body, among people, and they do not receive it, it will return back to its place."

Coming to Understanding

"Whoever does [not] know the work of perfection does not know anything.

"One who does not stand in the darkness cannot see the [134] light.

"One who does not [understand] how fire came to be will burn in it, not knowing its origin.[45]

"One who does not first understand water knows nothing. For what use is there for such a person to be baptized in it?

"One who does not understand how the wind that blows came to be will blow away with it.[46]

"One who does not understand how the body that a person wears came to be will perish with it.

"How will someone who does not know the son know the [father]?

"All things are hidden from one who does not know the root of all things.

"Whoever does not know the root of wickedness is no stranger to it.

"Those who do not understand how they came will not understand how they will go, and they are no strangers to this world, which will [exalt itself] and be humbled."

Judas, Matthew, and Mary Have an Apocalyptic Vision

He [took] Judas, Matthew, and Mary [135] [to show them the final] consummation of heaven and earth, and when he placed his [hand] on them, they hoped they might [see] it. Judas gazed up and saw a region of great height, and he saw the region of the abyss below.

Judas said to Matthew, "Brother, who can ascend to such a height or descend to the abyss below? For there is great fire there, and great terror."

At that moment a word[47] issued from the height. As Judas was standing there, he saw how the word came [down].

He asked the word, "Why have you come down?"

The child of humankind[48] greeted them and said to them, "A seed from a power was deficient, and it descended to the earth's abyss. The majesty remembered [it] and sent the [word to] it. The word brought the seed up into [the presence] of the majesty, so that [136] the first word might not be lost."[49]

[His] disciples marveled at everything he told them, and they accepted all of it in faith. And they understood that it was no longer necessary to keep an eye on evil.

Then he said to his disciples, "Did I not tell you that, like a visible flash of thunder and lightning, what is good will be taken up to the light?"

All his disciples praised him and said, "Master, before you appeared here, who was there to praise you, for all praises are because of you? Or who was there to bless [you], for all blessing comes from you?"

As they were standing there, he saw two spirits bringing a single soul with them, and there was a great flash of lightning. A word came from the child of humankind, saying, "Give them their garments," and the small became like the great. They were [like] those who were received up; [137] [there was no distinction] among them.[50]

The [words] he [spoke convinced the] disciples.

Mary Asks about the Vision

Mary [said to him, "Look, I] see the evil [that affects] people from the start, when they dwell with each other."

The master said [to her], "When you see them, [you understand] a great deal; they will [not stay there]. But when you see the one who exists eternally, that is the great vision."

They all said to him, "Explain it to us."

He said to them, "How do you wish to see it, [in] a passing vision or in an eternal vision?"

He went on to say, "Do your best to save what can come after [me], and seek it and speak through it, so that whatever you seek may be in harmony with you. For I [say] to you, truly the living God [is] in you, [138] [as you also are] in God."[51]

Judas Asks about the Rulers of the World and the Garments

Judas [said], "I really want [to learn everything]."

The [master] said to him, "The living [God does not] dwell [in this] entire [region] of deficiency."[52]

Judas [asked], "Who [will rule over us]?"

The master replied, "[Look, here are] all the things that exist [among] what remains. You [rule] over them."

Judas said, "But look, the rulers are over us, so they will rule over us."

The master answered, "You will rule over them. When you remove jealousy from yourselves, you will clothe yourselves in light and enter the bridal chamber."[53]

Judas asked, "How will [our] garments be brought to us?"

The master answered, "There are some who will provide them for you and others who will receive [them], [139] and they [will give] you your garments. For who can reach that place? It is very [frightening]. But the garments of life were given to these people because they know the way they will go.⁵⁴ Indeed, it is even difficult for me to reach it."⁵⁵

Mary Utters Words of Wisdom

Mary said, "So,

> The wickedness of each day <is sufficient>.⁵⁶
>
> Workers deserve their food.⁵⁷
>
> Disciples resemble their teachers."⁵⁸

She spoke this utterance as a woman who understood everything.⁵⁹

The Disciples Ask about Fullness
and Deficiency, Life and Death

The disciples asked him, "What is fullness and what is deficiency?"

He answered them, "You are from fullness and you are in a place of deficiency. And look, his light has poured down on me."

Matthew asked, "Tell me, master, how the dead die and how the living live." [140]

The master said, "[You have] asked me about a [true] saying that eye has not seen, nor have I heard it, except from you.⁶⁰ But I say to you, when what moves a person slips away, that person will be called dead, and when what is living leaves what is dead, it will be called alive."

Judas asked, "So why, really, do some <die> and some live?"

The master said, "Whatever is from truth does not die. Whatever is from woman dies."[61]

Mary asked, "Tell me, master, why have I come to this place, to gain or to lose?"[62]

The master replied, "You show the abundance of the one who reveals."

Mary asked him, "Master, then is there a place that is abandoned or without truth?"

The master said, "The place where I am not."

Mary said, "Master, you are awesome and marvelous, [141] and [like a devouring fire] to those who do not know [you]."

Matthew asked, "Why do we not go to our rest at once?"[63]

The master said, "When you leave these burdens behind."

Matthew asked, "How does the small unite with the great?"

The master said, "When you leave behind what cannot accompany you, then you will rest."[64]

Mary and the Other Disciples Discuss
True Life with the Master

Mary said, "I want to understand all things, [just as] they are."

The master said, "Whoever seeks life, this is their wealth. For the world's [rest] is false, and its gold and silver are deceptive."[65]

His disciples asked him, "What should we do for our work to be perfect?"

The master [said] to them, "Be ready, in every circumstance. Blessings on those who have found [142] the [strife and have seen] the struggle with their eyes. They have not killed nor have [they] been killed, but they have emerged victorious."

Judas asked, "Tell me, master, what is the beginning of the way?"[66]

He said, "Love and goodness. If one of these had existed among the rulers, wickedness would never have come to be."

Matthew said, "Master, you have spoken of the end of the universe with no difficulty."

The master said, "You have understood all the things I said to you and you have accepted them in faith. If you know them, they are yours. If not, they are not yours."

They asked him, "To what place are we going?"

The master said, "Stand in the place you can reach."

Mary asked, "Is everything established in this way visible?"

The master said, "I have told you, the one who can see reveals."

His twelve disciples asked him, "Teacher, [with] [143] serenity . . . teach us . . . ."

The master said, "[If you have understood] everything I have [told you], you will [become immortal, for] you . . . everything."[67]

Mary said, "There is only one saying I shall [speak] to the master, about the mystery of truth. In this we stand and in this we appear to those who are worldly."

Judas said to Matthew, "We want to understand what sort of garments we are to be clothed with when we leave the corruption of the [flesh]."

The master said, "The rulers and the administrators[68] have garments that are given only for a while and do not last. But you, as children of truth, are not to clothe yourselves with these garments that last only for a while. Rather, I say to you, you will be blessed when you strip off your clothing. For it is no great thing [144] [to lay aside what is] external."[69]

. . .[70] said, "Do I speak and do I receive . . . ?"

The master said, "Yes, [one who receives] your father in [a reflective way]."[71]

Mary Questions the Master about the Mustard Seed

Mary asked, "[Of what] kind is the mustard seed?[72] Is it from heaven or from earth?"

The master said, "When the father established the world for himself, he left many things with the mother of all. That is why he sows and works."[73]

Judas said, "You have told us this from the mind of truth. When we pray, how should we pray?"

The master said, "Pray in the place where there is no woman."

Matthew says, "He tells us, Pray in the place where there is no woman, which means, destroy the works of the female,[74] not because there is another form of birth[75] but because they should stop [giving birth]."

Mary said, "Will they never be destroyed?"

The master said, "[You] know they will perish [once again], [145] and [the works] of [the female here] will be [destroyed as well]."[76]

Judas said [to Matthew], "The works of the [female] will perish. [Then] the rulers will [call upon their realms], and we shall be ready for them."

The master said, "Will they see [you and will they] see those who receive you? Look, a true word[77] is coming from the father to the abyss, silently, with a flash of lightning, and it is productive.[78] Do they see it or overcome it? No, you know more fully [the way] that [neither angel] nor authority [knows]. It is the way of the father and the son, for the two are one. And you will travel the [way] you have come to know. Even if the rulers become great, they will not be able to reach it. I tell you the [truth], it is even difficult for me to reach it."[79] [146]

[Mary] asked [the master], "If the works [are destroyed, what actually] destroys a work?"

[The master said], "You know that [when] I destroy [it, people] will go to their own places."

Judas said, "How is the spirit disclosed?"

The master said, "How [is] the sword [disclosed]?"

Judas said, "How is the light disclosed?"

The master said, "[It is disclosed] through itself eternally."

Judas asked, "Who forgives whose works? Do the works [forgive] the world or does the world forgive the works?"

The master [answered], "Who [knows]? For it is the responsibility of whoever has come to know the works to do the [will] of the father.

Conclusion

"As for you, work hard to rid yourselves of [anger] and jealousy, and strip yourselves of your [works], and do not . . . [147] reproach . . . . For I say to [you], . . . you receive . . . many . . . one who has sought, having [found true life]. This person will [attain rest and] live forever. I say to [you, watch yourselves], so that you may not lead [your] spirits and your souls into error."[80]

[The Dialogue] of the Savior

PART TEN

The Second Discourse of Great Seth

T HE SECOND DISCOURSE of Great Seth, traditionally entitled the Second Treatise (or, Logos) of the Great Seth, is a
speech or message of Jesus about salvific knowledge and the true
meaning of the crucifixion in the face of the theology of the
emerging orthodox church. The title of the text, given entirely in
Greek at the end of the document, calls the text the second *logos*,
apparently in contrast to the first discourse, which may be referred
to near the opening of the text: "I have uttered a discourse for the
glory of the father. . . ." In both instances the discourse may be a
spoken word—here a spoken word that has been written down. If
that interpretation is correct, this text consists of a second speech
or message of great Seth. The title may also refer to the personified *logos*, the divine word, as in John 1 and many gnostic texts.
Great Seth, mentioned only in the title of the text, is a leading
character in other gnostic texts, especially Sethian texts such as the
Holy Book of the Great Invisible Spirit. In Christian Sethian traditions the heavenly figure of Seth can come to expression in the
person of Christ, who may be the incarnation of Seth. Thus, the
Second Discourse of Great Seth may be understood to be the second speech or message delivered by Jesus, the manifestation of
heavenly Seth.

The speaker throughout the Second Discourse of Great Seth is Jesus himself. Jesus proclaims the good news of salvation in the first-person singular, so that the text presents itself as the good news according to Jesus. Jesus explains that he is with the majesty of the spirit—that is, God—and that he came down to this world, "approached a bodily dwelling and evicted the previous occupant," and went in (51). The rulers of the world were confused and upset at the divine stranger in their midst, although at least one of the powers, whose name is Adonaios and who is known from other gnostic texts, including Sethian texts, did not join the other archons in their opposition to Jesus. Adonaios's name is taken from Adonai, Hebrew for "my lord," and Adonaios seems to be lord of the Jewish people in the Second Discourse of Great Seth. As in the gnostic text On the Origin of the World, Adonaios is a good archon.

The rest of the world rulers tried to kill Jesus, but in their ignorance they were unable to do so. Jesus says,

> *The death they think I suffered they suffered in their error and blindness. They nailed their man to their death. Their thoughts did not perceive me, since they were deaf and blind. By doing these things they pronounce judgment against themselves. As for me, they saw me and punished me, but someone else, their father, drank the gall and the vinegar; it was not I. They were striking me with a scourge, but someone else, Simon, bore the cross on his shoulder. Someone else wore the crown of thorns. And I was on high, poking fun at all the excesses of the rulers and the fruit of their error and conceit. I was laughing at their ignorance. (55–56)*

The leaders and members of the emerging orthodox church, Jesus goes on to say, mistakenly focus upon the story of the crucifixion, which they misunderstand, and they establish their theology upon it. Like Paul, they claim that baptism is dying with Christ, but Christ himself says, in the present text, that true baptism means people come to be in Christ and Christ in them: "The scripture regarding the ineffable water in use among us is this word: I am in you and you are in me, just as the father is in me <and in> you, with no guile at all" (49–50). In the emerging orthodox church people preach "the doctrine of a dead man" (60), and they behave in a legalistic fashion, so that they are in bondage, though some of them use the name of Christ and claim to be proponents of Christ. Actually, they serve two masters, Christ and Yaldabaoth the world ruler, and even more, probably Yaldabaoth's fellow cosmic bureaucrats. Further, Jesus says, Yaldabaoth is a joke, as are all those folks, from Adam to John the baptizer, who are Yaldabaoth's lackeys. The so-called Christians are the very people who, along with the ignorant, oppose the members of the perfect assembly or church. In this way the Second Discourse of Great Seth, like Valentinian texts, may suggest a threefold division of people into the ignorant (people of flesh), ordinary Christians (people of soul), and the members of the perfect assembly— gnostics (people of spirit).

According to the Second Discourse of Great Seth, Jesus teaches that he has come to his own and has united with them. He says, "Our thought was one with their thought, so they understood what I was saying" (59). In word and peace they have united in the *gnōsis* of Jesus, and Jesus concludes,

> They have come to know fully and completely that the one who is is one, and all are one. They have been taught about the One and the assembly and the members of the assembly. For the father of all is immeasurable and

immutable, mind, word, division, jealousy, fire, yet he is simply one, all in all in a single principle, because all are from a single spirit. (68)

The Second Discourse of Great Seth is to be found in Nag Hammadi Codex VII, tractate 2. It has been translated into Coptic but originally was composed in Greek. The Coptic is difficult to understand and translate, and many passages remain obscure. Gregory Riley posits that it may have been written in the latter half of the second century, perhaps in Alexandria, and that suggestion may be as good as any.

For further reading: Louis Painchaud, *Le Deuxième Traité du Grand Seth*; Silvia Pellegrini, "Der zweite Logos des großen Seth"; Gregory J. Riley, "Second Treatise of the Great Seth."

The Second Discourse
of Great Seth

or

The Second Treatise
of the Great Seth[1]

(*NHC VII,2*)

Perfect Majesty, the Mother, and the Savior

Perfect majesty is at rest in ineffable light, in truth, the mother of all things. Since I[2] alone am perfect, all of you attain to me on account of the word. For I dwell with all the majesty of the spirit, who is a friend equally to us and to our kin.

The Word and Baptism

I have uttered a discourse[3] for the glory of our father, through his goodness and imperishable thought, and this word comes from him. It is a matter fit for slavery to say, We shall die with Christ,[4] which means with imperishable and undefiled thought. What an incomprehensible wonder! The scripture regarding the ineffable water in use among us is this word: I am in you and you are in me, just as the father is in me <and in> you, [50] with no guile at all.[5]

The Call for the Salvation of Divine Thoughts

Let us call together an assembly.[6] Let us examine this creation of his[7] and send someone, just as he also examined thoughts[8] in the regions below.[9]

I said this to all the members of the whole vast assembly of the majesty, so that they rejoiced, and the entire household of the father of truth rejoiced. Since I am of them, I reminded them of the thoughts that had come from the undefiled spirit and had descended to the water—that is, to the regions below. A single thought was in all of them, since it came from a single source. They expressed their decision to me, and I concurred and went forth to reveal glory to my kin, my friends in spirit.

Those in the world had been prepared by the will of our sister Sophia,[10] whose indiscretion[11] was without guile. She was not sent out, nor did she request anything from the realm of all, the majesty of the assembly, and the fullness[12] when she first came [51] to prepare homes and habitations for the child of light. From the elements below she derived collaborators to construct bodily dwellings for them, but in their vainglory they fell into ruin. Yet it was in these dwellings that those in the world came to live.[13] And since they were prepared by Sophia, they are ready to receive the saving word of the ineffable One[14] and the majesty of the assembly of all those who still are in waiting and those who already are in me.

Coming to This World

I approached a bodily dwelling and evicted the previous occupant, and I went in.[15] The whole multitude of rulers was upset, and all the material stuff of the rulers and the powers born of earth began to tremble at the sight of the figure with a composite image.[16] I was in it, and I did not look like the previous occupant. He was a [52] worldly person, but I, I am from above the heavens. I did not defy them, and I became an anointed one,[17] but neither did I reveal myself to them in the love coming from me. Rather, I revealed that I am a stranger to the regions below.

Unrest and Confusion in the World

There was a great disturbance, with confusion and restlessness, in the whole world and in the council of the rulers.

Some were convinced when they saw the mighty deeds I accomplished. They are of the generation of Adonaios[18] and are descended from the one who fled from the throne to Sophia of hope, since she had previously given indication about us and all those with me.[19] They all were moving about.

Others hurried to inflict every sort of punishment on me from the world ruler and his accomplices. They were restless of mind about what they would plot against me. They thought their majesty was everything, and they also told lies about the human being[20] and all the majesty [53] of the assembly. They were incapable of knowing the father of truth, the human being of majesty. They usurped the name through corruption and ignorance, <through>[21] a flame of fire and a vessel created for the destruction of Adam, made to conceal all those who likewise are theirs.

The rulers from the realm of Yaldabaoth disclosed the circuit of the angels.[22] This is what humankind was seeking, that they might not know the true human, for Adam the modeled creature appeared to them. So, throughout their dwelling place there was agitation and fear that the angels surrounding them might take a stand against them.

For those offering praise I died, though not really, that their archangel might be useless.

The Arrogance of the World Ruler

Then the voice of the world ruler announced to the angels, "I am God, and there is no other beside me."[23] I laughed heartily when I reflected upon how conceited he was. He kept saying, over and over, "Who [54] is the human being?"[24] The whole host of his angels, who had seen Adam and his dwelling place, laughed at its insignificance. Thus their thought turned away from the heavenly majesty, who is the true human, whose name they perceived in the insignificance of a dwelling place. They are inferior, senseless in their empty thought, in their laughter, and so they were corrupted.

The entire majesty of the fatherhood of the spirit was at rest in his realms, and I was with him, since I have a thought of a single emanation from the eternal and unknowable ones, undefiled and immeasurable. I disturbed and frightened the whole multitude of the angels and their ruler, and I placed a small thought in the world. I examined all with flame and fire through my thought, and all they did they did through me.

There was trouble and strife around the seraphim and the cherubim, whose glory will perish, [55] and commotion around Adonaios, on every side, and around their dwelling place, all the way to the world ruler, who said, "Let us seize him." Others said, "This plan will never work out." For Adonaios knows me, through hope.[25]

In the Mouths of Lions

I was in the mouths of lions.[26] They hatched a plot against me, to counter the destruction of their error and foolishness, but I did not give in to them as they had planned. I was not hurt at all. Though they punished me, I did not die in actuality but only in appearance, that I might not be put to shame by them, as if they are part of me. I freed myself of shame, and I did not become fainthearted because of what they did to me. I would have become bound by fear, but I suffered only in their eyes and their thought, that nothing may ever be claimed about them. The death they think I suffered they suffered in their error and blindness. They nailed their man to their death. Their thoughts did not perceive [56] me, since they were deaf and blind. By doing these things they pronounce judgment against themselves. As for me, they saw me and punished me, but someone else, their father, drank the gall and the vinegar; it was not I. They were striking me with a scourge, but someone else, Simon,[27] bore the cross on his shoulder. Someone else wore the crown of thorns. And I was on high, poking fun at all the excesses of the rulers and the fruit of their error and conceit. I was laughing at their ignorance.[28]

Coming Down Past the Rulers

I brought all their powers into subjection. When I came down, no one saw me, for I kept changing my forms on high, transforming from shape to shape, so when I was at their gates, I assumed their likeness.[29] I passed by them quietly. I saw their realms, but I was not afraid or ashamed, because I was pure. I was speaking with them and mingling with them, through those who are mine. Jealously I trampled on those who [57] are harsh toward them, and I put out the fire. I was doing all this by my will, to complete what I willed in the will of the father above.

Bringing Up the Child of the Majesty from the Region Below

We brought the child of the majesty, hidden in the region below, to the height. There I am, in the eternal realms that no one has seen or understood, where the wedding of the wedding robe is. It is the new wedding, not the old, and it does not perish, for the new bridal chamber is of the heavens, and it is perfect.[30]

As I have revealed, there are three ways, and this is an undefiled mystery in the spirit of the eternal realm that is not destroyed or divided or even discussed, for it is indivisible, universal, and permanent.

The soul from on high will not discuss error here or carry herself[31] away from these realms that are here. She will be carried forth when she is liberated and treated nobly in the world, and she stands [58] before the father with no difficulty or fear, forever communing with the mind of ideal power. These will see me from every side with no animosity, for they see me, and they are seen, mingling with them. They did not put me to shame, and they were not ashamed. They were not afraid in my presence, and they will pass by every gate without fear and be perfected in the third glory.[32]

The Crucifixion Interpreted

The world was not receptive to my visible exaltation, my third immersion in an image that was perceptible.[33] The flame of the seven authorities was extinguished, the sun of the powers of the rulers set, darkness overcame them, and the world became impoverished. They bound this one with many bonds and nailed him to the cross, and they secured him with four bronze nails. He ripped the temple veil with his own hands. An earthquake shook earth's chaos, for the souls of the dead were released and resurrected, and they walked out in the open. They laid aside [59] ignorant jealousy and lack of insight by the dead tombs, and they put on the new person. They had come to know the blessed, perfect one of the eternal, incomprehensible father and the infinite light. That is what I am.[34]

When I came to my own and united them with me, there was no need for many words. Our thought was one with their thought, so they understood what I was saying. We made plans for the destruction of the rulers, and in this I did the will of the father. That is what I am.

Opposed and Persecuted in the World

When we left our home and came down to this world and became embodied in the world, we were hated and persecuted both by those who are ignorant[35] and by those who claim to be enriched with the name of Christ,[36] though they are vain and ignorant. Like irrational animals they do not know who they are. They hate and persecute those whom I have liberated.[37] If these people would only shut their mouths for once, they would start weeping and groaning in futility, because [60] they have not really known me. Rather, they have served two masters[38]—and even more.[39]

You, however, will be winners in everything, in combat, fights, and schism with jealousy and anger. In the uprightness of our love, we are innocent, pure, and good, and we have the mind of the father in an ineffable mystery.

The Opponents Are Insignificant and Ignorant

It was a joke, I tell you, it was a joke. The rulers do not know that all this is an ineffable unity of undefiled truth like what is among the children of light. They have imitated it, and they proclaim the doctrine of a dead man,[40] along with false teachings that mock the freedom and purity of the perfect assembly. In their doctrine they bind themselves to fear and slavery and worldly concerns and improper forms of worship, for they are ignorant and of no significance. They do not accept the nobility of truth. They hate the one to whom they belong and they love the one to whom they do not belong.

They do not have the [61] knowledge[41] of the majesty, that it is from above, from the fountain of truth and not from slavery, jealousy, fear, and love of the material world. Boldly and freely they make use of what is not theirs and what is theirs. They do not covet because of their authority and their law that addresses what they desire.[42] And those who are without the law are in dire straits: they do not have it and they still desire. These people mislead folks who through them resemble those who have the truth of their freedom, so as to place us under a yoke and coerce us with anxiety and fear.[43] One person is subjected to bondage, another is controlled by God through threats and violent force.

Noble people of the fatherhood, however, are not controlled, since they control themselves by themselves, without command or force. They belong to the thought of the fatherhood, and they are one with their will, that the fatherhood may be perfect and inexpressible through [62] the living water.

The Perfect People Who Live in Harmony and Friendship

Be wise among yourselves, not only in words that are heard but also in deeds, in words that are fulfilled. In this way those who are perfect are worthy to be established and united with me, and they will have no enmity. With good friendship I do everything through the one who is good, for this is the unity of truth, that people should have no adversary. If some cause division, they do not learn wisdom, because they cause division and are not friends. They are enemies. But those who live in the harmony and friendship of love of brother and sister, naturally and not only of necessity, completely and not merely in part, those truly reflect the will of the father. This is universal and perfect love.

Adam and His Descendants Were a Joke

Adam was a joke.[44] He was created by the ruler of the seventh realm[45] in a phony way, in the shape of a human, as though he had become stronger than I and my siblings.[46] We are blameless toward him, and we have not sinned.

Abraham was a joke, as were Isaac and Jacob, since they were called patriarchs in a phony way by the ruler of the seventh realm, as though [63] he had become stronger than I and my siblings. We are blameless toward him, and we have not sinned.

David was a joke, since his son was named child of humankind[47] and was put in power by the ruler of the seventh realm, as though he had become stronger than I and my kin. We are blameless toward him; we have not sinned.

Solomon was a joke, since he became arrogant through the ruler of the seventh realm and thought he was the anointed,[48] as though he had become stronger than I and my siblings. We are blameless toward him; I have not sinned.

The twelve prophets were a joke, since they appeared as imitations of the true prophets. They came in a phony way through the ruler of the seventh realm, as though he had become stronger than I and my siblings. We are blameless toward him, and we have not sinned.

Moses was a joke, called a faithful servant[49] and friend.[50] The testimony about him was wrong, since he never knew me. He did not know me, and none of those before him, from Adam to Moses and John the baptizer, knew me or [64] my siblings. They had instruction from angels to observe food laws and submit to bitter slavery. They never knew truth and they never will, because their souls are enslaved and they can never find a mind with freedom to know, until they come to know the child of humankind. On account of my father, I was the one the world did not know, and for this reason it rose up against me and my siblings. But we are blameless toward it; we have not sinned.

The Ruler of the World Is a Joke

The ruler was a joke, for he said, "I am God, and no one is greater than I. I alone am father and lord, and there is no other beside me. I am a jealous god, and I bring the sins of the fathers upon the

children for three and four generations,"[51] as though he had become stronger than I and my siblings. We are blameless toward him,
and we have not sinned. In this way we mastered his doctrine, but
he is conceited and does not agree with our father. So through our
friendship we overcame his doctrine, since he is arrogant and conceited and does not agree with our father. He was a joke, with his
[65] judgment and false prophecy.

I Am Christ

O you who cannot see! You do not perceive that on account of
your blindness this is one unknown. Neither did those people ever
know or understand him. They would not listen to an accurate account of him, and so they practiced their lawless justice and raised
their filthy, murderous hands against him as if they were beating
the air. Those who are mindless and blind are always mindless, always slaves of law and worldly fear.

I am Christ, child of humankind, one from you who is within
you. For you I am despised, that you may dismiss what is imper-
manent. Do not become female, lest you give birth to evil and what
is related, jealousy, dissension, anger, wrath, dishonesty, greed.[52]

To you I am an ineffable mystery. Once, before the foundation
of the world, when the whole multitude of the assembly in the
realm of the eight[53] came together [66] and made plans, they united
in spiritual marriage.[54] The marriage was consummated in these
ineffable places by means of a living word, through the mediator
Jesus, who dwells in all of them and rules over them with pure
profound love.[55] He transformed himself and appeared as a single
manifestation of all of them, as thought, father, One. He stands
apart from them, for he came forth all by himself.

He is life,
he from the father of truth,[56]
ineffable, perfect,
the father of those there,
the unity of peace,
friend of the good,
eternal life and spotless joy,
in complete harmony of life and faith,
through eternal life
of fatherhood, motherhood, sisterhood,
and wisdom
of the word.
These were one with mind
that extends itself,
that will extend itself,
in joyful union.
He is honored [67]
and listens faithfully
to the One.

This is
in fatherhood, motherhood, brotherhood
of the word,
and wisdom.
This is a wedding of truth,
incorruptible rest,
in a spirit of truth,
in every mind,
perfect light
in unnamed mystery.

This does not happen and will not happen among us in any regions and locales where there is dissension and disruption of peace. Rather, this is union, a feast of love,[57] and all are fulfilled in the one who is. This love also is to be found in the regions under heaven that are joined to the realms above. Those who have come to know me through salvation and unity, and those who have lived for the glory of the father and truth, once were separate, but they have been united with the One through the living word.

I Am with Those Who Are Friends

I am in the spirit and truth of motherhood, where unity is, and I am with those who are always friends to each other. They know nothing of enmity and wickedness, but they are united [68] by my knowledge[58] in word and peace, which dwells completely with everyone and in everyone. Those who have taken on the likeness of my form will take on the likeness of my word, and they will emerge in the light forever, in mutual friendship in the spirit. They have come to know fully and completely that the one who is is one, and all are one. They have been taught about the One and the assembly and the members of the assembly. For the father of all is immeasurable and immutable, mind, word, division, jealousy, fire, yet he is simply one, all in all in a single principle, because all are from a single spirit.

Why Did You Not Know the Mystery?

O you who cannot see, why really did you not know the mystery? The rulers around Yaldabaoth were disobedient because of the thought that came down to him from Sophia the sister of thought, and they got together with those who were with them in a conflagration of [69] fiery cloud, which was their jealousy, along with all the others produced by their own creatures. They acted as though they had brought together the noble pleasure of the assembly. Instead they showed their own collective ignorance through a phony image of fire and earth and murderer.[59] They are few, they are uneducated, and they are ignorant. They were bold to do these things, but they did not understand that light associates with light and darkness with darkness, and what is impure associates with what is perishable and what is imperishable with what is pure.

This Is What I Have Given You

This is what I have presented to you. I am Jesus the Christ, child of humankind, exalted above the heavens. You who are perfect and undefiled, I have presented this to you on account of the mystery that is undefiled and perfect and ineffable, that you understand that we ordained these things before the foundation of the world, so that when we appear throughout the world, we may present the symbols of incorruption from the spiritual union with [70] knowledge. You do not know this because of the cloud of flesh that overshadows you.

It is I who am the friend of Sophia.[60] From the beginning I have been close to the father, where the children of truth are, and the majesty.[61] Rest in me, my friends in spirit, my brothers and sisters, forever.

Second Discourse of Great Seth[62]

PART ELEVEN

The Book of Baruch
by Justin

THE BOOK OF BARUCH is a gnostic account of the origin and destiny of the universe that is thoroughly Jewish in character but still has a place for the person of Jesus of Nazareth as well as Greco-Roman mythological figures. Known only from passages that are excerpted and paraphrased by the heresiologist Hippolytus of Rome, the Book of Baruch is said to have been written by a gnostic teacher named Justin. Hippolytus calls it the most abominable book he has ever read, but he is hardly an objective observer. The book tells the story of divine powers and angelic beings with Hebrew names, and it does so by interpreting passages from the Jewish scriptures, including the opening chapters of Genesis. Nonetheless, Jesus plays a key role in the account, as do Greco-Roman gods, goddesses, and heroes, especially Heracles.

The Book of Baruch is a love story with a tragic cosmic twist but a satisfying conclusion. In the beginning there are three powers of the universe: the highest God, called the Good, and Elohim and Eden. Elohim is male and Eden is female, and Eden has, in part, a wild, serpent-like nature. Elohim and Eden fall in love and produce angelic children with names that, in many cases, are familiar from the Jewish heritage. Some of the names are also well known from gnostic texts—for example, Achamoth (the name for lower wisdom, especially in Valentinian texts) and Adonaios (a

Greek form of Adonai, a Hebrew name for God, and a name of a cosmic power, especially in Sethian texts). The angelic children of Elohim and Eden make up the world and all its features. Elohim breathes spirit into humankind, and Eden breathes soul.

When the world is fully formed, Elohim decides to ascend to highest heaven, but he does so without Eden. In heaven Elohim sees the Good and light that is brighter than the sun, and he is astonished. Initially Elohim wishes to destroy what he and Eden made, since the spirit of Elohim is trapped within human beings, but the Good does not allow it. The Good says, "You can do nothing evil when you are with me. You and Eden made the world through your love, so let Eden have creation as long as she wishes, and you stay with me" (26.18). Elohim never returns to Eden.

Meanwhile, according to the Book of Baruch, Eden recognizes that Elohim has abandoned her, and she is not pleased. She decides to use her angel Naas (from the Hebrew for "serpent") to torment people and the spirit of Elohim within people, so that they will feel the pain she feels. She and her angelic entourage instigate adultery and divorce on the earth. When Elohim sees what Eden is doing, he responds by sending one of his angels, Baruch (Hebrew for "blessed"), to come to the aid of the spirit in people and to oppose Naas. Baruch and Naas battle for the spirit, and Baruch approaches Moses, the prophets, Heracles, and Jesus to help in the struggle. The Book of Baruch says, "Baruch told Jesus everything that had happened, from the beginning, from Eden and Elohim, and all that would be thereafter" (26.29), and Jesus agrees to preach the word to people and proclaim "the things of the father and the Good" (26.30). In spite of the fierce opposition of Naas, Jesus stays faithful to Baruch and his message. Naas has

Jesus crucified. The account continues, "Jesus left the body of Eden on the cross and ascended to the Good" (26.31). The account concludes with several references to Greek mythology and Jewish literature. When these citations are interpreted allegorically, it is said, they tell the same story of Elohim and Eden.

The Book of Baruch is derived from the heresiological presentation of Hippolytus in Refutation of All Heresies. In Hippolytus the passages from the Book of Baruch are given in Greek. Hippolytus wrote his Refutation in the early third century, so clearly the Book of Baruch was written prior to that. However, the circumstances of composition are unknown.

For further reading: Willis Barnstone, "The Book of Baruch"; Ernst Haenchen, "The Book Baruch"; Ernst Haenchen, "Das Buch Baruch"; Kurt Rudolph, *Gnosis*, 144–47; Michael A. Williams, *Rethinking "Gnosticism,"* 18–23.

The Book of Baruch[1]

(Hippolytus, Refutation of All Heresies 5)

The Oath

[24.1] If you wish to know[2] what eye has not seen nor ear heard and what has not arisen in the human heart,[3] and who is the Good exalted over all things, swear to keep silent about the secrets of the instruction. Our father saw the Good and was made perfect with him, and he also kept silent about what must remain secret. He swore an oath, as it is written, "The lord has sworn and will not change his mind."[4]

[27.2] Here is the oath: I swear by the Good, who is over all, to keep these mysteries and to tell them to no one, and not to go back from the Good to creation.

When one swears this oath, one goes in to the Good and sees what eye has not seen nor ear heard and what has not arisen in the human heart.[5] One drinks from living water, which is the ritual washing, the spring of living water welling up.[6] [3] There is a difference between water and water.[7] The water beneath the firmament belongs to the evil creation, and earthly and psychical people wash in it. The water above the firmament is living water belonging to the Good, and spiritual, living people wash in it, as did Elohim, and he did not change his mind after washing.

Three Unconceived Powers in the Beginning

[26.1] There were three unconceived powers of the universe, two male, one female. One male power is called the Good, and he alone is called by that name[8] and knows everything in advance. The other male power, called father of all created things, has no such foreknowledge, and he is invisible. The female power likewise has no foreknowledge, and she is irritable. She is of two minds and two bodies, exactly like the female in the myth of Herodotus, a young woman above and a viper below.[9] [2] She is named Eden[10] and Israel.

These are the powers of the universe, the roots and wellsprings from which everything came. There was nothing else.

The Union of Elohim and Eden

When father Elohim,[11] without foreknowledge, saw Eden the half-woman, he came to desire her. Eden desired Elohim no less, and desire united them in mutual love. [3] From this union the father conceived twelve angels for himself through Eden. The names of the paternal angels are these:

Michael

Amen

Baruch

Gabriel

Esaddaios

. . .[12]

[4] Similarly, the names of the maternal angels, whom Eden produced, are as follows:

Babel

Achamoth[13]

Naas

Bel

Belias

Satan

Sael

Adonaios[14]

Kauithan

Pharaoth

Karkamenos

Lathen

[5] Of these twenty-four angels, the paternal angels assist the father and do everything according to his will, and the maternal angels do the same for mother Eden. The company of all these angels together constitutes paradise, of which Moses says, "God planted paradise in Eden, toward the east"[15]—in front of Eden—so that Eden might constantly look at paradise, the angels.

[6] The angels of paradise are called, allegorically, trees, and the tree of life is Baruch,[16] the third paternal angel, while the tree of the knowledge[17] of good and evil is Naas,[18] the third maternal angel. Moses spoke of these things in a veiled way, since not everyone can comprehend truth.

The Creation of Adam and Eve

[7] After paradise came to be from the love of Elohim and Eden, the angels of Elohim took some of the best earth and made human-kind.[19] They took it not from the bestial part of Eden but from the upper, human parts, the civilized regions of earth. From the bestial parts came wild animals and other creatures.

[8] They made humankind a symbol of their union and love, and they placed their powers within him. Eden contributed the soul, Elohim the spirit. The human being Adam became a kind of seal and token of their love, and an eternal symbol of the marriage of Eden and Elohim. [9] So also, as it is written by Moses, Eve be-came an image and symbol, a seal of Eden to be preserved forever. Eden put the soul in Eve the image, Elohim put the spirit in her.

Adam and Eve were commanded, "Be fruitful and multiply and inherit the earth"[20]—that is, Eden. [10] Eden brought all her power to Elohim, like a marriage dowry, and since then women come to their husbands with dowries in imitation of that first marriage, and they obey the divine hereditary law that came from Elohim and Eden.[21]

The Angels Are Divided into Four Astrological Groups

[11] When everything was created, as it is written by Moses, "heaven and earth and what is in them," the twelve angels of the mother were divided into four powers, and each of the four parts is called a river: Pishon, Gihon, Tigris, and Euphrates, as Moses said.[22] These twelve angels are organized in four groups, and they circle about and govern the world with sovereign authority over the world from Eden. [12] They do not stay in the same places,

but as in a circling chorus they move from place to place, and at appropriate times and intervals they leave the places assigned to them. When the angels of Pishon control a region, then famine, distress, and affliction break out in that part of the earth, for these angels rule with avarice. [13] In all four regions bad times and diseases come in accordance with each power and nature. This torrent of evil constantly flows around the world, under the control of the four rivers and by the will of Eden.

Elohim Ascends to the Good

[14] This is how, of necessity, evil came about. When Elohim had fashioned and formed the world through his love with Eden, he wished to ascend to the highest reaches of heaven to see if there was anything lacking in creation. He took his angels along. He was drawn up but he left Eden behind, for she is earth and decided not to follow her companion upward.

[15] When Elohim reached the upper limit of heaven, he saw a light brighter than the light he had created, and he said, "Open the gates for me, that I may enter and acknowledge the lord.[23] I thought I was the lord."

[16] A voice came to him from the light and said, "This is the lord's gate. The righteous enter through it."[24]

At once the gate opened, and the father, without his angels, went in to the Good, and he saw what eye has not seen nor ear heard and what has not arisen in the human heart.[25]

[17] The Good said to him, "Be seated at my right hand."[26]

The father said to the Good, "Lord, let me destroy the world I have made, for my spirit is imprisoned within human beings, and I want to take it back."[27]

[18] The Good replied to him, "You can do nothing evil when you are with me. You and Eden made the world through your love, so let Eden have creation as long as she wishes, and you stay with me."

Eden Punishes the Spirit of Elohim

[19] Then Eden knew she had been abandoned by Elohim. In her grief she gathered her angels around her and adorned herself in an attractive manner, in order to arouse the desire of Elohim and make him come back to her.

[20] Elohim, however, was restrained by the Good, and he did not come down to Eden again. So Eden ordered Babel, who is the same as Aphrodite, to provoke adultery and divorce among people, so that just as she had been separated from Elohim, so also the spirit of Elohim in people might feel the pain and torment of separation and suffer as had Eden, who was also abandoned. [21] Eden gave full authority to Naas, her third angel, to punish the spirit of Elohim in people with every sort of torment, so that through that spirit Elohim himself might be punished, because he abandoned his companion Eden in violation of the agreement he made with her.

Elohim Sends His Angel Baruch

When father Elohim saw this, he sent Baruch, his third angel, to come to the aid of the spirit in all people. [22] Baruch came and stood among the angels of Eden, in the middle of paradise, since paradise consisted of the angels among whom he stood.[28] He commanded humankind to eat from all the trees in paradise and enjoy them, but not to eat from the tree of the knowledge[29] of good and evil.[30] That tree is Naas.[31] In other words, they could obey the other eleven angels of Eden, because these eleven have passions but do not break the law, while Naas does break the law. [23] For Naas approached Eve and seduced her and committed adultery with her, and this is against the law, and he also approached Adam and fondled him as a boy, and this is also against the law. Adultery and pederasty came from these deeds.

Since then both evil and good have had power over people, and both come from a single source, the father. [24] By ascending to the Good the father showed the way for those who wish to ascend, and by leaving Eden he brought about the origin of evil for the spirit of the father in people.

Baruch Is Sent to Moses, the Prophets, Heracles

Baruch was sent to Moses, and through Moses he spoke to the children of Israel, that they might turn back to the Good. [25] But Naas, the third angel of Eden, concealed the commands of Baruch and made his own commands to be heard through the soul from Eden, which was in Moses as it is in all people. For this reason the soul is set against the spirit and the spirit against the soul. The soul is Eden and the spirit is Elohim, and both are in all people, women and men alike.

[26] Next Baruch was sent to the prophets, that through the prophets the spirit living in people might hear and flee from Eden and the evil creation as father Elohim had once fled. In the same way and with the same purpose as before, Naas deceived the prophets

through the soul that along with the father's spirit is in people, and they all were led astray and did not follow the words of Baruch that Elohim commanded.

[27] Then Elohim chose a prophet from the uncircumcised, Heracles, and sent him to overcome the twelve angels of Eden and free the father from the twelve evil angels of creation. These are the twelve labors of Heracles in which he struggled, from first to last, with the lion, the hydra, the boar, and the rest. [28] These names from the gentiles have been modified by the activity of the maternal angels. Just when it seemed that Heracles was triumphant, Omphale,[32] who is the same as Babel or Aphrodite, got involved with him and seduced him and stripped him of his strength, namely the orders of Baruch that Elohim commanded, and she clothed him in her own robe—that is, the power of Eden, the power below. So the prophecy and the deeds of Heracles came to nothing.

Baruch Finds Jesus of Nazareth

[29] Finally, in the days of Herod the king,[33] Baruch was sent once more by Elohim, and he came to Nazareth and found Jesus son of Joseph and Mary as he, a boy twelve years old,[34] was tending sheep. Baruch told Jesus everything that had happened, from the beginning, from Eden and Elohim, and all that would be thereafter.

[30] Baruch said, "All the prophets before you were led astray. Jesus, child of humankind,[35] try not to be led astray, but preach this word to people, and tell them about the things of the father and the Good, and ascend to the Good and be seated there with Elohim, father of us all."

[31] Jesus obeyed the angel and said, "Lord, I shall do everything." And he preached.

Naas also wanted to deceive Jesus, but he was unable to do so, because Jesus remained faithful to Baruch. Naas was furious that he could not lead him astray, and he had him crucified. But Jesus left the body of Eden on the cross and ascended to the Good.[36]

[32] Jesus said to Eden, "Woman, here is your son"[37]—the psychical and earthly person—and he yielded the spirit into the hands of the father[38] and ascended to the Good.[39]

The Myths of Priapos, Leda, Ganymede, Danae

The Good is Priapos, who created before anything was.[40] He is called Priapos because he prepared everything beforehand. [33] Thus he is set up in every temple and honored by all creation and in the streets, carrying fruit[41]—produce of the creation he brought about—since he prepared creation before anything was.

[34] When you hear people say that the swan came upon Leda and produced children from her, the swan is Elohim and Leda is Eden.[42]

When people say that an eagle came upon Ganymede, the eagle is Naas and Ganymede is Adam.[43]

[35] When it is said that gold came upon Danae and produced offspring from her, the gold is Elohim and Danae is Eden.[44]

In the same way all these stories are interpreted by comparing them to myths that resemble them.

The Accounts of the Prophets

[36] When the prophet says, "Hear, heaven, and listen, earth, for the lord has spoken,"[45] he means that heaven is the spirit of Elohim in people, earth is the soul that along with the spirit is in people, the lord is Baruch, and Israel is Eden, for Eden, the companion of Elohim, is also called Israel. [37] "Israel did not know me.[46] If she[47] had known that I[48] am with the Good, she would not have punished the spirit in people because the father ignored her."[49]

[27.4] When the prophet is said to take a wife who is a whore, because the land will play the whore behind the lord,[50] with these words the prophet clearly declares the whole mystery of what Eden does behind Elohim, but on account of the wickedness of Naas the prophet went unheeded.

PART TWELVE

The Round Dance
of the Cross

THE ROUND DANCE of the Cross, or the Hymn of Jesus, is a song Jesus is said to have taught his disciples before he was crucified. Included within the Acts of John, the song is accompanied by instructions for liturgical dance. This account of the hymn and dance has been incorporated into Marguerite Yourcenar's novel *L'oeuvre au noir* and Luis Buñuel's film *La voie lactée,* and Gustav Holst set it to music in *The Hymn of Jesus.* The Round Dance of the Cross employs themes from the Johannine tradition (e.g., Jesus is the word of God who describes the mystery of suffering), and it may reflect Valentinian motifs (e.g., it refers to word, mind, a realm of eight, wisdom, and grace—dancing grace). Jesus sings the verses of the hymn, which include "I am" statements, some of which are riddle-like and paradoxical; the disciples respond, antiphonally, by singing "Amen," and they dance in a circle around Jesus.

The hymn and dance conclude with an explanation of the meaning. The Round Dance of the Cross is about suffering—not only the suffering of Jesus but also that of the disciples, and of everyone else. Jesus says, "Yours is the human passion I am to suffer," but he adds that he is not what he seems to be, and, by implication, that suffering is likewise not what it seems to be. For if people come to understand suffering, they will be liberated from suffering:

> *If you knew how to suffer*
> *you would be able not to suffer.*
> *Learn how to suffer*
> *and you will be able not to suffer.*

Jesus declares, "Know the word of wisdom," and he ends with a few final observations and another verse of the hymn:

> *Glory to you, father.*
> *Glory to you, word.*
> *Glory to you, spirit.*
> *Amen.*

The textual history of the Acts of John is complex, but it is commonly assumed that the Acts of John was composed in the second half of the second century, or perhaps a little later. It was likely composed, at least in large part, in Greek, though portions may derive from Syriac. Syria is the probable place of composition.

For further reading: Barbara E. Bowe, "Dancing into the Divine"; Arthur J. Dewey, "The Hymn in the Acts of John"; Marvin Meyer, "The Round Dance of the Cross"; Knut Schäferdiek, "The Acts of John," 181–84.

The Round Dance
of the Cross

or

The Hymn of Jesus[1]

(Acts of John 94–96)

[94] Jesus told us to form a circle and hold each other's hands, and he stood in the middle and said,

> Respond to me with Amen.[2]

The Song

He began singing a hymn and declaring,

> Glory to you, father.

We circled around him and responded,

> Amen.

> Glory to you, word.[3]
> Glory to you, grace.
>> Amen.

Glory to you, spirit.
Glory to you, holy one.
Glory to your glory.
    Amen.

We praise you, father.
We thank you, light,
in whom no darkness lives.[4]
    Amen.

[95] I declare why we offer thanks:
I will[5] be saved and I will save.
    Amen.

I will be released and I will release.
    Amen.

I will be wounded and I will wound.
    Amen.

I will be born and I will bear.
    Amen.

I will eat and I will be eaten.
    Amen.

I will hear and I will be heard.
    Amen.

I will be in mind, I, pure mind.
    Amen.

I will be washed and I will wash.
    Amen.

Grace dances.[6]

> I will play the flute.
> Dance, everyone.
> > Amen.
>
> I will weep.
> Lament, everyone.
> > Amen.
>
> A realm of eight[7] sings with us.
> > Amen.
>
> The twelfth number[8] dances above.
> > Amen.
>
> The whole universe joins in dancing.
> > Amen.
>
> If you do not dance you do not know what is.
> > Amen.
>
> I will run away and I will remain.
> > Amen.
>
> I will adorn and I will be adorned.
> > Amen.
>
> I will be united and I will unite.
> > Amen.
>
> I am homeless and I have homes.
> > Amen.
>
> I have no place and I have places.
> > Amen.

I have no temple and I have temples.
>   Amen.

I am a lamp to you who see me.
>   Amen.

I am a mirror to you who recognize me.
>   Amen.

I am a door[9] to you who knock on me.
>   Amen.

I am a way[10] to you, passerby.[11]
>   Amen.

Understanding the Song

[96] If you follow my dance,
>   see yourself in me when I speak.
>   If you have seen what I do,
>   keep quiet about my mysteries.

You who dance, consider what I do.
>   Yours is the human passion I am to suffer.
>   You could never understand what you suffer
>   unless I the word was sent to you by the father.

You who have seen what I do
>   have seen me as suffering,
>   and when you saw it,
>   you did not stand still

but were utterly moved.
You were moved to wisdom,
and you have my help.

Rest in me.

Who I am
you will know when I go.
What I am seen to be now
I am not.
What I am
you will see when you come.

If you knew how to suffer
you would be able not to suffer.
Learn how to suffer
and you will be able not to suffer.

What you do not know
I shall teach you.
I am your God,
not the traitor's.
I wish holy souls
to be in harmony with me.
Know the word of wisdom.[12]

Say again with me,

Glory to you, father.
Glory to you, word.
Glory to you, spirit.
    Amen.

If you wish to know what I was,
I ridiculed everything with the word,
and I was not ridiculed[13] at all.[14]
I jumped for joy.
Understand everything,
and when you have understood, declare,
Glory to you, father.
    Amen.

Notes

Introduction

1. On the story of the discovery of the Nag Hammadi library, see James M. Robinson, "From the Cliff to Cairo: The Story of the Discoverers and Middlemen of the Nag Hammadi Codices"; James M. Robinson, "Nag Hammadi: The First Fifty Years."

2. In this volume the codices are sometimes identified with the abbreviation NHC, for Nag Hammadi Codex.

3. On the story of the discovery of Berlin Gnostic Codex 8502, see Karen L. King, *The Gospel of Mary of Magdala*, 7–12.

4. In addition to these Coptic and gnostic texts, Stephen Emmel and James M. Robinson have reported that more such texts have been identified in a codex that currently is neither published nor available for study. Cf. James M. Robinson, "Introduction," in *The Facsimile Edition of the Nag Hammadi Codices: Introduction*, 21. Rodolphe Kasser has announced that a text entitled the Gospel of Judas is included in this codex. See note 32, below.

5. For other testimonia to the Gospel of Thomas in early Christian literature, cf. Harold W. Attridge, "The Greek Fragments," in *Nag Hammadi Codex II,2–7*, ed. Bentley Layton, 1:103–9.

6. Cf. Bentley Layton, "Prolegomena to the Study of Ancient Gnosticism," 348–49.

7. Michael A. Williams, *Rethinking "Gnosticism,"* 263.

8. Michael A. Williams, *Rethinking "Gnosticism,"* 51–52.

9. Karen L. King, *What Is Gnosticism?* 15.

10. Karen L. King, *What Is Gnosticism?* 235–36. See my review of King's book in *Review of Biblical Literature*.

11. Cf. Bentley Layton, *The Gnostic Scriptures*, 5–8; Michael A. Williams, *Rethinking "Gnosticism,"* 31–43.

12. No fewer than four copies of the Secret Book of John survive, three in the Nag Hammadi library (NHC II,1; III,1; IV,1) and one in BG 8502 (BG 8502,2). In his discussion of the Barbelognostics in Against Heresies 1.29.1–4, Irenaeus of Lyon also includes citations that closely parallel portions of the Secret Book of John.

13. In *Drudgery Divine*, Jonathan Z. Smith reminds us that comparisons and classifications are an inevitable part of the scholarly enterprise, and they tell us as much about those doing the comparisons as the phenomena being compared. Smith also writes that comparisons are triadic, with an implicit "more than" and an additional "with respect to" (i.e., A resembles B more than C with respect to a set of traits N). Hence, Smith indicates that statements of comparison and classification are always relative and contextual. Smith's observations may be helpful in the application of the terms *gnōsis*, "gnostic," and "gnosticism" to particular texts and traditions, and in the determination of the extent to which such terms are appropriate.

14. This argument is developed more fully in my essay "Gnosticism, Gnostics, and *The Gnostic Bible*," in *The Gnostic Bible*, ed. Willis Barnstone and Marvin Meyer, 1–16. See also Birger Pearson, "Gnosticism as a Religion," in *Gnosticism and Christianity in Roman and Coptic Egypt*, 201–23.

15. Several of these gospels, like the New Testament gospels, are attributed to apostles and other famous people in the Jesus movement. Such attribution of authorship follows the practice of pseudepigraphy—the fictitious suggestion that the author of a text is a person of renown. The actual authors of these texts remain unknown.

16. Marcion of Sinope, the second-century Christian dualist and fervent Paulinist, took Paul's discussion as a literal reference to a written gospel, and so he concluded that Paul's gospel was the Gospel of Luke, though he was convinced that proponents of the Jewish God had perverted the text of the Gospel of Luke by writing in words favorable to the Jewish God and the Jewish scriptures. Cf. Marvin Meyer, "Gnosticism, Gnostics, and *The Gnostic Bible*," in *The Gnostic Bible*, ed. Willis Barnstone and Marvin Meyer, 18–19.

17. The New Testament Gospels of Mark, Matthew, and Luke are called synoptic gospels because they see Jesus in a similar way and are literarily dependent upon one another.

18. Cf. Martin Kähler, *Der sogenannte historische Jesus und der geschichtliche, biblische Christus*, 60.

19. Karen L. King, "The Apocryphon of John: Part II of the Gospel of John?"

20. Q, from the German *Quelle*, "source," is the source of Jesus sayings that was most likely used by Matthew and Luke in the compilation of their gospels. Cf. John S. Kloppenborg, *Excavating Q*; John S. Kloppenborg, *The Formation of Q*; Burton L. Mack, *The Lost Gospel*; James M. Robinson, Paul Hoffman, and John S. Kloppenborg, *The Critical Edition of Q*.

21. On the Sethians, cf. John D. Turner, "Sethian Gnosticism: A Literary History"; John D. Turner, *Sethian Gnosticism and the Platonic Tradition*.

22. On the Valentinians, cf. Christoph Markschies, *Valentinus Gnosticus?*; Antonio Orbe, *Estudios Valentinianos*; Elaine H. Pagels, *The Johannine Gospel in Gnostic Exegesis*; Kurt Rudolph, *Gnosis*; François Sagnard, *La Gnose valentinienne et le témoignage de Saint Irénée*.

23. Wisdom is also personified as Athena or Metis in the Greek world. Cf. the Secret Book of John, included in this volume, and the accompanying notes.

24. Marvin Meyer, *The Gospel of Thomas*, 10.

25. On Jesus in the Gospel of Thomas, cf. Marvin Meyer, "Albert Schweitzer and the Image of Jesus in the Gospel of Thomas," in *Secret Gospels*, 17–38; Stephen J. Patterson, *The Gospel of Thomas and Jesus.*

26. For a discussion of these sorts of metaphors used to describe the state of ignorance of people in this world, cf. Hans Jonas, *The Gnostic Religion*, 48–99.

27. Elaine H. Pagels, *Beyond Belief*, 164.

28. The feminine pronoun is used for the soul here and throughout this volume because in Greek the word *psychē*, "soul," is feminine in gender and typically is personified as the young female Psyche, about whom many mythic stories are told in Greek and gnostic literature. Compare the myth of Psyche and Eros (or Cupid, love) in Apuleius's Metamorphoses, books 4–6, as well as On the Origin of the World and Exegesis on the Soul.

29. This quotation from the Gospel of Mary may also be translated with masculine pronouns: "Follow him. Those who seek him will find him." See the translation and notes for the Gospel of Mary.

30. The issue of the suffering and death of Jesus and the meaning of the crucifixion of Jesus in gnostic texts remains complicated. Cf. Kurt Rudolph, *Gnosis*, 148–71. Rudolph refers to what Adolph von Harnack once observed: "It is not Docetism (in the strict sense) which is the characteristic of gnostic Christology, but the two-nature doctrine, i.e. the distinction between Jesus and Christ, or the doctrine that the redeemer as redeemer did not become man" (162). Occasionally a gnostic text may be emphatic in affirming that Jesus did in fact suffer. In the text Melchizedek (NHC IX,*1*), for instance, it is said that some deny that Jesus suffered when in actuality he did (5). On Jesus laughing at the mistake made at the crucifixion, compare Revelation of Peter (NHC VII,*3*) 81–83; Basilides according to Irenaeus of Lyon, Against Heresies 1.24.4; perhaps Round Dance of the Cross 96. On the crucifixion of Jesus in Islamic traditions, cf. Geoffrey Parrinder, *Jesus in the Qur'an*, 105–21; F. E. Peters, "Jesus in Islam," in *Jesus Then and Now*, ed. Marvin Meyer and Charles Hughes, 267–68.

31. Elaine H. Pagels, *Beyond Belief*, 125.

32. Theoretically, more texts might also be included in such a volume, but the twelve texts presented here are meant to provide a substantial and manageable collection of gnostic gospels and other texts that are related to each other in important ways. One such text may be the Gospel of the Savior, which includes elements that may be understood as gnostic; cf. Charles W. Hedrick and Paul A. Mirecki, *Gospel of the Savior*; Stephen Emmel, "The Recently Published *Gospel of the Savior*"; Stephen Emmel, "Unbekanntes Berliner Evangelium = the Strasbourg Coptic Gospel"; Charles W. Hedrick, "Caveats to a 'Righted Order' of the *Gospel of the Savior.*" An additional text, entitled the Gospel of Judas, is included, along with a version of the Letter of Peter to Philip and a revelation of James, in a codex that is not yet available but is being prepared for publication. The formal announcement of the existence of the Gospel of Judas was made by Rodolphe Kasser at the 8ème Congrès International d'Études Coptes, in Paris, in July 2004. Both Irenaeus of Lyon, Against Heresies 1.31.1, and Epiphanus of Salamis, Panarion ("Medicine Chest") 38.1.5, confirm that there was a Gospel of Judas in use in the early church. Further, Charles W. Hedrick has indicated

that he has had access to photographs of pages that derive from the Gospel of Judas and other texts in the collection, and he reports as follows: "The second-century Christian theologian Irenaeus attributed a gospel in the name of Judas the betrayer to the gnostic sect that he calls the Cainites. Later Epiphanius in the late fourth century also mentioned the Gospel of Judas and associated the Cainites, a libertine sect, with the Sethians, who also produced books in the name of Allogenes. In 1983, Stephen Emmel, then a graduate student, saw a fourth-century Coptic codex being offered for sale containing, as he then reported in an unpublished note, 'a dialogue between Jesus and his disciples (at least Judas [presumably Judas Thomas]) . . . .' He also reported that the text contained a copy of 'The First Apocalypse of James' and 'The Letter of Peter to Philip,' both known from the Nag Hammadi library. There is a report on the Judas codex to the same effect by James M. Robinson in 1984 (*The Facsimile Edition of the Nag Hammadi Codices: Introduction* [Leiden: E. J. Brill, 1984], 21). The codex was later purchased by an anonymous foundation in Zurich, Switzerland, and the distinguished Coptologist Rodolphe Kasser is commissioned to publish it. The date of publication has been announced as 2005. I am in possession of photographs taken of the codex while it was still on the market (ca. September 2001). There are at least two subscript titles in the codex (measuring 12½ inches tall and 7⅛ inches wide): '[The Letter] of Peter to Philip' and 'The Gospel of Judas.' Judas is not the disciple of Jesus, Judas Thomas, but rather Judas the betrayer, as is made clear in the last line of the text. Judas is described as a 'disciple of Jesus,' as taking 'money,' and the last line of the text concludes, 'and he delivered him over.' The two leaves preceding the final leaf appear to reflect some sort of heavenly setting in which Allogenes is addressed by a heavenly voice from a cloud and is pressured for some action by Satan. In the final leaf Judas receives instructions from a cloud and 'delivers Jesus over.' The association with Allogenes, a figure in Sethian texts, argues that this gospel is the same as that seen in the second century by Irenaeus."

Part One: The Gospel of Thomas

1. Editions: *The Facsimile Edition of the Nag Hammadi Codices: Codex II*; Helmut Koester, Bentley Layton, Thomas O. Lambdin, and Harold W. Attridge, "The Gospel According to Thomas," in *Nag Hammadi Codex II,2–7*, ed. Bentley Layton, 1:37–128; Marvin Meyer, *The Gospel of Thomas*. Translations: Beate Blatz, "The Coptic Gospel of Thomas," in *New Testament Apocrypha*, ed. Wilhelm Schneemelcher, 1:110–33; Helmut Koester and Thomas O. Lambdin, "The Gospel of Thomas," in *The Nag Hammadi Library in English*, ed. James M. Robinson, 124–38; Bentley Layton, *The Gnostic Scriptures*, 376–99; Jacques-É. Ménard, *L'Évangile selon Thomas*; Stephen J. Patterson, James M. Robinson, and Hans-Gebhard Bethge, *The Fifth Gospel*; Jens Schröter and Hans-Gebhard Bethge, "Das Evangelium nach Thomas," in *Nag Hammadi Deutsch*, ed. Hans-Martin Schenke, Hans-Gebhard Bethge, and Ursula Ulrike Kaiser, 1:151–81. The present translation is based on an ultraviolet collation of the Coptic text, by Marvin Meyer, at the Coptic Museum in 1988. I include the traditional numbers for 114 sayings, and I also provide numbers of subdivisions of sayings, in keeping with an increasingly common convention.

2. Didymos.

3. Cf. Secret Book of James 2; Book of Thomas 138.

4. Probably Jesus, possibly Judas Thomas.

5. Cf. Sir. 39:1–3; John 8:51–52.

6. Or, "Jesus says," for such a quotation formula here and elsewhere in the text. In the Greek Gospel of Thomas the quotation formulas are given in the present tense.

7. Papyrus Oxyrhynchus 654.8–9 adds "and [having reigned], one will rest." For the saying in general cf. Gospel of the Hebrews 4a, 4b; Book of Thomas 140–41; 145; Matt. 7:7–8 (Q); Luke 11:9–10 (Q); Dialogue of the Savior 129; Wisd. of Sol. 6:12, 17–20.

8. Papyrus Oxyrhynchus 654.13 reads "under the earth."

9. Cf. Luke 17:20–21; Gospel of Thomas 113; Manichaean Psalm Book 160.

10. "Know yourself" was among the Greek inscriptions at Delphi. On knowing and being known, cf. Gal. 4:8–9; 1 Cor. 8:1–3; 13:12; Gospel of Truth 19.

11. Probably an uncircumcised child. (Jewish boys were circumcised on the eighth day.)

12. Cf. Hippolytus, Refutation of All Heresies 5.7.20, a saying said to derive from the Gospel of Thomas: "One who seeks will find me in children from seven years, for there, hidden in the fourteenth age, I am revealed."

13. Cf. Matt. 20:16 (Q); Luke 13:30 (Q); Matt. 19:30; Mark 10:31; Barnabas 6:13.

14. Cf. Manichaean Kephalaia 65 163,26–29, where a nearly identical version of this saying of Jesus is cited.

15. Cf. Mark 4:22; Luke 8:17; Matt. 10:26 (Q); Luke 12:2 (Q). On the last portion of the saying, cf. Gospel of Thomas 6:5–6. Papyrus Oxyrhynchus 654.31 adds "and nothing buried that [will not be raised]."

16. Cf. Matt. 6:1–18; Didache 8:1–3. Saying 14 provides a more direct answer to these questions.

17. This is the negative formulation of the golden rule.

18. Papyrus Oxyrhynchus 654.38 reads "truth" (Greek *alētheia*, equivalent to Coptic *me*; here the Coptic for "heaven" is *pe*).

19. Cf. Gospel of Thomas 5:2.

20. Or, "foul."

21. Here the lion seems to symbolize what is passionate and bestial in human experience. A person may consume the lion or be consumed by it. Cf. Plato, Republic 588E–589B.

22. Or, "The human," "The man."

23. Cf. Matt. 13:47–50; Babrius, Fable 4.

24. Cf. Matt. 13:3–9; Mark 4:2–9; Luke 8:4–8.

25. Cf. Luke 12:49 (Q?); Pistis Sophia 141.

26. Cf. Matt. 24:35; Mark 13:31; Luke 21:33; Matt. 5:18 (Q); Luke 16:17 (Q).

27. Cf. Hippolytus, Refutation of All Heresies 5.8.32: "So they say, 'If you ate dead things and made them living, what will you do if you eat living things?'" In the light of this citation, it is possible to imagine (as does Hans-Martin Schenke, in an unpublished note) that the original wording of the saying may have been as follows:

"During the days when you ate what is dead, you made it alive. <When you eat what is alive, what will you do? During the days when you were in the darkness, you saw the light.> When you are in the light, what will you do?"

28. On James the righteous, cf. the New Testament Acts of the Apostles; Gospel of the Hebrews 7; the Secret Book of James; the First and Second Revelations of James; Hegisippus, in Eusebius, Ecclesiastical History 2.23.4–7; Josephus, Antiquities of the Jews 20.200.

29. Or, "angel."

30. Or, "three words." The three sayings or words are unknown, and they may be mentioned as a device for the reflection of the reader. For examples of three words, cf. Hippolytus, Refutation of All Heresies 5.8.4 (Kaulakau, Saulasau, Zeesar, from the Hebrew of Isa. 28:10, 13); Pistis Sophia 136 (Yao Yao Yao, the ineffable name of God).

31. Cf. Gospel of Bartholomew 2:5.

32. Cf. the questions in Gospel of Thomas 6.

33. Literally, "walk in the places."

34. Cf. Matt. 10:8 (Q); Luke 10:8–9 (Q); 1 Cor. 10:27.

35. Cf. Matt. 15:11; Mark 7:15.

36. Cf. John 10:30.

37. Or, "as solitaries" (Coptic *monakhos*). Cf. Matt. 10:34–36 (Q); Luke 12:49 (Q?), 50, 51–53 (Q).

38. Cf. 1 Cor. 2:9; Isa. 64:4; Apocalypse of Elijah or Secrets (Apocrypha) of Elijah; Plutarch, How the Young Person Should Study Poetry 17E.

39. Cf. Matt. 24:3; Mark 13:3–4; Luke 21:7.

40. Cf. Gospel of Thomas 49.

41. Cf. Gospel of Philip 64; Lactantius, Divine Institutes 4.8; Irenaeus, Proof of the Apostolic Preaching 43.

42. Cf., for example, Gospel of Thomas 77:3.

43. Five trees in paradise are mentioned elsewhere in gnostic and Manichaean literature. Cf. Gen. 2:9.

44. The Coptic text reads *sobᶜk*, emended to read <s>sobᶜk.

45. Cf. Matt. 13:31–32 (Q); Luke 13:18–19 (Q); Mark 4:30–32.

46. Here the editors of the Gospel of Thomas in Kurt Aland, ed., *Synopsis Quattuor Evangeliorum*, 525, understand *šēre šēm* ("children") to be a translation of the Greek word *pais*, "child, servant," and they assume the latter meaning of *pais* and hence translate the passage as follows: "They are like servants entrusted with a field that is not theirs."

47. Cf. Gospel of Thomas 37.

48. Cf. Gospel of Thomas 103; Matt. 24:43 (Q); Luke 12:39 (Q).

49. The editors of the Gospel of Thomas in *Synopsis Quattuor Evangeliorum*, ed. Kurt Aland, 525, translate this clause "For the necessities for which you are waiting (with longing) will be found." (An additional possible translation is given in a note: "For the possession you are watching out for they will find.")

50. Cf. Mark 4:29; Joel 3:13.

51. Cf. Gal. 3:27–28; Gospel of the Egyptians; 2 Clement 12:2–6; Martyrdom of Peter 9; Acts of Philip 140; Gospel of Thomas 114.

52. Cf. Deut. 32:30; Eccles. 7:28; Pistis Sophia 134.

53. Or, "he," here and below.

54. In general, cf. Matt. 6:22–23 (Q); Luke 11:34–35 (Q), 36 (Q?); Dialogue of the Savior 125–26.

55. Or, "your life," "yourself."

56. Cf. Matt. 22:39; Mark 12:31; Luke 10:27; Lev. 19:18; Gospel of the Hebrews 5; Didache 2:7.

57. Cf. Matt. 7:3–5 (Q); Luke 6:41–42 (Q).

58. Cf. Clement of Alexandria, Miscellanies 3.15.99.4; Tertullian, Against the Jewish People 4.

59. Cf. John 1:14; 1 Tim. 3:16; Prov. 1:20–33; Bar. 3:37.

60. Or, "sons of men."

61. Cf. Gospel of Thomas 7.

62. Papyrus Oxyrhynchus 1.23–30 has been reconstructed to read as follows: "[Jesus says], 'Where there are [three, they are without] God, and where there is only [one], I say, I am with that one. Lift up the stone, and you will find me there. Split the piece of wood, and I am there." On the conclusion of this version of the saying, cf. Gospel of Thomas 77:2–3. On the saying in general, cf. Matt. 18:19–20; Ephraem Syrus, Exposition on the Harmony of the Gospel 14.

63. Cf. Matt. 13:57; Mark 6:4; Luke 4:23–24; John 4:44.

64. Cf. Matt. 5:14; 7:24–25 (Q); Luke 6:47–48 (Q).

65. The phrase "in the other ear" may be a case of dittography (i.e., accidental duplication by the author or copyist), or it may refer to someone else's ear or even one's own "inner" ear.

66. Cf. Matt. 5:15 (Q); Luke 11:33 (Q); Mark 4:21; Luke 8:16.

67. Cf. Matt. 15:14 (Q); Luke 6:39 (Q).

68. Cf. Matt. 12:29 (Q?); Mark 3:27; Luke 11:21–22 (Q?).

69. Cf. Matt. 6:25–33 (Q), 34; Luke 12:22–31 (Q), 32. Papyrus Oxyrhynchus 655.1–17 presents the following expanded saying: "[Jesus says, 'Do not worry], from morning [to nightfall nor] from [evening to] morning, either [about] your [food], what [you will] eat, [or] about [your robe], what clothing you [will] wear. [You are much] better than the lilies, which do not card or [spin]. And since you have one article of clothing, what (or, why) . . . you . . . ? Who might add to your stature? That is the one who will give you your clothing.'" See the notes for Greek Gospel of Thomas 36.

70. Cf. Gospel of the Egyptians; Gospel of Philip 75; Hippolytus, Refutation of All Heresies 5.8.44; Manichaean Psalm Book 99,26–30.

71. Cf. Matt. 13:17 (Q); Luke 10:24 (Q); 17:22; John 7:33–36; Prov. 1:23–28.

72. Or, "have received."

73. In Coptic, from Greek, *gnōsis*.

74. Cf. Matt. 23:13 (Q); Luke 11:52 (Q); Pseudo-Clementine Recognitions 2.30.1; Abu Hamid Muhammad al-Ghazali, Revival of the Religious Sciences 1.49.

75. Cf. Matt. 10:16.

76. Cf. Matt. 15:13; John 15:5–6; Isa. 5:1–7; Gospel of Thomas 57; Matt. 13:24–30; Book of Thomas 144.

77. Cf. Matt. 13:12; Mark 4:24–25; Luke 8:18; Matt. 25:29 (Q); Luke 19:26 (Q).

78. Cf. an Arabic inscription at the site of a mosque at Fatehpur Sikri, India; Petrus Alphonsi, Clerical Instruction.

79. Cf. John 14:8–11.

80. Cf. Luke 6:43–44 (Q); Matt. 7:16a, 16b (Q), 19–20; 12:33a–b, 33c (Q).

81. Cf. Matt. 12:31–32 (Q); Luke 12:10 (Q); Mark 3:28–29.

82. Cf. Luke 6:43–45 (Q); Matt. 7:16a, 16b (Q), 17, 18 (Q), 19–29; 12:33a–b, 33c (Q), 34a, 34b–35 (Q); James 3:12.

83. Most likely the person's eyes, possibly John's.

84. Literally, "be broken."

85. Cf. Matt. 11:11 (Q); Luke 7:28 (Q).

86. Cf. Matt. 6:24 (Q); Luke 16:13 (Q).

87. Cf. Matt. 9:17; Mark 2:22; Luke 8:37–39.

88. Cf. Matt. 9:16; Mark 2:21; Luke 5:36.

89. Cf. Gospel of Thomas 106; Matt. 18:19; 17:20b (Q); Luke 17:6b (Q); Matt. 21:21; Mark 11:23; 1 Cor. 13:2.

90. Or, "solitary" (Coptic *monakhos*).

91. Cf. Gospel of Thomas 18.

92. This may possibly be emended to read "<Who> are you?" (*ᵉntōtᵉn <nim>*).

93. This saying recalls the accounts of the career of the soul or of the person in the Secret Book of John, the Hymn of the Pearl, and the Exegesis on the Soul.

94. Instead of "rest" (*anapausis*), the editors of the Gospel of Thomas in *Synopsis Quattuor Evangeliorum*, ed. Kurt Aland, 532, emend to read "<resurrection>" (*ana<sta>sis*).

95. Cf. Luke 17:20–21; Gospel of Thomas 113:4; John 3:18–19; 5:25; 2 Tim. 2:17–18; Treatise on Resurrection 49.

96. 2 Esd. 14:45 gives twenty-four as the number of books in the Jewish scriptures.

97. Cf. Augustine, Against the Adversary of the Law and the Prophets 2.4.14.

98. Cf. Rom. 2:25–29.

99. Cf. Matt. 5:3 (Q); Luke 6:20 (Q).

100. Cf. Matt. 10:37–38 (Q); Luke 14:26–27 (Q); Matt. 16:24; Mark 8:34; Luke 9:23; Gospel of Thomas 101.

101. Cf. Gospel of Thomas 80. This saying reads "carcass" (Coptic, from Greek, *ptōma*); saying 80 reads "body" (Coptic, from Greek, *sōma*).

102. Cf. Matt. 13:24–30.

103. Or, "who has suffered."

104. Cf. Prov. 8:34–36; Sir. 51:26–27; Gospel of Thomas 68–69.

105. Cf. Luke 17:22; John 7:33–36; 8:21; 13:33; Gospel of Thomas 38.

106. The emendation assumes Coptic letters were omitted due to haplography (i.e., accidental omission of similar letters or words by the author or copyist)—

hence the opening of the saying is restored to read <*afnau*>, "<He saw>." Also possible is <*aunau*>, "<They saw>."

107. Probably Jesus, possibly the Samaritan.

108. Literally, the Coptic text may be translated, "That person is around the lamb." Possibly emend to read, "<Why does> that person <carry> around the lamb?" or the like. The editors of the Gospel of Thomas in *Synopsis Quattuor Evangeliorum*, ed. Kurt Aland, 534, offer a different interpretation of the Coptic and translation of the saying: "<He saw> a Samaritan who was trying to take away a lamb while he was on his way to Judea. He said to his disciples, 'That (person) is pursuing the lamb.' They said to him, 'So that he may kill it (and) eat it.'"

109. Or, more literally, "So that he may kill it and eat it."

110. Cf. Gospel of Thomas 7; 11:3.

111. Cf. Luke 17:34–35 (Q); Matt. 24:40–41 (Q).

112. Or, "bed."

113. Literally, "as from one." Bentley Layton, *Nag Hammadi Codices II,2–7*, 1:74, notes two other possibilities. The Greek for "as a stranger" (*hōs xenos*) may have been mistranslated "as from one" (*hōs ex henos*), or the Greek for "as from whom" (*hōs ek tinos*) may have been mistranslated "as from someone" (*hōs ek tinos*, with a different accent). The editors of the Gospel of Thomas in *Synopsis Quattuor Evangeliorum*, ed. Kurt Aland, 534, opt for the translation "as a <stranger>."

114. Cf. Matt. 11:27 (Q); Luke 10:22 (Q); John 3:35; 6:37–39; 13:3–4.

115. Here the Coptic text reads *efšēf*, "desolate." It is emended to read *efšē<š>*, "<whole>."

116. Cf. John 8:12.

117. Cf. Matt. 13:11; Mark 4:11; Luke 8:10.

118. Cf. Matt. 6:3.

119. Cf. Luke 12:16–21 (Q?); Sir. 11:18–19.

120. Cf. Matt. 22:1–10 (Q); Luke 14:16–24 (Q); Deut. 20:5–7; 24:5.

121. Cf. Sir. 26:29.

122. Or, "A creditor." The Coptic text reads *khrē[st.]s*, which may be restored to read either "A [usurer]" (*khrē[stē]s*), as here, or "A [good person]" (*khrē[sto]s*).

123. Possibly emend to read "Perhaps <they> did not know <him>."

124. Cf. Matt. 21:33–41; Mark 12:1–9; Luke 20:9–16.

125. Cf. Ps. 118:22; Matt. 21:42; Mark 12:10; Luke 20:17; Acts 4:11; 1 Pet. 2:7.

126. Cf. Book of Thomas 138. The editors of the Gospel of Thomas in *Synopsis Quattuor Evangeliorum*, ed. Kurt Aland, 536, translate this saying as follows: "Whoever knows all, if he is lacking one thing, he is (already) lacking everything."

127. Cf. Matt. 5:10, 11 (Q); Luke 6:22 (Q); Gospel of Thomas 58; 69.

128. Cf. Gospel of Thomas 68.

129. Cf. Matt. 5:6 (Q); Luke 6:21 (Q).

130. Cf. Gospel of Thomas 41; 67.

131. Cf. Matt. 26:61; Mark 14:58; Matt. 27:40; Mark 15:29; Acts 6:14; John 2:19. The restoration "[again]" is tentative (*ⁿ[kesop]*) and may require a small blank space at the end of the line. For this reason the editors of the Gospel of Thomas in

Synopsis Quattuor Evangeliorum, ed. Kurt Aland, 537, prefer to restore to read "[except me]" (*ᵉn[sabᶜllai]*).

132. Cf. Luke 12:13–14 (Q?); ʿAbd al-Jabbar, Book on the Signs of Muhammad's Prophecy.

133. Or, "lord."

134. Cf. Matt. 9:37–38 (Q); Luke 10:2 (Q); Pirke Avot 2.20.

135. Literally, "He said."

136. Or, "Lord."

137. Or, "no one."

138. The Coptic text has *šōne*, "illness," here emended to read *šō<t>e*, "<well>."

139. Or, "solitary" (Coptic *monakhos*).

140. Sayings 73–75 most likely constitute a small dialogue. Cf. Heavenly Dialogue, in Origen, Against Celsus 8.15. For saying 75 cf. Matt. 25:1–13.

141. Cf. Matt. 13:45–46.

142. Cf. Matt. 6:19–20 (Q); Luke 12:33 (Q); Matt. 13:44.

143. Cf. John 8:12; Wisd. of Sol. 7:24–30.

144. Cf. Rom. 11:36; 1 Cor. 8:6; Martyrdom of Peter 10.

145. Cf. Eccles. 10:9; Hab. 2:18–20; Lucian of Samosata, Hermotimus 81. Also cf. Gospel of Thomas 30 and the note.

146. Cf. Matt. 11:7–8 (Q); Luke 7:24–25 (Q).

147. Cf. Luke 11:27–28 (Q?); Petronius, Satyricon 94.

148. Cf. John 13:17; James 1:25.

149. Cf. Luke 23:29; Matt. 24:19; Mark 13:17; Luke 21:23; Gospel of the Egyptians.

150. Cf. Gospel of Thomas 56 and the note.

151. Cf. 1 Cor. 4:8; Gospel of Thomas 110; Dialogue of the Savior 129.

152. Cf. Ignatius, Smyrnaeans 4:2; Greek proverbs. Versions of this saying are also known from Origen, from Didymus the Blind, from an Armenian text from the Monastery of St. Lazzaro, and from the Gospel of the Savior: "If someone is near me, that person will [burn]. I am the fire that blazes. Whoever is [near me] is near the fire; whoever is far from me is far from life" (Berlin 22220 107,39–48).

153. For sayings 83–84 cf. Gen. 1:26–28 and discussions in Philo of Alexandria and gnostic accounts of creation.

154. Simon Magus was called the great power of God. Cf. Acts 8:9–10; Concept of Our Great Power.

155. Or, "son of man."

156. Cf. Matt. 8:20 (Q); Luke 9:58 (Q); Plutarch, Life of Tiberius Gracchus 9.4–5; Abu Hamid Muhammad al-Ghazali, Revival of the Religious Sciences 3.153.

157. Cf. Gospel of Thomas 29; 112.

158. Or, "angels."

159. Cf. Secret Book of John II, 25; Authoritative Teaching 32.

160. Cf. Matt. 23:25–26 (Q); Luke 11:39–41 (Q); Babylonian Talmud, Berakoth 51a; Kelim 25.1–9.

161. Or, "lordship."

162. Cf. Matt. 11:28–30; Sir. 51:26–27.

163. Cf. Matt. 16:1, 2–3 (Q); Luke 12:54–56 (Q).

164. Cf. Gospel of Thomas 2; 94; Matt. 7:7–8 (Q); Luke 11:9–10 (Q).

165. Cf. John 16:4–5, 12–15, 22–28.

166. Cf. Matt. 7:6. The restoration at the end of the saying is tentative (*šina je nouaaf ⁽ᵉ⁾nla[jte]*), but it fits the context. Bentley Layton, *Nag Hammadi Codex II,2–7,* 1:86–87, notes the following additional suggestions for restoration: "or they might bring it [to naught]"; "or they might grind it [to bits]."

167. Cf. Gospel of Thomas 2; 92; Matt. 7:7–8 (Q); Luke 11:9–10 (Q).

168. Cf. Matt. 5:42 (Q); Luke 6:30 (Q), 34–35b (Q?), 35c (Q); Didache 1:5.

169. Cf. Matt. 13:33 (Q); Luke 13:20–21 (Q).

170. The editors of the Gospel of Thomas in *Synopsis Quattuor Evangeliorum,* ed. Kurt Aland, 542, prefer to emend (with Peter Nagel) to read "she had not noticed (anything) while <she> toiled" (*e<s>hise*).

171. This parable is known only here in early Christian literature, though a somewhat similar story is found in "Macarius" of Syria.

172. This parable is known only here in early Christian literature. In general cf. Gospel of Thomas 35; Matt. 11:12–13 (Q); Luke 16:16 (Q).

173. Cf. Matt. 12:46–50; Mark 3:31–35; Luke 8:19–21; Gospel of the Ebionites 5.

174. Cf. Matt. 22:15–22; Mark 12:13–17; Luke 20:20–26.

175. This restoration is tentative (*⁽ᵉ⁾ntas[ti naei ⁽ᵉ⁾mpc]ol*). Another possibility: "For my mother, who has [given birth to me, has destroyed me]" (see the note in Kurt Aland, ed., *Synopsis Quattuor Evangeliorum,* 543). It may even be possible, though more difficult, to restore to read saying 101:3 as follows: "For my mother [gave birth to me], but my true [mother] gave life to me."

176. Perhaps the holy spirit; cf. Gospel of the Hebrews 3; Secret Book of James 6; Gospel of Philip 55.

177. Cf. Matt. 10:37–38 (Q); Luke 12:26–27 (Q); Gospel of Thomas 55.

178. Cf. Matt. 23:13 (Q); Luke 11:52 (Q); Gospel of Thomas 39:1–2; Aesop, Fable 702.

179. This may refer to either the time or the place of entry.

180. Cf. Gospel of Thomas 21:5–9; Matt. 24:43 (Q); Luke 12:39 (Q).

181. Cf. Matt. 9:14–15; Mark 2:18–20; Luke 5:33–35; Gospel of the Nazoreans 2.

182. On despising physical connections, cf. Gospel of Thomas 55; 101; Book of Thomas 144. On Simon Magus, Helena, and the soul's prostitution, cf. Irenaeus, *Against Heresies* 1.23.2; *Exegesis on the Soul.* On the tradition of Jesus as the illegitimate child of Mary, cf. Origen, *Against Celsus* 1.28, 32; perhaps John 8:41.

183. Or, "sons of man."

184. Cf. Gospel of Thomas 48; Matt. 18:19; 17:20b (Q); Luke 17:6b (Q); Matt. 21:21; Mark 11:23; 1 Cor. 13:2.

185. Cf. Matt. 18:12–13 (Q); Luke 15:4–7 (Q); Ezek. 34:15–16.

186. Cf. Gospel of Thomas 13; John 4:13–14; 7:37–39; Sir. 24:21.

187. Cf. Prov. 2:1–5; Sir. 20:30–31; Matt. 13:44; Midrash Rabbah, Song of Songs 4.12.1; Aesop, Fable 42.

188. Cf. Gospel of Thomas 27:1; 81.

189. Cf. Isa. 34:4; Ps. 102:25–27 (some ancient texts); Heb. 1:10–12; Rev. 6:13–14.

190. This may be a later comment incorporated into the saying.

191. Cf. Gospel of Thomas 29; 87.

192. Or, "They will not say."

193. Cf. Mark 13:21–23; Matt. 24:23–25, 26–27 (Q); Luke 17:20–22, 23–24 (Q); Gospel of Thomas 3:1–3; Gospel of Mary 8.

194. The editors of the Gospel of Thomas in *Synopsis Quattuor Evangeliorum*, ed. Kurt Aland, 546, understand this ("For," Coptic *je*) as an introduction to direct speech, and they read "(But I say to you): Every woman . . . ."

195. While the language of this saying may be shocking to our sensitivities, the intent of the saying seems to be liberating. Here the female may symbolize what is earthly and perishable and the male what is heavenly and imperishable, so that the female becoming male means that all who are mortal and of this world, men and women alike, become immortal and divine. Gospel of Thomas 22 uses gender categories in a somewhat different way but for similar purposes. Cf. Hippolytus, Refutation of All Heresies 5.8.44; Clement of Alexandria, Excerpts from Theodotus 79; First Revelation of James 41; Zostrianos 131; also Second Word of Great Seth 65, and Gospel of Philip 58, in this volume, on the Valentinian concept of the female images of all of us being joined to the male angels in final union.

196. Edition: Harold W. Attridge, "The Greek Fragments," in *Nag Hammadi Codex II,2–7*, ed. Bentley Layton, 1:95–128. On saying 36, see below.

197. The text of the Prologue and sayings 1–7 and 24 are from P. Oxy. 654.

198. The text of sayings 26–30, 77, and 31–33 are from P. Oxy. 1.

199. Or, "why."

200. A previous reading of the Greek text of this saying allowed for the following translation: "As for you, when you have no garment, what [will you put] on?" (cf. Harold W. Attridge, "The Greek Fragments," 1:121; but now see James M. Robinson, "A Written Greek Sayings Cluster Older Than Q: A Vestige").

201. The text of sayings 36–39 are from P. Oxy. 655.

202. In Greek, [*gnōseōs*], a form of *gnōsis*.

203. In Greek, *aiōn*, "aeon."

204. This version of saying 4 is from Hippolytus, Refutation of All Heresies 5.7.20.

205. This version of saying 11 is from Hippolytus, Refutation of All Heresies 5.8.32.

Part Two: The Gospel of Mary

1. Editions: Anne Pasquier, *L'Évangile selon Marie;* Walter C. Till and Hans-Martin Schenke, *Die gnostischen Schriften des koptischen Papyrus Berolinensis 8502;* R. McL. Wilson and George W. MacRae, "The Gospel According to Mary," in *Nag Hammadi Codices V,2–5 and VI with Papyrus Berolinensis 8502,1 and 4*, ed. Douglas M. Parrott, 453–71. Translations: Esther A. de Boer, *The Gospel of Mary;* Judith Hartenstein, "Das Evangelium nach Maria," in *Nag Hammadi Deutsch*, ed. Hans-Martin Schenke, Hans-Gebhard Bethge, and Ursula Ulrike Kaiser, 2:833–44; Karen L. King, *The Gospel of Mary of Magdala;* Karen L. King, George W. MacRae, R. McL. Wilson, and Douglas

M. Parrott, "The Gospel of Mary," in *The Nag Hammadi Library in English*, ed. James M. Robinson, 523–27; Marvin Meyer, *The Gospels of Mary*, 16–22.

2. The first six pages are missing from the Coptic manuscript, and the extant text begins in the middle of a dialogue between Jesus and his disciples on the nature of matter. This dialogue includes reflections upon Stoic themes. Cf. Esther A. de Boer, *The Gospel of Mary*.

3. Cf. Gospel of Philip 53.

4. Literally, "act adulterously."

5. In the Gospel of Mary adultery is understood to be improper mingling with the world. Cf. the similar perspective in the Exegesis on the Soul, from the Nag Hammadi library, Heracleon's Commentary on the Gospel of John, and Gospel of Philip 61.

6. Cf. the discussion of sin in Romans 7.

7. Cf. Luke 24:38; John 14:27.

8. Or, "images of nature." On truth being present in symbols and images, cf. Gospel of Philip 67.

9. Cf. John 14:27; 20:19, 21, 26.

10. Or, "son of man," here and below.

11. Cf. Luke 17:21; Gospel of Thomas 113.

12. Or, "him," here and in the next sentence.

13. The departure of Jesus could be either his crucifixion or his resurrection and ascension.

14. Most likely Mary of Magdala, throughout the text, since this portrayal of Mary resembles Mary of Magdala as presented elsewhere.

15. In Papyrus Oxyrhynchus 3525 it is added that Mary also kissed them tenderly.

16. Or perhaps, with Karen L. King, "brothers and sisters," here and below, though no other women are mentioned in the text.

17. On the special love of Jesus for Mary of Magdala, see Gospel of Mary 17–18, as well as Gospel of Philip 59; 63–64; also Pistis Sophia 17; 19.

18. Or, "lord," here and below.

19. Here Karen L. King, *The Gospel of Mary of Magdala*, 196, suggests that the Greek of Papyrus Oxyrhynchus 3525 may imply that Jesus appeared more than once ("*Once* when the Lord appeared to me in a vision . . .").

20. Cf. Matt. 6:21.

21. The text on page 10 of the Coptic manuscript concludes with these words (before the text breaks off): "and that is [what] . . . ."

22. Pages 11–14 are missing from the Coptic manuscript. The text resumes as Mary is recounting her vision of the ascent of the soul beyond the cosmic powers. In the translation feminine pronouns are used for the soul, because in Greek the word *psychē*, "soul," is feminine in gender, and the soul is typically personified in Greek literature as the young female Psyche. Here the vision apparently describes four stages of ascent, and these stages seem to depict the liberation of the soul from the four elements of this world. The name of the first power is missing from the text, but it may have been "darkness," according to the list of the forms of the

fourth power. The names of the other powers are "desire," "ignorance," and, apparently, "wrath," a deadly composite power. As in other texts relating to gnosticism and the career of the soul, the soul ascends through the realms of the powers and is interrogated by them. The soul is successful in her ascent from this world of matter and body, and she is set free at last. Cf. also Gospel of Thomas 50.

23. This garment, which clothes the soul, is made up of all the features that characterize bodily existence in this world. The soul puts on this garment upon entering the world and takes it off when leaving the world.

24. Compare the seven heavenly spheres (often for the sun, moon, and five planets) described by ancient astronomers and astrologers. On the names of the seven powers of wrath, compare the Secret Book of John.

25. Or, "from," here and later in the sentence.

26. On the hostility of Peter toward Mary Magdalene, cf. Gospel of Thomas 114; Pistis Sophia 36; 72; 146.

27. Levi was a disciple of Jesus, named Levi son of Alphaeus in the Gospel of Mark and said to be a tax collector from Capernaum. Sometimes Levi is identified with the disciple Matthew, but the identification is uncertain. (In the Dialogue of the Savior Matthew is one of the three main disciples with whom Jesus is in dialogue.)

28. On the love of Jesus for Mary, see Gospel of Mary 10; Gospel of Philip 59; 63–64; Pistis Sophia 17; 19.

29. Or, "nurture."

30. In Papyrus Rylands 463 only Levi is said to leave in order to preach.

Part Three: The Gospel of Philip

1. April D. DeConick, "The Great Mystery of Marriage," 342.

2. Editions: *The Facsimile Edition of the Nag Hammadi Codices: Codex II;* Wesley W. Isenberg and Bentley Layton, "The Gospel According to Philip," in *Nag Hammadi Codex II,2–7,* ed. Bentley Layton, 1:129–217; Jacques-É. Ménard, *L'Évangile selon Philippe.* Translations: Wesley W. Isenberg, "The Gospel of Philip," in *The Nag Hammadi Library in English,* ed. James M. Robinson, 139–60; Bentley Layton, *The Gnostic Scriptures,* 325–53; Hans-Martin Schenke, "Das Evangelium nach Philippus," in *Nag Hammadi Deutsch,* ed. Hans-Martin Schenke, Hans-Gebhard Bethge, and Ursula Ulrike Kaiser, 1:183–213; Hans-Martin Schenke, "The Gospel of Philip," in *New Testament Apocrypha,* ed. Wilhelm Schneemelcher, 1:179–208. A number of the textual restorations incorporated here derive from these editions, and particularly from the work of Hans-Martin Schenke.

3. Or, "proselyte," here and in the next sentence.

4. Or, "the dead will not die and will live all the more." Cf. Gospel of Thomas 11:2–3.

5. Cf. Gospel of Thomas 99; 101; 105.

6. Cf. Gospel of Thomas 14:2.

7. Cf. Gospel of Thomas 57.

8. Literally, "brothers," or more generally, "are related to one another."

9. Or, "words," here and below.

10. In gnostic texts the forces are among the rulers of this world. Here they are identified with the ancient gods and goddesses, to whom sacrifices were made.

11. Ancient gods and goddesses were often depicted as animals.

12. Perhaps humankind in general, or perhaps Christ.

13. Cf. John 6:31, 50–51; Exod. 16:4; Ps. 78:23–24.

14. Or, "the realm of all."

15. Cf. 1 Cor. 2:8.

16. Cf. Matt. 1:18, 20; Luke 1:35.

17. In Hebrew and other Semitic traditions the word for *spirit* is feminine in gender, and the spirit may be considered to be the divine mother. Cf. Secret Book of James 6; Gospel of Thomas 101; especially Gospel of the Hebrews 3, in which Jesus refers to his mother as the holy spirit.

18. The restoration is tentative (cf. Hans-Martin Schenke, "The Gospel of Philip," 190).

19. Or, "lord," here and below.

20. Matt. 16:17. Cf. also Matt. 6:9; Luke 11:2 (the Lord's Prayer).

21. Or, "private name, personal name" (so Bentley Layton, *The Gnostic Scriptures*, 332).

22. Or, "public name" (so Bentley Layton, *The Gnostic Scriptures*, 332).

23. The restored letters (Coptic *nam<ou>*) are suggested for a blank space on the papyrus.

24. Literally, an assarius, a Roman coin of little value.

25. 1 Cor. 15:50.

26. John 6:53.

27. The text employs the term *logos* for "word," as above, where it is said that the flesh of Jesus in the eucharist is the word. Here the indefinite article is used with *logos*, and thus a more general translation of *logos* may be preferred.

28. Baptismal water.

29. Philip? Jesus?

30. Literally, "the eucharist."

31. In Valentinian thought, this language means uniting the female images of all of us with the male angels in final union, as a result of the sacrament of the bridal chamber.

32. Or, "the door" (perhaps the door of the sheepfold, as in John 10). Translating this passage as "the king" assumes a slight emendation of the Coptic text (from *ro* to *<ͤr>ro*).

33. Literally, "brothers."

34. The Coptic text reads "her sister" (Coptic *tessōne*) here, and the translation may reflect that reading (but see the reading "his sister" just below).

35. This may be a reference to the father and the son, in contrast to the spirit, mentioned next, or it may be a reference to the spirit, or even to father, son, and spirit together.

36. Or, "Sophia," here and below.

37. Cf. Lev. 2:13; Mark 9:49 (with the variant reading); Col. 4:6.

38. The suggested restoration is tentative and includes a possible reference to Lot's wife (cf. Hans-Martin Schenke, "The Gospel of Philip," 192, 207).

39. This passage seems to reflect the Valentinian distinction between a higher wisdom (often called Sophia) and a lower wisdom (often called Achamoth). In Hebrew and Aramaic *'ekh-moth* means "like death."

40. Adam.

41. Cain.

42. Such gnostic texts as the Secret Book of John and the Nature of the Rulers describe how the ruler of this world, sometimes with his powers, seduced or raped Eve and thus produced Cain.

43. Abel.

44. Or, "baptizes."

45. Or, "baptized."

46. For another meditation on dyeing, cf. Gospel of Philip 63.

47. The text suggests an eschatological perspective with a present realization of spiritual union with Christ and an anticipation of future union with the father. Such an eschatological perspective is also found in the letters of Paul.

48. Compare the discussion of faith and love in 1 Cor. 13 and Secret Book of James 8.

49. The Greek word *nazōraios* can indicate someone from Nazareth or someone who is an observant Jewish Christian.

50. The Greek word *nazarēnos* indicates someone from Nazareth.

51. In Greek *christos* means "anointed."

52. In Syriac *mšiha* can have both meanings.

53. "Jesus" comes from the Hebrew and Aramaic names Yeshua and Yehoshua (Joshua), which mean "The lord (Yahweh) is salvation" (or the like).

54. Hans-Martin Schenke, "Das Evangelium nach Philippus," 198, emends to read "<the man of> the truth."

55. That is, "truth" and "redemption."

56. Here God is the ruler of this world. On this passage cf. Testimony of Truth 32.

57. Or, "spirit," here and below.

58. Jesus was "spread out" on the cross.

59. Seventy-two is a traditional number of nations in the world according to Jewish lore.

60. Or, "son of man," here and below.

61. For another meditation on dyeing, see Gospel of Philip 61.

62. Or, "Sophia."

63. Or, dividing the sentences differently, "Wisdom, who is called barren, is the mother of the angels and the companion of the [savior]. The [savior loved] Mary of Magdala . . . ."

64. On the blind person in darkness, cf. Gospel of Thomas 34.

65. Cf. Gospel of Thomas 19:1.

66. The reference is to baptism.

67. This meditation suggests that the state of salvific androgyny (the union of female image and male angel) protects against unclean spirits. Cf. Gospel of Philip 58.

68. The person described in this paragraph seems to be one who has not left the world.

69. The middle is the region between the fullness of the divine above and this world below.

70. That is, when we die.

71. The translation of this paragraph remains tentative.

72. For a similar apocalyptic vision of hell, cf. Book of Thomas 142–43.

73. The water of baptism.

74. Probably the name "Christian."

75. Jesus.

76. Cf. Gospel of Thomas 22:4.

77. Perhaps cf. Gospel of Thomas 11:1.

78. Literally, "what is outside the outer."

79. Matt. 8:12; 22:13; 25:30.

80. Matt. 6:6.

81. Christ brings people from the material world back to the realm of fullness.

82. Emended. The Coptic text may read, without emendation, "If he again becomes complete and attains his former self, death will cease to be." This meditation suggests that death will be undone in the oneness of androgyny.

83. Matt. 27:46 and Mark 15:34, citing Ps. 22:1.

84. Or, "bridal chamber," here and below.

85. Cf. John 4:23.

86. On the restorations here, cf. Hans-Martin Schenke, "Das Evangelium nach Philippus," 203; "The Gospel of Philip," 197–98. On the curtain of the temple being torn, cf. Matt. 27:51; Mark 15:38; Luke 23:45; Heb. 10:19–20; Gospel of Philip 85.

87. Cf. Gen. 2:7 and gnostic accounts of creation.

88. Cf. Secret Book of John II, 19–20.

89. In Gen. 2:7 the name of Adam is connected to the Hebrew word 'adamah, "earth," from which Adam is made.

90. That is, people worship gods depicted in the form of animals, as in Egypt. Cf. Gospel of Philip 54–55.

91. Possibly emend to read "worship God."

92. "Rest" is the term commonly employed in gnostic texts to describe the state of ultimate bliss.

93. Cf. Gen. 1:26–27.

94. Matt. 3:15.

95. Literally, "a paradise."

96. Or, "paradise."

97. Cf. Gospel of Thomas 11:2–3.

98. Or, "paradise," here and below.

99. Cf. Gen. 3:1–7. Here the speaker seems to be Adam. The word for "knowledge" in Coptic, from Greek, is *gnōsis*, here and below.

100. That is, "The anointed one."

101. Or, "lord."

102. This is the body worn as a garment, here a garment of rags.

103. Bread, the cup, and oil are elements in the sacraments of the eucharist and chrism.

104. Or, "children."

105. Or, "a child."

106. That is, the cup of the eucharist.

107. This is baptismal imagery. Living or running water was commonly used in baptism, and a person being baptized was thought to take off the old and put on the new—namely, Christ.

108. "Know yourself" is the well-known Greek maxim from Delphi.

109. The middle is the place between the fullness above and this world below.

110. The restorations here remain tentative.

111. Or, "priest."

112. The references are to the eucharist.

113. Or, "filled." Hans-Martin Schenke, "The Gospel of Philip," 201, understands this to mean "Jesus filled the water of baptism with spirit."

114. Or, "wind."

115. The text has *gnōsis* in Coptic, from Greek, here and below.

116. Cf. John 8:32.

117. John 8:34.

118. Or, "puffs them up." Cf. 1 Cor. 8:1.

119. 1 Cor. 8:1.

120. Cf. Luke 10:34.

121. 1 Pet. 4:8.

122. Or, "lord," here and below.

123. *Logos,* here and below.

124. Or, "wind, spirit," here and below.

125. In Coptic, from Greek, *gnōsis,* here and below.

126. On faith, hope, love, and knowledge, cf. 1 Cor. 13 and Secret Book of James 8.

127. Literally, "The *logos*," perhaps "Reason."

128. Or, "rest," here and below.

129. Bentley Layton, *The Gnostic Scriptures,* 350, translates as follows: "If slaves, a first course (that is, a single dish); if children, a complete meal."

130. Cf. Matt. 15:27; Mark 7:28.

131. Or, "[rejoiced]"; cf. John 8:56.

132. Or, "scripture."

133. Matt. 3:10; Luke 3:9.

134. Or, "scripture."

135. John 8:32.

136. In Coptic, from Greek, *gnōsis.*

137. The word "<not>" (Coptic <*an*>) presumably was omitted in the text, and it is supplied here.

138. A curtain or veil separates the realm of fullness from the world below in Valentinian thought, and a curtain separates the holy of holies from the holy place in the temple in Jerusalem.

139. On the curtain being torn, cf. Gospel of Philip 69–70, with references.

140. That is, the lesser godhead, the realm of demiurge and demigod. Here and

elsewhere in Valentinian literature, the ruler of this world can be a somewhat kinder and gentler demiurge who is not entirely diabolical.

141. This refers to the cross of Christ as source of salvation.

142. This refers to Noah's ark as source of salvation.

143. Or, with a slight correction, "the upper realm was opened for us, <along with> the lower realm."

144. Or, "offspring," here and below.

145. Or, "be anointed."

146. Matt. 15:13.

Part Four: The Gospel of Truth

1. *The Gnostic Scriptures*, 251.

2. Editions: *The Facsimile Edition of the Nag Hammadi Codices: Codex I*; Harold W. Attridge and George W. MacRae, "The Gospel of Truth," in *Nag Hammadi Codex I*, ed. Harold W. Attridge, 1:55–122, 2:39–135; Jacques-É. Ménard, *L'Évangile de Vérité*. Translations: Harold W. Attridge and George W. MacRae, "The Gospel of Truth," in *The Nag Hammadi Library in English*, ed. James M. Robinson, 38–51; Bentley Layton, *The Gnostic Scriptures*, 250–64; Hans-Martin Schenke, "Evangelium Veritatis," in *Nag Hammadi Deutsch*, ed. Hans-Martin Schenke, Hans-Gebhard Bethge, and Ursula Ulrike Kaiser, 1:27–44.

3. Cf. John 1:1.

4. *Plērōma*, here and elsewhere in the text.

5. Here error is personified and feminine in gender. Compare her role with that of wisdom and the demiurge elsewhere in gnostic texts.

6. As in the Gospel of Philip, the middle is the region between the fullness of the divine above and this world below.

7. Here Bentley Layton translates this clause "and surely then not because of him!" (continuing the negative from the previous clause; see *The Gnostic Scriptures*, 254).

8. Cf. John 14:6.

9. This reference to the tree recalls both the tree on which Jesus was crucified and the tree of the knowledge of good and evil in the Garden of Eden (described in Genesis and gnostic texts).

10. Cf. Heb. 2:17; Mark 10:45; 1 Tim. 2:6.

11. Cf. Phil. 2:5–11. The reference to the perishable rags describes the physical body of Jesus.

12. Literally, "He."

13. Coptic *me*. Or, "thought" (correct to read *me<eue>*).

14. Cf. 1 Pet. 2:2–3.

15. On the two-edged sword cf. Heb. 4:12; Rev. 2:12, 16; 19:15; Philo of Alexandria, Who Is the Heir of Divine Things? 130–40.

16. Or, "and cried out that she understood nothing" (Bentley Layton, *The Gnostic Scriptures*, 258).

17. Coptic *petšōp eimēti*. Or, "who exists" (read *petšōpe imēti*).

18. The author, writing in the first-person singular, notes that they have potential if not actual existence.

19. Descriptions of the nightmares follow in the text.

20. Cf. Matt. 11:5; Luke 7:21–22; John 9:10–11; 11:37.

21. Compare the portrayal of Jesus as word in the Gospel of John, especially chap. 1.

22. Cf. Matt. 18:12–14; Luke 15:4–7; Gospel of Thomas 107.

23. In the Roman system of counting on the fingers, numbers 1–99 were counted on the left hand, and number 100 switched to the right.

24. On Jesus and the father both working, cf. John 5:17.

25. Or, "sun."

26. Cf. Matt. 7:16; 12:33; Luke 6:44.

27. Or, "breath" (Coptic *pna*, for *pneuma*).

28. The author is employing a pun, in Greek, by comparing *psychē* ("psychical form, soul") and *psychos* ("cold").

29. That is, "anointed one."

30. Probably the word.

31. Literally, "it."

32. Or, "nor is it possible for them to study him."

33. The meaning of the Coptic is uncertain. Perhaps correct to read: "<and he> alone <is in the position> to give him a name" (Hans-Martin Schenke, "Evangelium Veritatis," 42–43).

34. Literally, "He."

35. Probably the son.

36. Again, probably the son.

37. This restoration remains tentative; cf. Hans-Martin Schenke, "Evangelium Veritatis," 43.

38. Or, "who exists there for them" (Coptic *petoei ᶜmmeu neu*).

39. Or, "true siblings"; literally, "true brothers."

Part Five: The Holy Book of the Great Invisible Spirit

1. Editions: *The Facsimile Edition of the Nag Hammadi Codices: Codex III; The Facsimile Edition of the Nag Hammadi Codices: Codex IV;* Alexander Böhlig and Frederik Wisse, eds., *Nag Hammadi Codices III,2 and IV,2.* Translations: Alexander Böhlig and Frederik Wisse, "The Gospel of the Egyptians," in *The Nag Hammadi Library in English,* ed. James M. Robinson, 208–19; Bentley Layton, *The Gnostic Scriptures,* 101–20; Marvin Meyer, "The Baptismal Ceremony of the Gospel of the Egyptians," in *The Gnostic Bible,* ed. Willis Barnstone and Marvin Meyer, 218–23; Uwe-Karsten Plisch, "Das heilige Buch des großen unsichtbaren Geistes," in *Nag Hammadi Deutsch,* ed. Hans-Martin Schenke, Hans-Gebhard Bethge, and Ursula Ulrike Kaiser, 1:293–321. This translation is based primarily on the Codex III version of the Holy Book of the Great Invisible Spirit, though the Codex IV version has also been used. Where lacunae in one version may be confidently restored on the basis of readings preserved in the other version, they are not placed within brackets.

2. This is the reading of the Codex IV version. The Codex III version reads "The book of the holy . . . of the great invisible [spirit]." Possibilities for restoring the lacuna in the Codex IV version: "[prayers]" or "[prayers of the] great invisible [spirit]."

3. The text reads "father" (*eiōt*), here and below, for the transcendent great invisible spirit as well as for the lower manifestations of the divine.

4. Compare the role of silence in the Secret Book of John.

5. *Autogenēs* (Coptic, from Greek), here and below.

6. Or, "son," here and below.

7. "Domedon" may mean "lord of the house"; "Doxomedon," "lord of glory." Cf. Alexander Böhlig and Frederik Wisse, eds., *Nag Hammadi Codices III,2 and IV,2*, 41.

8. This constitutes a second trinity.

9. Literally, "from the bosom," here and below.

10. Or, "ogdoad," here and below.

11. On Barbelo, cf. the Secret Book of John.

12. The Codex IV version reads ". . . kaba."

13. "Adone," added here from the Codex IV version.

14. The Codex IV version includes ". . . akroboriaor . . . ."

15. Literally, "voices."

16. On this epithet, here and below, compare the Secret Book of John.

17. The mystery seems to be in the sequence of the vowels: IĒOU, E, A, Ō. Iēou, or Ieou, or Yeu, is the true name of God (cf. Yao) according to the gnostic Book of Yeu; E, epsilon, may have the numerical value of five and is used later in the text, or conceivably it may represent the Greek word *estin*, "is"; A and Ō are alpha and omega, the first and last letters of the Greek alphabet. If E means "is," then the vowel series may read "Ieou is alpha and omega." Here each of the vowels is written twenty-two times; there are twenty-two letters in the Hebrew alphabet. Cf. Bentley Layton, *The Gnostic Scriptures*, 107.

18. The Codex IV version reads "She (that is, Barbelo) asked for power."

19. These lines are added from Codex IV, 55.

20. On Ainon, perhaps compare the site named in John 3:23 and on the Madaba mosaic map. In Greek ainon means "praise" (accusative case).

21. Pages 45–48 are missing in the Codex III version. The following pages are added from Codex IV, 55–60.

22. On five seals, here and below, compare the baptismal reference in Secret Book of John II, 31.

23. The text may be restored to read "[An emanation]" (*[apohr]oia*) or "[Forethought]" (*[pron]oia*) or "[A thought]" *[enn]oia*). On forethought, compare the Secret Book of John.

24. The Codex III version resumes with page 49.

25. The text reads "Mirothoe." Mirothea is a Sethian name or epithet for the divine in several texts. The meaning is uncertain, but it may mean "divine destiny" (from Greek *moiro-theos*—compare Moira, "destiny," in Greek mythology) or "divine anointed one" (from Greek *myro-theos*). Mirothea is feminine in form; Mirotheos is masculine. Here Mirothea denotes the mother of Adamas (compare

Pigeradamas in the Secret Book of John). See John D. Turner, *Sethian Gnosticism and the Platonic Tradition*, 211.

26. The utterance is from the Codex IV version. "EA EA EA" may represent the Greek *ei a, ei a, ei a*, "You are one, you are one, you are one." The Codex III version reads "IEN IEN EA EA EA, three times." "IEN IEN" may be Greek, *ei hen, ei hen*, "You are one, you are one." E (epsilon) and A (alpha) may also be taken as numbers: "O five, one, five, one, five, one." The following lines are from Codex IV, 61.

27. Here the Codex III version resumes.

28. Cf. John 1:3.

29. "[Barbelo]" is restored in the Codex IV version.

30. Or, "Prophania" (Coptic, from Greek).

31. On the four great luminaries, compare the Secret Book of John.

32. Here the Codex IV version reads "Samblo" and the Codex III version reads "Samlo."

33. Abrasax, here and below, is the name of a cosmic power in several traditions, including gnostic traditions. The numerical value of the name Abrasax in Greek is 365, and thus it corresponds to the number of days in the solar year. The name Abrasax may come from the Hebrew *Arba* ("four," for the tetragrammaton or four-letter name of God, YHWH) *Sabaoth* ("hosts," "armies," shortened in the name), and thus Abrasax may reflect the meaning "lord of hosts."

34. The meaning of "the fourth" is uncertain; the Codex III version originally read "the seventy-fourth," and this reading was corrected to the present reading. Perhaps compare the trinities or divine triads in the Holy Book of the Great Invisible Spirit with the present father as the fourth after a trinity; Heracleon, Commentary on John 16 (on the Valentinian concept of forty and four, and the realm of four, or tetrad); Secret Book of James 12 (on "a fourth one in heaven").

35. Or, "offspring," here and below.

36. This reading follows the Codex IV version; the Codex III version reads "The triple male children."

37. Or, "church" (*ekklēsia*).

38. Several phrases are inserted from the Codex IV version, page 67.

39. The name Plesithea may mean "full goddess" or "nearby goddess." Cf. Alexander Böhlig and Frederik Wisse, eds., *Nag Hammadi Codices III,2 and IV,2*, 182; Bentley Layton, *The Gnostic Scriptures*, 113.

40. On the stories of Sodom and Gomorrah, cf. Holy Book of the Great Invisible Spirit III, 60–61, and Gen. 18–19. Here and in other gnostic texts—for example, the Paraphrase of Shem—Sodom and Gomorrah can be considered to be locales inhabited by gnostics who are persecuted by the ruler of this world.

41. Or, correct "with him" (Coptic *ᶜnmmaf*) to read "with <her>" (Coptic *ᶜnmma<s>*).

42. This reading follows the Codex IV version; the Codex III version reads "in the fourth realm."

43. Or, "monads."

44. Sakla, whose name means "fool" in Aramaic, is the creator of this world, especially in Sethian texts.

45. In Manichaean thought the female Nebroel and the male Sakla are demons who create the creatures of the material world through sexuality.

46. Adonaios is also mentioned in the Secret Book of John and the Second Discourse of Great Seth.

47. Several of these names are restored from the similar list in the Secret Book of John II, 10–11. For a possible restoration of the lacuna for the first angel Athoth, see the tentative restoration in the Secret Book of John.

48. Exod. 20:5; Deut. 5:9; Isa. 46:9.

49. Or, "Man." Here this is Adamas.

50. Or, "son of man." Here this is great Seth.

51. *Metanoia* (Coptic, from Greek).

52. The name Hormos means "refuge, shelter, haven."

53. Literally, "vessel."

54. A reference to the seed of Seth coming into this world, within bodies formed through sexual intercourse.

55. Here the Codex III version has *sooun*, the Codex IV version *gnōsis*.

56. Sakla.

57. The text of the Codex III version reads "Barbelon," here and below.

58. The Codex IV version reads "Selmelchel."

59. In Coptic, *hōtb*; or read *hōtp*, "reconciliation."

60. Or, "the reconciliation of world with world."

61. Compare the thirteen kingdoms in Revelation of Adam 77–82.

62. Cf. Gospel of Thomas Prologue.

63. Cf. Colossians 2:8–15; Revelation of Adam 77–82.

64. Literally, "Through it (or, him)," with reference to baptism, or else to Seth, Jesus, or the act of nailing.

65. This may refer to actions undertaken in the rite of baptism.

66. The name Yesseus Mazareus Yessedekeus, here and below, may be related to the name of Jesus (compare Jesus of Nazareth or Jesus the Nazarene [*nazōraios*] and Jesus the righteous [*ho dikaios*]).

67. This line is added from the Codex IV version.

68. The traditional spelling of a word or name of power, found in the Codex IV version. (The Codex III version omits "bar.") Known from magical texts, the name Sesengenbarpharanges probably derives from Aramaic (S. son of [bar-] Ph.?). John G. Gager, *Curse Tablets and Binding Spells*, 269, refers to a drug from a fig tree in "the Baaras ravine" (Greek, *pharangos* [in the genitive case]).

69. The Codex IV version reads "Umneos" or "Hymneos."

70. Coptic, from Greek, *prutanis*; the Codex IV version reads "Phritanis."

71. The Codex IV version reads "slain souls."

72. The Codex IV version reads "Telmachael Telmachael Eli Eli Machar Machar Seth."

73. Cf. Gal. 4:4–5.

74. This name resembles the name Poimandres in Hermetic literature, and Poimandres probably derives from the Greek for "shepherd of men." The name Poimael may suggest Hermetic themes in the Holy Book of the Great Invisible Spirit; see the work of Régine Charron, Université Laval.

75. Or, "the baptism of living water"; literally, "spring baptism."

76. Cf. Gospel of Thomas 1; 3.

77. The translation of the baptismal hymn includes materials drawn from the Codex IV version.

78. Possibly compare Greek: *ei aaaa, ōōōō*, "You are alpha (four times), omega (four times)." Alpha and omega, as the first and last letters of the Greek alphabet, can symbolize the first and the last, the beginning and the end; cf. Rev. 1:8; 21:6; 22:13, and other texts.

79. The Greek vowels in sequence; five omicrons are expected after four iotas, to maintain the sequence. In texts of ritual power such vowels may be arranged for visual effect—in this case, perhaps to form a pyramid.

80. Greek *aiōn*, for "aeon, eternal realm"?

81. Greek *huie*, for "son, child"?

82. These three lines are Greek: *aei eis aei, ei ho ei, ei hos ei.*

83. "In another voice" seems to be a liturgical rubric to indicate that the following portion of the baptismal hymn is to be chanted in a different voice.

84. If this is Greek *sou*, it may be translated "yours" or "it is yours." Otherwise it may be left as glossolalia, "SOU." The following lines also are Greek: *IĒS. Ide aei ō, aei e, ō IS.*

85. The numerical value of the letter epsilon is five, a number which plays a prominent role in Sethian texts. Cf. also Plutarch, On the E at Delphi.

86. Greek for "Be. Be"? Perhaps a reference to Esephech, twice?

87. Possibly read "it"—that is, the book.

88. Literally, "in the flesh my name is Gongessos." The Latin form of this name is Concessus.

89. ICHTHYS, a Greek word meaning "fish," is a famous Greek acronym for "Jesus Christ, Son of God, Savior."

Part Six: The Secret Book of John

1. Editions: *The Facsimile Edition of the Nag Hammadi Codices: Codex II; The Facsimile Edition of the Nag Hammadi Codices: Codex III; The Facsimile Edition of the Nag Hammadi Codices: Codex IV;* Walter C. Till and Hans-Martin Schenke, *Die gnostischen Schriften des koptischen Papyrus Berolinensis 8502;* Michael Waldstein and Frederik Wisse, eds., *The Apocryphon of John: Synopsis of Nag Hammadi Codices II,1; III,1; and IV,1 with BG 8502,2.* Translations: Bentley Layton, *The Gnostic Scriptures,* 23–51; Marvin Meyer, "The Secret Book of John," in *The Gnostic Bible,* ed. Willis Barnstone and Marvin Meyer, 135–65; Michael Waldstein, "Das Apokryphon des Johannes," in *Nag Hammadi Deutsch,* ed. Hans-Martin Schenke, Hans-Gebhard Bethge, and Ursula Ulrike Kaiser, 1:95–150; Frederik Wisse, "The Apocryphon of John," in *The Nag Hammadi Library in English,* ed. James M. Robinson, 104–23. The present translation is based

mainly on the Coptic text of Nag Hammadi Codex II (the longer version of the Secret Book of John). Where lacunae in the Codex II version may be confidently restored on the basis of readings preserved in the other texts, they are not placed within brackets. A few lines omitted from the Codex II text are added from the Codex IV text, the other text representing the longer version of the Secret Book of John. References to the texts of BG 8502 and Nag Hammadi III, which represent the shorter version, are also included.

2. Or restore to read "[that are]."

3. This name recalls the evil Zoroastrian deity Ahriman.

4. The speaker is John.

5. Perhaps from the Coptic [*ourōme*]; here the shorter version in BG 8502, 20, reads *oualou*, "a child."

6. Coptic *hal*, "servant," probably is a translation of the Greek *pais*, which can mean "youth" or "servant." In the present context "youth" is much more likely.

7. Coptic, from Greek, *monas*, "monad." The following lines offer a classic statement of divine transcendence formulated in terms of negation. This statement in the Secret Book of John is very similar to another Nag Hammadi text, the Foreigner (Allogenes), and reminiscent also of the *via negativa* of the Hindu Upanishads, with the insistence that the ultimate is *neti neti*, "not this, not that."

8. The text reads "father" (*eiōt*), here and below, for the transcendent great invisible spirit. The translation "parent" is incorporated here to emphasize that the divine parent transcends gender categories.

9. The last clause is restored from Nag Hammadi Codex IV,4.

10. The parallel passages in the shorter version of the Secret Book of John in BG 8502, 24, and Nag Hammadi Codex III,5, and in the Foreigner 63, read "he is not a creature." The differences here may be related to a confusion of the Greek terms *poion*, "what kind," and *poiēton*, "creature."

11. In Coptic, from Greek, *gnōsis*.

12. Here and elsewhere the word "father" is used for clarity of translation when the Coptic uses only a personal pronoun.

13. The father gazes into the water and falls in love with its own image in a manner that calls to mind Narcissus in Greek mythology (see Ovid, Metamorphoses 3.402–510).

14. Through this love of the father for its own image the father's thought (*ennoia*, from Greek, here and below) emanated, and the first thought or forethought (*pronoia*, from Greek, here and throughout the text) comes from the mind of the father: the divine mother, Barbelo. The father thus produces an entity independently, without the aid of a lover. Other gods who are credited with acts of independent procreation include the Greek god Zeus, who produces Athena, the daughter of Metis (wisdom or skill), from his head alongside the River (or Lake) Triton (see Hesiod, Theogony 886–900, 924–29), or the Egyptian god Atum, who mates with his hand and spits— that is, he produces the seed of life by means of masturbation. On Sophia conceiving independently, cf. Secret Book of John II, 9–10.

15. Barbelo is the divine mother and the first emanation of the father of all in Sethian texts. She is also described as the forethought (Greek, *pronoia*) of the

invisible spirit. The name Barbelo may derive from Hebrew, and a possible translation is "God (compare *el*) in (*b-*) four (*arb[a]*)," with reference to the tetragrammaton, the ineffable four-letter name of God.

16. Coptic, from Greek, *mētropatōr*, probably a term for an androgynous parent.

17. This is a term of praise, in which maleness symbolizes all that is heavenly, like the divine father, and maleness is amplified by being male three times over. Similar themes occur in Gospel of Thomas 114, the Holy Book of the Great Invisible Spirit, the Three Steles of Seth, and other texts.

18. Or, throughout this section, "looked on," "looked on in agreement," or "nodded in agreement." Cf. the Holy Book of the Great Invisible Spirit.

19. The one who comes from the spirit's thought is most likely forethought, or possibly foreknowledge.

20. Or, "thinking," "mind."

21. The five in Coptic, from Greek, is *pentas*, "pentad" or "quintet." It consists of Barbelo and the four spiritual attributes Barbelo requested. Since they are androgynous, they can also be called the ten (Coptic *dekas*, from Greek). The five or the ten are the same as the father in emanation.

22. Spiritual intercourse between the father and Barbelo produces a child of light. In the longer version of the Secret Book of John, the father is considered to be the active procreative force. In the shorter version found in BG 8502 and Nag Hammadi Codex III, Barbelo is the one who gazes into the father or the pure light, and then she gives birth.

23. M^{c}ntkhrs, here and below, from the Greek *chrēstos* ("good") or *christos* ("anointed"). The text apparently maintains that the divine child is both good and anointed.

24. *Nous* (from Greek), here and below. (The Coptic *meeue* is also used.)

25. Or, "Christ," here and below (Coptic, from Greek, *pekhrs*).

26. Coptic, "it" or "him"; possibly "the anointed."

27. Here begins creation by the word, as in Gen. 1 and John 1, as well as in the Egyptian creation text, the Memphite cosmogony, in which Ptah is described creating by means of the spoken word.

28. Coptic, from Greek, *autogenēs*, here and below.

29. Or, "whom the spirit honored."

30. Or, "appeared" (in BG 8502, 33).

31. Or, "and is the first angel."

32. Or, "afterthought," *epinoia* (from Greek), here and throughout. On *pronoia* and *epinoia*, compare, in Greek mythology, the Titans Prometheos ("forethought") and Epimetheos ("afterthought"), who create human beings, though Epimetheos does his job imperfectly. Prometheos makes the humans stand upright, after the manner of the gods, and he takes fire from the gods and brings it down to earth. For his actions he is punished by being chained to a pillar in the mountains, where a bird of prey eats his liver. Eventually Heracles frees him.

33. Pigeradamas? Perhaps read "the great self-conceived child, the anointed." See also Secret Book of John II, 9.

34. Or, "Geradamas," here and below. Here BG 8502, 35, reads "Adam" and

Nag Hammadi Codex III, 13, reads "Adamas." The name Pigeradamas or Geradamas may mean "Adam the stranger" (Hebrew, *gēr 'adam*), "holy Adam" (Greek, *hier-adamas*), or "old (Greek, *gerōn*) Adam."

35. Sophia tries to imitate the original procreative act of the father. This account of Sophia bringing forth by herself seems to reflect ancient gynecological theories about women's bodies and reproduction. In Greek mythology the goddess Hera also imitates Zeus and brings forth a child by herself. According to one version of the myth, the child is the monster Typhon (Homeric Hymn to Pythian Apollo 300–362). According to another, it is the lame deity Hephaistos, whom Hera evicts from Olympus and sends down to the world below (Hesiod, Theogony 924–29). Hephaistos is the artisan among the gods, and is represented in Egypt by his counterpart Khnum, a ram-headed creator who molds creatures on a potter's wheel. In the Secret Book of John all the evils and misfortunes of this world derive from Sophia's blunder.

36. Or, "was amazed in the mindlessness." Yaldabaoth mating with his mindlessness (*aponoia*, from Greek, here and below) probably suggests that he masturbated.

37. The reading (*p[jaio]b‘s*) remains tentative.

38. That is, the evil eye (Coptic *pbal ‘mpkōh*). BG 8502, 40, and Nag Hammadi Codex III, 16, read "the eye of fire" (Coptic *pbal ‘mpkōht*).

39. Adonaios is also mentioned in the Holy Book of the Great Invisible Spirit and the Second Discourse of Great Seth.

40. The twelve cosmic authorities probably correspond to the signs of the zodiac. On this list of names, cf. Holy Book of the Great Invisible Spirit III, 58.

41. The seven kings probably correspond to the seven planetary spheres (for the sun, the moon, Mercury, Venus, Mars, Jupiter, and Saturn) described by ancient astronomers.

42. In Aramaic Yaldabaoth probably means "child of chaos" or "child of (S)abaoth," Sakla means "fool," and Samael means "blind god." Here the first two names are spelled "Yaltabaoth" and "Saklas."

43. Isa. 45:5–6, 21; 46:9.

44. The number of angels corresponds to the days in the solar year.

45. Yao (*Iaō*) is a form of Yahweh, the name of God, especially in Greek. Yao is a power of this world in some gnostic texts and a son of Yaldabaoth in On the Origin of the World. In this section several of the names derive from Hebrew words, especially words that designate God.

46. Here the name is spelled "Sabbede." Other versions give the name as Sabbataios or Sabbadaios. Throughout the text the spelling of the names varies in the manuscripts, but only a few of the variant spellings are given here.

47. The seven powers correspond to the days of the week.

48. The seraphim are a class of angels, here angels of Yaldabaoth.

49. Here the name is spelled "Eloaio." Another version gives the name as Eloaios.

50. Here the name is spelled "Astraphaio." Another version gives the name as Astaphaios.

51. Here the name is spelled "Sanbaoth." Other versions give the name as Sabaoth.

52. Here the name is spelled "Sabbateon." Another version gives the name as Sabbataios.

53. Isa. 45:5–6, 21; 46:9.

54. John.

55. Or, "Lord," here and below.

56. Gen. 1:2.

57. This sentence is restored from Nag Hammadi Codex IV, 21.

58. Coptic *thbsō ꜥmpkake*; BG 8502, 46, reads "aborted fetus of darkness" (*phouhe mpkake*), with reference to Yaldabaoth.

59. This clause is restored from Nag Hammadi Codex IV, 22.

60. Sophia dwells in the ninth sphere, above Yaldabaoth, who occupies the eighth sphere (sometimes called the "ogdoad" and identified as the sphere of the fixed stars). Yaldabaoth himself is thus positioned over the seven kings in their seven spheres (sometimes called the "hebdomad"). See also the Discourse on the Eighth and Ninth, and other gnostic texts.

61. Or, "Man."

62. Or, "son of man," here and below.

63. In the longer version of the Secret Book of John, the figure that appears is that of forethought; in the shorter version it is that of the father or first human Pigeradamas.

64. Yaldabaoth and his authorities look at the waters above the earth, and from underneath they see the reflection of a human shape in the water.

65. Gen. 1:26. In the Secret Book of John a distinction is made between the image of God and the likeness of the creators.

66. Yaldabaoth and his authorities create a psychical man with a psychical body—that is, they create a soul-man, his body composed entirely of the animating soul. His physical body of flesh and blood will be constructed later.

67. Or, "and these seven psychical substances were taken by the authorities."

68. Or, "The first one began by creating the head, Eteraphaope-Abron created the skull."

69. These words are restored from Nag Hammadi Codex IV, 25.

70. These words are restored from Nag Hammadi Codex IV, 25.

71. The translation is tentative.

72. The last three names are restored from Nag Hammadi Codex IV, 26.

73. "Sense-perception is not in an excited state" (from Greek, *aisthēsis ouch epi ptoē*), a philosophical saying (see Bentley Layton, *The Gnostic Scriptures*, 43).

74. "The 7 senses are (or, Sense-perception is) not in an excited state" (from Greek, again), another version of the philosophical saying (Bentley Layton, *The Gnostic Scriptures*, 43).

75. The angels assembling the psychical body parts correspond to the days in the solar year, as above.

76. The precise identification of the Book of Zoroaster remains uncertain, but the title calls to mind the text Zostrianos, or else Porphyry's Life of Plotinos 16, where Porphyry refers to other texts written under the name of Zoroaster, including a book of Zoroaster.

77. Gen. 2:7.

78. Perhaps parallel to Gen. 2:25.

79. Zoe (from Greek). Cf. Gen. 3:20: Eve is named Zoe in the Septuagint.

80. Or, "offspring."

81. Cf. Three Steles of Seth 127.

82. Here fiery winds replace air as the fourth element.

83. The scene recalls a workshop in which a statue or a fetter is being forged.

84. Here material spirit replaces air as the fourth element.

85. The description of a human being and a shadow in a cave may derive from the allegory of the cave in Plato's Republic, Book 7. The body as the prison or tomb of the soul is also a well-known Platonic and Orphic teaching.

86. Gen. 2:16–17.

87. Literally, "the tree of their life" (in Nag Hammadi Codex II).

88. The savior, here Jesus.

89. Insight assumes the form of a tree, just as in Greek mythology Daphne changes into a laurel tree (see Nature of the Rulers 89, On the Origin of the World 116–17, and Ovid, Metamorphoses 1.452–562). Like Daphne, insight is not to be apprehended.

90. Or, "his fullness."

91. The savior, here Jesus.

92. John.

93. Literally, "He" or "It." This probably refers to the first ruler, possibly the snake.

94. Moses's first book is thought to be Genesis.

95. Gen. 2:21.

96. Isa. 6:10.

97. Gen. 2:21–22.

98. Gen. 2:23.

99. Gen. 2:24. The manuscript includes an instance of dittography here.

100. Zoe, as in Gen. 3:20.

101. This clause is restored from Nag Hammadi Codex IV, 36.

102. In Coptic, from Greek, *gnōsis*.

103. The savior appears as a heavenly bird; the eagle is the bird of Zeus. Compare the Hymn of the Pearl, in which the royal letter flies as an eagle and becomes a voice of revelation.

104. Gen. 3:7, 10–11.

105. Gen. 3:22–24.

106. Zoe.

107. *Eloim* and *Yawe*, two names of God in the Hebrew Bible. Elohim is a word that means God (though plural in form and ending); Yahweh is the name of God (based on the tetragrammaton, the ineffable four-letter name).

108. Gen. 4:1–2.

109. That is, Elohim and Yahweh.

110. Or "the tomb" (as above).

111. Gen. 4:25; 5:3.

112. The water of forgetfulness recalls the water of the River Lethe in the Greek conception of the underworld. If a thirsty soul drinks of the water of this river, it forgets about its previous lives and thus may be reincarnated in another body.

113. Coptic, from Greek, *pathlon*, as in all the manuscripts except Codex II, which reads, apparently erroneously, "what is good" (*pagathon*).

114. Coptic *senašo[one]*, restored from Nag Hammadi Codex IV, 40; BG 8502, 66, and Nag Hammadi Codex III, 34, read "be saved" (*senaoujai*).

115. These clauses are restored from Nag Hammadi Codex IV, 40.

116. This description of every person is like that of Adam moving and standing after receiving spirit from Yaldabaoth in Secret Book of John II, 19.

117. Feminine pronouns are used for the soul in the translation of this part of the Secret Book of John, since the soul (*psychē*) is commonly depicted as being female in Greek and gnostic literature.

118. The soul is thrown into another body and thus is reincarnated.

119. Literally "nature," Coptic *phusis* (from Greek). Returning to the mother's womb is also a theme encountered in John 3:4.

120. In the Greco-Roman world, fate (in Greek, *heimarmenē*, as here; in Coptic, *šimarmenē*) was considered to be the overwhelming force that determines the destiny of all that is earthly and heavenly.

121. Cf. Gen. 6:5–8:22.

122. Gen. 7:7.

123. Cf. Gen. 6:1–4; 1 Enoch 6–11.

124. The concluding hymn of the savior is found only in the longer version of the Secret Book of John (Nag Hammadi Codices II and IV). It reflects a hymn sung by heavenly forethought, the divine mother, as savior. In the present Christianized version of the Secret Book of John the reader may understand the savior to be Jesus. Three descents of the savior are also described in Three Forms of First Thought.

125. The call to awaken addresses a prototypical sleeper—any person who may awaken to knowledge and salvation.

126. Or, "enclosure," even "garment."

127. The shorter versions of the Secret Book of John in BG 8502 and Nag Hammadi Codex III do not include this overtly Christian concluding statement.

Part Seven: The Secret Book of James

1. Editions: *The Facsimile Edition of the Nag Hammadi Codices: Codex I;* Donald Rouleau, *L'Épître apocryphe de Jacques;* Francis E. Williams, "The Apocryphon of James," in *Nag Hammadi Codex I,* ed. Harold W. Attridge, 1:13–53, 2:7–37. Translations: Judith Hartenstein and Uwe-Karsten Plisch, "Der Brief des Jakobus," in *Nag Hammadi Deutsch,* ed. Hans-Martin Schenke, Hans-Gebhard Bethge, and Ursula Ulrike Kaiser, 1:11–26; Dankwart Kirchner, *Epistula Jacobi Apocrypha;* Dankwart Kirchner and Einar Thomassen, "The Apocryphon of James," in *New Testament Apocrypha,* ed. Wilhelm Schneemelcher, 1:285–99; Marvin Meyer, "The Secret Book of James," in *The Gnostic Bible,* ed. Willis Barnstone and Marvin Meyer, 341–50; Francis E.

Williams, "The Apocryphon of James," in *The Nag Hammadi Library in English*, ed. James M. Robinson, 29–37.

2. Thought to be James the righteous, brother of Jesus and leader of the Jerusalem church (cf. Gospel of Thomas 12; First and Second Revelations of James).

3. Coptic *ᵉm[pšēre kērin]thos;* literally, "the [son (or, child) Cerinthos]." A person named Cerinthos was a well-known second-century Christian teacher who was considered one of the first gnostics by the heresiologists. This restoration is tentative; cf. Judith Hartenstein and Uwe-Karsten Plisch, "Der Brief des Jakobus," 18. The existing Coptic letters *-thos* could also be from such words as *pathos, sympathos,* or *agathos,* and the restoration could be "to [one who embraces suffering]," "to [his companion in suffering]," "to [one who is good]," or the like.

4. Or, "lord," here and below.

5. Coptic (from Greek, preserving the Greek dative plural ending) *hᵉn hensheei mmᵉnthebraiois;* literally, "in Hebrew letters." No such Hebrew text is known.

6. No additional secret book of James is known.

7. The restoration of these lines remains tentative. Cf. Judith Hartenstein and Uwe-Karsten Plisch, "Der Brief des Jakobus," 18.

8. Cf. Gospel of Thomas Prologue; Book of Thomas 138.

9. Other texts, including gnostic texts, also suggest long periods of time for appearances of Jesus—for example, eighteen months (540 days), 545 days (eighteen months plus five intercalary days?), or even twelve years. On eighteen days (or months), cf. Secret Book of James 8.

10. Perhaps restore to read "[like deaf people]." Cf. Dankwart Kirchner and Einar Thomassen, "The Apocryphon of James," 297.

11. The restoration of these lines remains tentative. Cf. Judith Hartenstein and Uwe-Karsten Plisch, "Der Brief des Jakobus," 19.

12. Or, "son of man," here and below.

13. Cf. Secret Book of James 12–13; John 20:29.

14. This paragraph is difficult to translate, but a significant distinction is made here between spirit (*pneuma*) and soul (*psychē*).

15. Coptic *pronoia.*

16. The text is emended here (*hᵉnn oumᵉnt<a>logos*). The manuscript reads "with reason."

17. Coptic *hᵉnn oušou;* burial in sand is characteristic of Egypt. It is also possible to emend to read *hᵉnn ouš<ōs>,* "in <shame>."

18. Coptic *tmᵉntᵉr[r]o . . . ᵉmpmou.* The text may well be emended to read *tmᵉntᵉr[r]o . . . ᵉmp<n>ou<te>,* "<God's> kingdom."

19. Or, "who put themselves to death," as voluntary martyrs.

20. Here the holy spirit may be understood to be God the mother. Cf. Gospel of Thomas 101; Gospel of Philip 55.

21. John the baptizer; cf. Gospel of Thomas 46.

22. This parable of the date palm shoot remains difficult to translate, and the translation given here is somewhat tentative. The reference to "it" in the last sentence apparently indicates the kingdom.

23. Coptic *ph[is]e*, which may also be translated "my suffering."

24. Or perhaps emend to read "eighteen months" (cf. Secret Book of James 2).

25. These are titles of or references to parables.

26. In Coptic, from Greek, *gnōsis*.

27. In Coptic, from Greek, *gnōsis*, here and below.

28. Coptic *ē at^{e}meire*; literally, "or not to do so."

29. Or, "I would never ascend from the earth."

30. Perhaps emend to read "he."

31. That is, "The father."

32. Or, "herself"; "soul," *psychē*, is feminine in gender. Here it is assumed that a person is composed of a body of flesh, an animating soul, and a vivifying spirit, as in Valentinian thought. Cf. also 1 Thess. 5:23.

33. This seems to be a way of saying that few are saved, and it may indicate one who is alone as a fourth one with God the father, mother, and child, and thus is as close as one can get to the divine.

34. "Know yourself" was a maxim from the oracular center at Delphi, Greece.

35. Cf. Secret Book of James 3; John 20:29.

36. Or, "will be able to stand alongside" (Coptic *naš ōhe aret^{e}f*).

37. On existing and not existing, cf. Secret Book of John II, 2–4; Three Steles of Seth 121–24; Foreigner 61–64.

38. On Jesus riding a chariot into heaven, compare accounts of Elijah and Enoch traveling into heaven, in 2 Kings 2 and 1 Enoch 70, as well as figures ascending to heaven in chariots on Roman commemorative coins.

39. The verbs "strip" and "clothe" refer to shedding the flesh as a garment and sometimes, as here, putting on a new heavenly garment.

40. Apocalyptic images.

41. This paragraph describes the dispersal of the apostles to preach throughout the world; cf. Letter of Peter to Philip 140. James stays in Jerusalem to lead the church there. The "loved ones who are to appear" are future believers, like the readers of the Secret Book of James.

Part Eight: The Book of Thomas

1. Editions: *The Facsimile Edition of the Nag Hammadi Codices: Codex II*; Raymond Kuntzmann, *Le Livre de Thomas*; John D. Turner and Bentley Layton, "The Book of Thomas the Contender Writing to the Perfect," in *Nag Hammadi Codex II,2–7*, ed. Bentley Layton, 2:171–205. Translations: Bentley Layton, *The Gnostic Scriptures*, 400–409; Marvin Meyer, "The Book of Thomas," in *The Gnostic Bible*, ed. Willis Barnstone and Marvin Meyer, 396–403; Hans-Martin Schenke, "Das Buch des Thomas," in *Nag Hammadi Deutsch*, ed. Hans-Martin Schenke, Hans-Gebhard Bethge, and Ursula Ulrike Kaiser, 1:279–91; Hans-Martin Schenke and Einar Thomassen, "The Book of Thomas," in *New Testament Apocrypha*, ed. Wilhelm Schneemelcher, 1:232–47; John D. Turner, "The Book of Thomas the Contender," in *The Nag Hammadi Library in English*, ed. James M. Robinson, 199–207.

2. Here Judas Thomas is thought to be the twin brother of Jesus; cf. Gospel of Thomas Prologue. The name of Mathaias resembles that of the original disciple Matthew and the replacement apostle Matthias, but his identity is unclear.

3. Cf. the Delphic maxim "Know yourself," and Gospel of Thomas 3:4–5.

4. Or, "lord," here and below.

5. This contrast between the visible and the invisible is a contrast between the lower world of body, change, perishability, and animal nature, and the higher world of soul, constancy, immortality, and spiritual nature. Compare the discussion of the soul in Plato's Phaedo.

6. The restoration of these lines is somewhat tentative. Cf. Hans-Martin Schenke, "Das Buch des Thomas," 285.

7. Coptic *e[u]onh*. Or, restore as "they are visible" (Coptic *e[uou]onh*).

8. That is, the sun.

9. The restoration of these lines is somewhat tentative. Cf. Hans-Martin Schenke, "Das Buch des Thomas," 286.

10. Sophia.

11. Cf. Ps. 1:3.

12. On the imprisonment of these people see the discussion in Plato's Phaedo, especially Phaedo 81C–82A; 83DE.

13. Cf. Gospel of Thomas 2.

14. This passage refers to the death and decay of the body and the punishment and reincarnation of ignorant people.

15. On phantoms cf. Plato's Phaedo 81C–E.

16. Or, "these people."

17. The Coptic is partially restored: *tm^en t^e r[ro]*.

18. The restoration of these lines is partial and somewhat tentative. Cf. Hans-Martin Schenke, "Das Buch des Thomas," 288.

19. On what sows and is sown, cf. Plato's Phaedo 83DE and other descriptions comparing the life cycles of plants and humans.

20. The underworld, or hell. This description includes features typical of other descriptions in Hesiod, Plato, Christian apocalypses, and Dante.

21. Tartarouchos is the angel or power who controls Tartaros.

22. The restoration of these lines is somewhat tentative. Cf. Hans-Martin Schenke, "Das Buch des Thomas," 289.

23. The body is the perishable prison of the soul in Platonic and Orphic thought. Compare also the prisoners bound in caves in Book of Thomas 143 and the allegory of the cave in Plato's Republic.

24. The garment is the body, which can be put on or taken off like an article of clothing.

25. The restoration of these lines is somewhat tentative. Cf. Hans-Martin Schenke, "Das Buch des Thomas," 290.

26. The four elements, with spirit replacing fire, since here fire is characteristic of passion, lust, and destruction. For "spirit" perhaps read "wind."

27. Cf. Dan. 6:16–18; Bel and the Dragon 31–32; Second Discourse of Great Seth 55.

28. The restoration of these lines is somewhat tentative. Cf. Hans-Martin Schenke, "Das Buch des Thomas," 291.

29. Literally, "that they may rise from death."

30. Cf. Gospel of Thomas 2.

31. Literally, "my brothers."

32. Or, "saints."

33. The scribal note probably applies to the entire codex.

Part Nine: *The Dialogue of the Savior*

1. Editions: *The Facsimile Edition of the Nag Hammadi Codices: Codex III*; Stephen Emmel, ed., *Nag Hammadi Codex III,5: The Dialogue of the Savior*; Pierre Létourneau, *Le Dialogue du Sauveur*. Translations: Beate Blatz and Einar Thomassen, "The Dialogue of the Saviour," in *New Testament Apocrypha*, ed. Wilhelm Schneemelcher, 1:300–312; Helmut Koester, Elaine H. Pagels, and Stephen Emmel, "The Dialogue of the Savior," in *The Nag Hammadi Library in English*, ed. James M. Robinson, 244–55; Silke Petersen and Hans-Gebhard Bethge, "Der Dialog des Erlösers," in *Nag Hammadi Deutsch*, ed. Hans-Martin Schenke, Hans-Gebhard Bethge, and Ursula Ulrike Kaiser, 1:381–97. A substantial number of textual restorations have been incorporated here, and many of them come from these editions, particularly from *Nag Hammadi Deutsch*, and also from *Le Dialogue du Sauveur*. More speculative restorations are given in the notes.

2. Literally, "brothers." Here in the Dialogue of the Savior the circle of disciples includes Judas (probably Judas Thomas), Matthew (compare the disciple Matthew, or Matthias the replacement apostle according to Acts 1:23–26, or Mathaias the scribe of the Book of Thomas), and Mary (probably Mary of Magdala).

3. Or, "suffering." Cf. Gospel of Thomas 58.

4. Cf. Gospel of Thomas 50; 90.

5. Here and below the text reads "it," but the translation follows *Nag Hammadi Deutsch* and reads "anger," for the sake of clarity.

6. Or, "solitary." Here and below, cf. Gospel of Thomas 16:4; 49:1; 75.

7. Cf. John 16:23; Letter of Peter to Philip 133–34.

8. *Logos.*

9. Or, "solitary."

10. Cf. Gospel of Thomas 3:1–3; 22:4–7; 89.

11. On the phrase "pass by," cf. Gospel of Thomas 42.

12. Compare the disciple Matthew, or Matthias the replacement apostle according to Acts 1:23–26, or Mathaias the scribe of the Book of Thomas.

13. Probably Judas Thomas. Cf. the Gospel of Thomas and the Book of Thomas.

14. Or, "Lord," here and below.

15. Or, "[your nature]," "[your belief]."

16. Cf. Gospel of Thomas 24.

17. Cf. John 16:5–7.

18. Probably Mary of Magdala.

19. Or restore to read "[the strength]." On the fruits of the spirit, cf. Gal. 5:22–23.

20. It is also possible to restore this sentence without the negative, but compare a few lines below, and Dialogue of the Savior 133.

21. Here Silke Petersen and Hans-Gebhard Bethge, "Der Dialog des Erlösers," 389, restore to read "[If you resemble] one [who never existed]."

22. Cf. Gen. 1:1.

23. Cf. Gen. 1:2.

24. Literally, "from [it]."

25. Here Silke Petersen and Hans-Gebhard Bethge, "Der Dialog des Erlösers," 390, restore to read "[wickedness thus has no existence]."

26. Or, "[Judas] said [to him]."

27. Or, "[movement]," "[mind]."

28. Here and below Silke Petersen and Hans-Gebhard Bethge, "Der Dialog des Erlösers," 390, restore to read "circumcision."

29. Here and below the restoration is tentative. If the saying discusses physical circumcision and spiritual circumcision, then cf. Gospel of Thomas 53; Rom. 2:25–29.

30. Perhaps read "[are circumcised]."

31. Cf. Gospel of Thomas 81:2.

32. Cf. Gospel of Thomas 2.

33. *Logos*, here and below. The text reflects upon the primal water of creation and the place of the word in the creative process, according to Genesis 1. Apparently the water is both below and above, as in much of ancient cosmological thought.

34. Or, "He"—that is, the word—here and below.

35. These are the constellations and stars that rule over what happens on the earth, according to astronomical and astrological theory.

36. The restoration is tentative. This may simply be a continuation of the discussion in the previous section.

37. Probably the sun.

38. That is, the dome of the sky, around the earth, on which the sun, moon, and stars are set. Cf. Gen. 1:6–8.

39. Or, "worshipped."

40. Cf. Gospel of Thomas 3:5.

41. Cf. the Delphic maxim "Know yourself," and Gospel of Thomas 3:4–5.

42. Literally, "it." This refers to the place of life under discussion in the context.

43. Literally, "his goodness" or "its goodness"—the goodness of that person or the goodness of that place.

44. It is also possible to translate this sentence as follows: "The word established the world, and the world came to be through the word, and the world received fragrance from the word." The Coptic text employs ambiguous pronouns throughout the sentence.

45. Literally, "root."

46. On the wind blowing, compare spirit. On the entire passage, cf. Gen. 1:2.

47. *Logos.* On the role of the word or *logos,* and Jesus as the incarnate word, compare John 1, earlier passages in the Dialogue of the Savior, and other gnostic texts. In the Gospel of John, as here, the word descends from the realm above, comes to this world below, and acts in a revelatory manner.

48. Or, "son of man," here and below.

49. These references to seed, power, and deficiency are typical of gnostic texts.

50. On garments clothing the soul, and on putting on perfect humanity as a garment, cf. Gospel of Mary 15; 18. On garments of light and life given to those who enter the bridal chamber, cf. Dialogue of the Savior 138–39.

51. For similarly mystical statements, cf. Gospel of Thomas 77; 108.

52. The region of deficiency is this world below, where the light is obscured in darkness.

53. On the rulers or archons who govern this world, cf. 1 Cor. 6:3. On the bridal chamber, cf. the Gospel of Philip; Gospel of Thomas 75.

54. On the garments of the soul and the garments of light and life, cf. Dialogue of the Savior 136–37; Gospel of Mary 15; 18.

55. Cf. Dialogue of the Savior 145.

56. Cf. Matt. 6:34.

57. Cf. Matt. 10:10 (Q); Luke 10:7 (Q); 1 Tim. 5:18.

58. Cf. Matt. 10:25. If this third saying is emended by adding a negation ("Disciples do <not> resemble their teachers"; cf. Silke Petersen and Hans-Gebhard Bethge, "Der Dialog des Erlösers," 394), then cf. John 13:16. Here in the Dialogue of the Savior it is Mary who utters these three sayings of wisdom.

59. Or, "She spoke this utterance as a woman who understood completely."

60. Cf. Gospel of Thomas 17; 1 Cor. 2:9.

61. Cf. Dialogue of the Savior 144–45; Gospel of the Egyptians.

62. This place is the present world of deficiency and mortality.

63. Going to one's rest at once means dying now, so this question may be about why we do not experience the transformation from death to life now, or even why we do not commit suicide now.

64. Leaving the burden of the body behind and ascending to the fullness of the divine means attaining final rest.

65. Cf. James 5:3.

66. Cf. John 14:5.

67. Here Silke Petersen and Hans-Gebhard Bethge, "Der Dialog des Erlösers," 395, restore to read "you [will sustain] everything."

68. The archons and other powers of the cosmos.

69. On putting on the garment of the body and taking it off, cf. Dialogue of the Savior 136–39; Gospel of Mary 15; Gospel of Thomas 21:2–4; 37:2–3.

70. Possibly restore to read "Judas" (Silke Petersen and Hans-Gebhard Bethge, "Der Dialog des Erlösers," 395).

71. The restoration is tentative; cf. Silke Petersen and Hans-Gebhard Bethge, "Der Dialog des Erlösers," 395.

72. Cf. the parable of the mustard seed in Gospel of Thomas 20; Matt. 13:31–32 (Q); Luke 13:18–19 (Q); Mark 4:30–32.

73. Or, "speaks and acts." Here the father is God the father, and the mother may be Sophia (wisdom) or another female manifestation of the divine.

74. Or, "womanhood," here and below.

75. This statement seems to deny the possibility of being born again.

76. Cf. Dialogue of the Savior 140; Gospel of the Egyptians; Gospel of Thomas 114.

77. Coptic *šaje*; cf. *logos*.

78. Cf. Dialogue of the Savior 135.

79. Cf. Dialogue of the Savior 139.

80. The concluding restorations are tentative.

Part Ten: *The Second Discourse of Great Seth*

1. Editions: *The Facsimile Edition of the Nag Hammadi Codices: Codex VII;* Louis Painchaud, *Le Deuxième Traité du Grand Seth;* Gregory J. Riley, "Second Treatise of the Great Seth," in *Nag Hammadi Codex VII,* ed. Birger A. Pearson, 129–99. Translations: Roger A. Bullard and Joseph A. Gibbons, "The Second Treatise of the Great Seth," in *The Nag Hammadi Library in English,* ed. James M. Robinson, 362–71; Silvia Pellegrini, "Der zweite Logos des großen Seth," in *Nag Hammadi Deutsch,* ed. Hans-Martin Schenke, Hans-Gebhard Bethge, and Ursula Ulrike Kaiser, 2:569–90. Matyas Havrda and Steven Johnson provided valuable assistance in the completion of my translation of this text.

2. Throughout the Second Discourse of Great Seth the speaker uses the first-person singular ("I"), and the speaker identifies himself as Christ. Thus the text presents itself as the discourse of Christ himself.

3. Or, "word, speech, message," here, above, and below, including in the title. It is also possible to translate the title "The Second Treatise of the Great Seth." This reference to a discourse previously uttered, however, suggests a spoken discourse, and this reference may indicate the first discourse or speech or message of great Seth, given prior to the present second discourse of great Seth.

4. This is a reference to Paul's understanding of baptism as dying with Christ (cf. Rom. 6), an interpretation the present text vigorously rejects in favor of an understanding of baptism as union with Christ, who is "imperishable and undefiled thought." See also below, Second Discourse of Great Seth 60.

5. Cf. John 17:21–23. The emendation is proposed by Louis Painchaud, *Le Deuxième Traité du Grand Seth,* 24.

6. In Coptic, from Greek, *ekklēsia,* which may also be translated "church," here and below.

7. Probably the creation or realm of the heavenly father; possibly the creation, here below, of the world ruler.

8. Coptic, from Greek, *ennoia,* here and below.

9. Or, "send someone from him to examine thoughts in the regions below." This is a declaration of the heavenly decision to send someone from the realms above to seek out and save spiritual people ("thoughts") in the world below.

10. Personified wisdom, here and throughout the text.

11. Coptic, from Greek, *pronikos* (for *prounikos*).

12. Coptic, from Greek, *plērōma*.

13. The antecedents of pronouns in this section are vague, and the translation suggests a probable interpretation.

14. Coptic, from Greek, *monas*, "monad." God is called "the One" several times in the Second Discourse of Great Seth. Cf. the divine "One" in the Secret Book of John and other texts.

15. A reference to the incarnation of Christ.

16. The human figure now has a different and alien appearance because of the entry of the heavenly Christ into the earthly body.

17. That is, a Christ.

18. In some texts Adonaios, whose name derives from Adonai (Hebrew for "my lord") and who is also called Sabaoth, is the son of Yaldabaoth who turns against his father and gives his loyalty to Sophia (cf. On the Origin of the World 101–7). Here those of the generation of Adonaios (the people of Adonai) seem to be the Jewish people. Adonaios is also mentioned in the Holy Book of the Great Invisible Spirit III, 58, Secret Book of John II, 10, and Book of Baruch 26.4.

19. Those through whom Sophia offers insights into the future seem to be Hebrew prophets.

20. The heavenly human, here and below, is equated with the father of truth.

21. The text is emended here to read *et<b>e* "<through>," rather than *ete*, "which" (for "which [is]"?). Cf. Silvia Pellegrini, "Der zweite Logos des großen Seth," 582.

22. This is the heavenly circuit of the planets in astronomy and astrology.

23. Cf. Isa. 45:5–6, 21; 46:9. In the Secret Book of John and other texts Yaldabaoth makes the same arrogant claim.

24. Cf. Ps. 8:4.

25. Cf. Sophia of hope, above.

26. Cf. Ps. 22:13. Yaldabaoth is often said to resemble a lion in appearance; cf. Secret Book of John II, 10.

27. Cf. Simon of Cyrene in Mark 15:21. In the present text it is unclear who is crucified, Simon of Cyrene or the body Christ adopted.

28. Cf. Revelation of Peter 81–83; Round Dance of the Cross 96; Irenaeus of Lyon, Against Heresies 1.24.4 (on Basilides); Qur'an sura 4.

29. Christ passes through the heavenly gates, guarded by cosmic powers, on his way from the realms above to the world below.

30. The bridal chamber is referred to in Gospel of Thomas 75 and Dialogue of the Savior 138, and it is discussed extensively in the Gospel of Philip.

31. In Greek the word *psychē*, "soul," is feminine in gender, and the soul is typically personified as the young female Psyche.

32. The souls of those who are liberated pass through the heavenly gates in their ascent to the realms above. Cf. Gospel of Mary 15–17.

33. The three immersions are probably birth, water baptism, and baptism in blood, and the crucifixion is the "third immersion." Cf. Gregory J. Riley, "Second Treatise of the Great Seth," 171.

34. This passage provides a gnostic interpretation of the account of the crucifixion of Jesus in Matthew 27.

35. These people are unbelievers, people who are not Christians. They may recall the material people, people of body and flesh, in Valentinian texts, and this description in general resembles the Valentinian threefold designation of people as *hylics, psychics,* and *pneumatics* (people of fleshly body, soul, and spirit).

36. These people are ordinary believers, who claim to be Christians, in the emerging orthodox church. They may recall the people of soul, or *psychics,* in Valentinian texts.

37. These people are the gnostics of the Second Discourse of Great Seth, who are opposed and persecuted by people in the emerging orthodox church. They may recall the people of spirit, or *pneumatics,* in Valentinian texts.

38. Cf. Matt. 6:24. Here Christ seems to suggest that ordinary believers actually serve both Christ and Yaldabaoth, the ruler of the world.

39. Probably all the powers of Yaldabaoth.

40. This is the proclamation of Christ crucified, the gospel of the cross, in the emerging orthodox church. See above, Second Discourse of Great Seth 49.

41. In Coptic, from Greek, *gnōsis.*

42. The opponents make use of the law, including the Ten Commandments, one of which states, "You shall not covet." On the food laws, cf. Second Discourse of Great Seth 64.

43. The law, or Torah, is sometimes referred to as a yoke, comparable to the yoke placed upon an animal to guide it; hence being under the law is said to resemble being under a yoke.

44. Adam and the rest of the prominent characters in the Jewish scriptures, along with John the baptizer, are said to be laughingstocks, because they are understood to be mere servants of the world ruler.

45. The ruler of the seventh realm, or hebdomad, is Yaldabaoth, the world ruler.

46. Literally, "my brothers," here and below.

47. Or, "son of man," here and below.

48. Christ.

49. Cf. Num. 12:7; Heb. 3:5.

50. Cf. Isa. 41:8; James 2:23.

51. Cf. Isa. 44:6; 45:5–6, 21; 46:9; Exod. 20:5. Similar claims are made by Yaldabaoth in the Secret Book of John and other texts.

52. Cf. Gospel of Thomas 114.

53. The realm of the eight, or ogdoad, is the heavenly region of the fixed stars. In the Second Discourse of Great Seth the heavenly assembly lives there.

54. On the bridal chamber and spiritual marriage, cf. Second Discourse of Great Seth 57.

55. Or, "will."

56. Cf. John 14:6.

57. Cf. the *agapē* meal or love feast or eucharist in Christian tradition.

58. In Coptic, from Greek, *gnōsis.*

59. The murderer may be Yaldabaoth or Cain. Cf. Gospel of Philip 61.
60. Or, "It is I who am the friend of wisdom."
61. Cf. John 1:18.
62. The concluding title is given entirely in Greek in the manuscript. Great Seth is also referred to by that name in the Holy Book of the Great Invisible Spirit.

Part Eleven: The Book of Baruch

1. Editions: Miroslav Marcovich, *Hippolyti refutationis omnium haeresium;* Paul Wendland, *Refutatio omnium haeresium.* Translations: Willis Barnstone, "The Book of Baruch," in *The Gnostic Bible,* ed. Willis Barnstone and Marvin Meyer, 119–33; Robert M. Grant, *Gnosticism,* 94–100; Robert Haardt, ed., *Gnosis,* 108–16; Ernst Haenchen, "The Book *Baruch,*" in *Gnosis,* ed. Werner Foerster, 1:48–58. For purposes of clarity, the present translation of the text follows the arrangement of the sections in Hippolytus suggested in the translation of Robert M. Grant (Hippolytus, Refutation of All Heresies 5.24.1; 27.2–3; 26.1–37; 27.4). The exact portions in Hippolytus that derive from the Book of Baruch are sometimes difficult to identify, and judicious decisions have been made for this translation.
2. In Greek, *gnōnai.*
3. Cf. Gospel of Thomas 17; 1 Cor. 2:9.
4. Ps. 110:4.
5. Cf. Gospel of Thomas 17; 1 Cor. 2:9.
6. Cf. John 4:10, 14.
7. Or, "There was a separation of water from water" (cf. Gen. 1:6–7, on the water above the firmament and the water below the firmament).
8. Cf. Luke 18:19.
9. Cf. Herodotus, History 4.8–10, on Heracles and the viper woman of the Scythians.
10. Or, "Edem," here and throughout the text. The Greek reads *Edem* here and in the Septaugint of Genesis 2–3. In Hebrew "Eden" means "delight," but the term may derive from the Sumerian word for "plain," and "Edem" resembles Hebrew words for "earth, ground" (cf. *'adam* and *'adamah*).
11. In Hebrew "Elohim" means "God." (The Hebrew ending is plural, and occasionally the word retains the plural meaning "gods.")
12. Seven names of paternal angels are missing.
13. Achamoth is often described as the lower figure of wisdom in Valentinian texts. Cf. Gospel of Philip 60.
14. Adonaios is described in the Second Discourse of Great Seth (52–55) and elsewhere as the son of Yaldabaoth who remains loyal to Sophia. His name derives from Adonai, Hebrew for "my lord."
15. Gen. 2:8.
16. In Hebrew "Baruch" means "blessed."
17. In Greek, *gnōsin,* a form of *gnōsis.*
18. In Hebrew "Naas" (*nahaš*) means "serpent" or "snake." Cf. the gnostics who

are termed Naassenes or Ophites (from the Greek *ophis*, which also means "serpent" or "snake").

19. Cf. Gen. 2:7.

20. Gen. 1:28.

21. Cf. Gen. 2:24.

22. Cf. Gen. 2:10–14.

23. Ps. 118:19.

24. Ps. 118:20.

25. Cf. Gospel of Thomas 17; 1 Cor. 2:9.

26. Ps. 110:1.

27. Cf. Gen. 6:7.

28. Cf. Gen. 2:9.

29. The Greek infinitive *ginōskein* is used here.

30. Cf. Gen. 2:16–17.

31. Here Naas is both the source of temptation and the tree of the knowledge of good and evil.

32. In Greek mythology Omphale is the queen of Lydia to whom Heracles was enslaved and by whom he was compelled to do women's work for a period of time.

33. Cf. Luke 1:5.

34. Cf. Luke 2:42.

35. Or, "son of man."

36. Cf. Second Discourse of Great Seth 55–56; Revelation of Peter 81–83.

37. John 19:26.

38. Cf. Luke 23:46.

39. Cf. Luke 24:51; Acts 1:9.

40. In Greek mythology Priapos is the fertility god known for his huge phallus.

41. Literally, "carrying fruit above him."

42. In Greek mythology Leda is the woman with whom Zeus, in the form of a swan, has sexual intercourse. Leda becomes pregnant, and eventually she gives birth to Pollux and Helen, who is to become Helen of Troy.

43. In Greek mythology Ganymede is the handsome Trojan prince who is kidnapped by Zeus's eagle and taken up to Olympus to become a cupbearer to the gods and goddesses.

44. In Greek mythology Danae is the beautiful princess of Argos who is imprisoned by her father but becomes pregnant when she is embraced by Zeus in a shower of gold. From this union Danae gives birth to Perseus, slayer of the gorgon Medusa and grandfather of Heracles.

45. Isa. 1:2.

46. Isa. 1:3.

47. Eden (Israel).

48. Elohim.

49. Or, "because of the father's ignorance (*dia tēn patrikēn agnoian enteuthen*)," or "that was imprisoned (*endethen*) because of the father's ignorance."

50. Cf. Hos. 1:2.

Part Twelve: The Round Dance of the Cross

1. Editions: André-Jean Festugière, *Les Actes apocryphes de Jean et de Thomas*, 199–207; Eric Junod and Jean-Daniel Kaestli, *Acta Johannis*. Translations: Barbara E. Bowe, "Dancing into the Divine"; Marvin Meyer, "The Round Dance of the Cross," in *The Gnostic Bible*, ed. Willis Barnstone and Marvin Meyer, 351–55; Knut Schäferdiek, "The Acts of John," in *New Testament Apocrypha*, ed. Wilhelm Schneemelcher, 2:181–84.

2. In the Acts of John it is said that Jesus taught the Round Dance of the Cross to his disciples prior to his crucifixion. Just before this opening, the circumstances of the Round Dance of the Cross are explained in strongly polemical terms, and reference is made to the "lawless Jews" who were inspired by the serpent.

3. *Logos*, here and below.

4. Cf. 1 John 1:5.

5. Here and throughout this section the English translation employs the emphatic future "I will" for the Greek *thelō*, literally, "It is my will to . . . ."

6. "Grace dances" is an instruction in the text for liturgical dance.

7. This may refer to the realm of eight (ogdoad) in Valentinian thought—that is, the seven planetary spheres plus the eighth sphere (of the stars). Sometimes the eighth sphere is considered the abode of the ruler of the cosmos; sometimes it is thought to be a higher level for spiritual advancement. Compare the Secret Book of John and the Discourse on the Eighth and Ninth.

8. Compare the twelve signs of the zodiac.

9. Cf. John 10:9.

10. Cf. John 14:6.

11. Cf. Gospel of Thomas 42.

12. In Greek, *ton logon gnōthi tēs sophias*.

13. Or, "put to shame."

14. Perhaps compare Second Discourse of Great Seth 55–56; Revelation of Peter 81–83.

Bibliography

Aland, Kurt, ed. *Synopsis Quattuor Evangeliorum: Locis parallelis evangeliorum apocryphorum et partum adhibitis.* 15th ed. Stuttgart: Deutsche Bibelgesellschaft, 1996. Corrected printing, with an appendix by the Berliner Arbeitskreis für koptisch-gnostische Schriften: "Das Thomas-Evangelium / The Gospel According to Thomas," 517–46.

Alberry, C. R. C., ed. *Manichaean Manuscripts in the Chester Beatty Collection.* Vol. 2, part 2, *A Manichaean Psalm-Book.* Stuttgart: W. Kohlhammer, 1938.

Asgeirsson, Jon Ma., Kristin De Troyer, and Marvin W. Meyer, eds. *From Quest to Q: Festschrift James M. Robinson.* Leuven, Belgium: Leuven Univ. Press and Peeters, 2000.

Attridge, Harold W. "The Greek Fragments." In *Nag Hammadi Codex II,2–7*, edited by Bentley Layton, 1:95–128.

———, ed. *Nag Hammadi Codex I (The Jung Codex).* 2 vols. Nag Hammadi Studies 22–23. Leiden: E. J. Brill, 1985.

Attridge, Harold W., and George W. MacRae. "The Gospel of Truth." In *Nag Hammadi Codex I,* edited by Harold W. Attridge, 1:55–122.

———. "The Gospel of Truth." In *The Nag Hammadi Library in English,* edited by James M. Robinson, 38–51.

Barnstone, Willis. "The Book of Baruch." In *The Gnostic Bible,* edited by Willis Barnstone and Marvin Meyer, 119–33.

Barnstone, Willis, and Marvin Meyer, eds. *The Gnostic Bible.* Boston: Shambhala, 2003.

Bauer, Walter. *Orthodoxy and Heresy in Earliest Christianity.* 2nd ed. Philadelphia: Fortress Press, 1971.

Bethge, Hans-Gebhard. " 'Zweite Logos des großen Seth': Die zweite Schrift aus Nag-Hammadi-Codex VII eingeleitet und übersetzt vom Berliner Arbeitskreis für koptisch-gnostische Scriften." *Theologische Literaturzeitung* 100 (1975): 97–110.

Bianchi, Ugo, ed. *Le Origini dello Gnosticismo: Colloquia di Messina, 13–18 Aprile 1966.* Studies in the History of Religions (Supplements to *Numen*) 12. Leiden: E. J. Brill, 1970.

Blatz, Beate. "The Coptic Gospel of Thomas." In *New Testament Apocrypha,* edited by Wilhelm Schneemelcher, 1:110–33.

Blatz, Beate, and Einar Thomassen. "The Dialogue of the Saviour." In *New Testament Apocrypha,* edited by Wilhelm Schneemelcher, 1:300–312.

Böhlig, Alexander, and Frederik Wisse. "The Gospel of the Egyptians." In *The Nag Hammadi Library in English*, edited by James M. Robinson, 208–9.

————, eds. *Nag Hammadi Codices III,2 and IV,2: The Gospel of the Egyptians*. Nag Hammadi Studies 4. Leiden: E. J. Brill, 1975.

Bowe, Barbara E. "Dancing into the Divine: The Hymn of the Dance in the *Acts of John*." *Journal of Early Christian Studies* 7 (1999): 83–104.

Bullard, Roger A., and Joseph A. Gibbons. "The Second Treatise of the Great Seth." In *The Nag Hammadi Library in English*, edited by James M. Robinson, 362–71.

Cameron, Ron. *Sayings Traditions in the Apocryphon of James*. Harvard Theological Studies 34. Philadelphia: Fortress Press, 1984.

Charron, Régine. *Concordance des textes de Nag Hammadi: Le Codex III*. Bibliothèque copte de Nag Hammadi, Section "Concordances" 3. Québec, Louvain, and Paris: Les Presses de l'Université Laval, 1995.

Crossan, John Dominic. *The Cross That Spoke: The Origins of the Passion Narrative*. San Francisco: Harper & Row, 1988.

————. *Four Other Gospels: Shadows on the Contours on Canon*. Minneapolis: Winston (Seabury), 1985.

Culianu, Ioan. "The Gnostic Revenge: Gnosticism and Romantic Literature." In *Religionstheorie und politische Theologie, Band 2: Gnosis und Politik*, edited by Jacob Taubes, 290–306. Munich, Paderborn, Vienna, and Zurich: Wilhelm Fink/Ferdinand Schöningh, 1984.

————. *The Tree of Gnosis: Gnostic Mythology from Early Christianity to Modern Nihilism*. Translated by H. S. Wiesner. San Francisco: HarperCollins, 1992.

Davies, Stevan. *The Gospel of Thomas and Christian Wisdom*. New York: Seabury, 1983.

de Boer, Esther A. *The Gospel of Mary: Beyond a Gnostic and a Biblical Mary Magdalene*. New York and London: T. & T. Clark International, 2004.

————. *Mary Magdalene: Beyond the Myth*. Translated by John Bowden. Harrisburg, PA: Trinity Press International, 1997.

————. "Mary Magdalene and the Disciple Jesus Loved." *Lectio Difficilior* 1 (2000): electronic journal (http://www.lectio.unibe.ch).

DeConick, April D. "The Great Mystery of Marriage: Sex and Conception in Ancient Valentinian Traditions." *Vigiliae Christianae* 57 (2003): 307–42.

Dewey, Arthur J. "The Hymn in the Acts of John." *Semeia* 38 (1986): 67–80.

Doresse, Jean. *The Secret Books of the Egyptian Gnostics: An Introduction to the Gnostic Coptic Manuscripts Discovered at Chenoboskion*. Translated by Philip Mairet. London: Hollis & Carter, 1960.

Emmel, Stephen, ed. *Nag Hammadi Codex III,5: The Dialogue of the Savior*. Nag Hammadi Studies 26. Leiden: E. J. Brill, 1984.

Emmel, Stephen. "The Recently Published *Gospel of the Savior* ('Unbekanntes Berliner Evangelium'): Righting the Order of Pages and Events." *Harvard Theological Review* 95 (2002): 45–72.

————. "Unbekanntes Berliner Evangelium = the Strasbourg Coptic Gospel: Prolegomena to a New Edition of the Strasbourg Fragments." In *For the Children, Perfect Instruction: Studies in Honor of Hans-Martin Schenke on the Occasion of the Berliner Arbeitskreis für koptisch-gnostische Schriften's Thirtieth Year*, edited by Hans-Gebhard

Bethge, Stephen Emmel, Karen L. King, and Imke Schletterer, 353–74. Nag Hammadi and Manichaean Studies 54. Leiden: E. J. Brill, 2002.

The Facsimile Edition of the Nag Hammadi Codices. Published under the auspices of the Department of Antiquities of the Arab Republic of Egypt in conjunction with the United Nations Educational, Scientific, and Cultural Organization. 12 vols. Leiden: E. J. Brill, 1972–84.

Fallon, Francis T. *The Enthronement of Sabaoth: Jewish Elements in Gnostic Creation Myths.* Nag Hammadi Studies 10. Leiden: E. J. Brill, 1978.

Festugière, André-Jean, ed. *Les Actes apocryphes de Jean et de Thomas.* Cahiers d'orientalisme 6. Geneva: Cramer, 1983.

Foerster, Werner, ed. *Gnosis: A Selection of Texts.* Translated by R. McL. Wilson. 2 vols. Oxford: Clarendon Press, 1974.

Gager, John G., ed. *Curse Tablets and Binding Spells from the Ancient World.* New York and Oxford: Oxford Univ. Press, 1992.

Grant, Robert M. *Gnosticism and Early Christianity.* 2nd ed. New York: Columbia Univ. Press, 1966.

———, ed. *Gnosticism: An Anthology.* New York: Harper, 1961.

Grobel, Kendrick. *The Gospel of Truth: A Valentinian Meditation on the Gospel, Translation from the Coptic and Commentary.* Nashville and New York: Abingdon, 1960.

Haardt, Robert, ed. *Gnosis: Character and Testimony.* Leiden: E. J. Brill, 1971.

Haenchen, Ernst. "The Book Baruch." In *Gnosis,* edited by Werner Foerster, 1:48–58.

———. "Das Buch Baruch: Ein Beitrag zum Problem der christlichen Gnosis." *Zeitschrift für Theologie und Kirche* 50 (1953): 123–58.

Halm, Heinz. *Die islamische Gnosis: Die extreme Schia und die 'Alawiten.* Die Bibliothek des Morgenlandes. Zurich: Artemis Verlag, 1982.

Hartenstein, Judith. "Das Evangelium nach Maria." In *Nag Hammadi Deutsch,* edited by Hans-Martin Schenke, Hans-Gebhard Bethge, and Ursula Ulrike Kaiser, 2:833–44.

Hartenstein, Judith, and Uwe-Karsten Plisch. "Der Brief des Jakobus." In *Nag Hammadi Deutsch,* edited by Hans-Martin Schenke, Hans-Gebhard Bethge, and Ursula Ulrike Kaiser, 1:11–26.

Hedrick, Charles W. "Caveats to a 'Righted Order' of the *Gospel of the Savior.*" *Harvard Theological Review* 96 (2003): 229–38.

Hedrick, Charles W., and Robert Hodgson, Jr., eds. *Nag Hammadi, Gnosticism, and Early Christianity.* Peabody, MA: Hendrickson, 1986.

Hedrick, Charles W., and Paul A. Mirecki. *Gospel of the Savior: A New Ancient Gospel.* California Classical Library. Santa Rosa, CA: Polebridge Press, 1999.

Hills, Julian V. "The Dialogue of the Savior." In *The Complete Gospels: Annotated Scholars Version,* edited by Robert J. Miller, 336–50.

Isenberg, Wesley W. "The Gospel According to Philip." In *The Nag Hammadi Library in English,* edited by James M. Robinson, 139–60.

Isenberg, Wesley W., and Bentley Layton. "The Gospel According to Philip." In *Nag Hammadi Codex II,2–7,* edited by Bentley Layton, 1:129–217.

Jeremias, Joachim. *Unknown Sayings of Jesus.* 2nd ed. Translated by Reginald H. Fuller. London: SPCK, 1964.

Jonas, Hans. *The Gnostic Religion: The Message of the Alien God and the Beginnings of Christianity.* 2nd ed. Boston: Beacon, 1963.

———. *Gnosis und spätantiker Geist. I. Die mythologische Gnosis.* 3rd ed. Forschungen zur Religion und Literatur des Alten und Neuen Testaments 51. Göttingen: Vandenhoeck & Ruprecht, 1964.

Jones, F. Stanley, ed. *Which Mary? The Marys of Early Christian Tradition.* Symposium 19. Atlanta: Society of Biblical Literature, 2002.

Junod, Eric, and Jean-Daniel Kaestli. *Acta Johannis.* Corpus Christianorum, series apocryphorum 1, 2. Turnhout, Belgium: Brepols, 1983.

Kähler, Martin. *Der sogenannte historische Jesus und der geschichtliche, biblische Christus.* Leipzig: Deichert, 1956.

King, Karen L. "The Apocryphon of John: Part II of the Gospel of John?" Paper presented at the annual meeting of the Society of Biblical Literature, Denver, CO, Nov. 2001.

———. "The Gospel of Mary." In *The Complete Gospels: Annotated Scholars Version,* edited by Robert J. Miller, 351–60.

———. *The Gospel of Mary of Magdala: Jesus and the First Woman Apostle.* Santa Rosa, CA: Polebridge Press, 2003.

———, ed. *Images of the Feminine in Gnosticism.* Studies in Antiquity and Christianity. Philadelphia: Fortress Press, 1988.

———. *Revelation of the Unknowable God: With Text, Translation, and Notes to NHC XI,3 Allogenes.* Santa Rosa, CA: Polebridge Press, 1995.

———. "Sophia and Christ in the Apocryphon of John." In *Images of the Feminine in Gnosticism,* edited by Karen L. King, 158–76.

———. *What Is Gnosticism?* Cambridge, MA: Belknap Press and Harvard Univ. Press, 2003.

———. "Why All the Controversy? Mary in the *Gospel of Mary.*" In *Which Mary?* edited by F. Stanley Jones, 53–74.

King, Karen L., George W. MacRae, R. McL. Wilson, and Douglas M. Parrott. "The Gospel of Mary." In *The Nag Hammadi Library in English,* edited by James M. Robinson, 523–27.

Kirchner, Dankwart. *Epistula Jacobi Apocrypha: Die zweite Schrift aus Nag-Hammadi-Codex I.* Texte und Untersuchungen 136. Berlin: Akademie Verlag, 1989.

Kirchner, Dankwart, and Einar Thomassen. "The Apocryphon of James." In *New Testament Apocrypha,* edited by Wilhelm Schneemelcher, 1:285–99.

Klijn, A. F. J. *Seth in Jewish, Christian, and Gnostic Literature.* Leiden: E. J. Brill, 1977.

Kloppenborg, John S. *Excavating Q: The History and Setting of the Sayings Gospel.* Minneapolis: Fortress Press, 2000.

———. *The Formation of Q: Trajectories in Ancient Wisdom Collections.* Philadelphia: Fortress Press, 1987.

———. *Q Parallels: Synopsis, Critical Notes, and Concordance.* Sonoma, CA: Polebridge Press, 1988.

Kloppenborg, John S., Marvin W. Meyer, Stephen J. Patterson, and Michael G. Steinhauser. *Q-Thomas Reader.* Sonoma, CA: Polebridge Press, 1990.

Koester, Helmut. *Ancient Christian Gospels: Their History and Development.* Philadelphia: Trinity; London: SCM, 1990.

Koester, Helmut, and Thomas O. Lambdin. "The Gospel of Thomas." In *The Nag Hammadi Library in English*, edited by James M. Robinson, 126–38.

Koester, Helmut, Bentley Layton, Thomas O. Lambdin, and Harold W. Attridge. "The Gospel According to Thomas." In *Nag Hammadi Codex II,2–7*, edited by Bentley Layton, 1:37–128.

Koester, Helmut, and Elaine H. Pagels. "Introduction." In *Nag Hammadi Codex III,5: The Dialogue of the Savior*, edited by Stephen Emmel, 1–17.

Koester, Helmut, Elaine H. Pagels, and Stephen Emmel. "The Dialogue of the Savior." In *The Nag Hammadi Library in English*, edited by James M. Robinson, 244–55.

Kuntzmann, Raymond. *Le Livre de Thomas (NH II,7): Texte établi et présenté*. Bibliothèque copte de Nag Hammadi, Section "Textes" 16. Québec: Les Presses de l'Université Laval, 1986.

Layton, Bentley. *The Gnostic Scriptures: A New Translation with Annotations and Introductions*. Garden City, NY: Doubleday, 1987.

———, ed. *Nag Hammadi Codex II,2–7, Together with XIII,2*, Brit. Lib. Or. 4926(1), and P. Oxy. 1, 654, 655*. 2 vols. Nag Hammadi Studies 20–21. Leiden: E. J. Brill, 1989.

———. "Prolegomena to the Study of Ancient Gnosticism." In *The Social World of the First Christians: Essays in Honor of Wayne A. Meeks*, edited by L. Michael White and O. Larry Yarbrough, 334–50.

———, ed. *The Rediscovery of Gnosticism: Proceedings of the International Conference on Gnosticism at Yale, New Haven, Connecticut, March 28–31, 1978*. Studies in the History of Religions (Supplements to *Numen*) 41. Leiden: E. J. Brill, 1980–81.

Létourneau, Pierre. *Le Dialogue du Sauveur (NH III, 5): Texte établi, traduit, et présenté*. Bibliothèque copte de Nag Hammadi, Section "Textes" 29. Québec: Les Presses de l'Université Laval, 2003.

Lüdemann, Gerd, and Martina Janssen. *Bibel der Haretiker: Die gnostischen Schriften aus Nag Hammadi*. Stuttgart: Radius, 1997.

Mack, Burton L. *Logos und Sophia: Untersuchungen zur Weisheitstheologie im hellenistischen Judentum*. Göttingen: Vandenhoeck & Ruprecht, 1973.

———. *The Lost Gospel: The Book of Q and Christian Origins*. San Francisco: HarperSanFrancisco, 1993.

MacRae, George W., and R. McL. Wilson. "The Gospel of Mary." In *Nag Hammadi Codices V,2–5 and VI*, edited by Douglas M. Parrott, 453–71.

Marcovich, Miroslav, ed. *Hippolyti refutationis omnium haeresium librorum decem quae supersunt*. New York and Berlin: Walter de Gruyter, 1986.

Markschies, Christoph. *Valentinus Gnosticus? Untersuchungen zur valentinianischen Gnosis mit einem Kommentar zu den Fragmenten Valentins*. Tübingen: J. C. B. Mohr (Paul Siebeck), 1992.

Ménard, Jacques-É. *L'Évangile de Vérité: Rétroversion grecque et commentaire*. Paris: Letouzey et Ané, 1962.

———. *L'Évangile selon Philippe: Introduction, texte, traduction, commentaire*. Strasbourg and Paris: Letouzey & Ané, 1967.

———. *L'Évangile selon Thomas*. Nag Hammadi Studies 5. Leiden: E. J. Brill, 1975.

Meyer, Marvin. "The Book of Thomas." In *The Gnostic Bible*, edited by Willis Barnstone and Marvin Meyer, 396–403.

———. *The Gospel of Thomas: The Hidden Sayings of Jesus.* San Francisco: HarperSan-Francisco, 1992.

———. "*Gospel of Thomas* Logion 114 Revisited." In *For the Children, Perfect Instruction: Studies in Honor of Hans-Martin Schenke on the Occasion of the Berliner Arbeitskreis für koptisch-gnostische Schriften's Thirtieth Year,* edited by Hans-Gebhard Bethge, Stephen Emmel, Karen L. King, and Imke Schletterer, 101–11. Nag Hammadi and Manichaean Studies 54. Leiden: E. J. Brill, 2002. Also in *Secret Gospels,* edited by Marvin Meyer, 96–106.

———. *The Gospels of Mary: The Secret Tradition of Mary Magdalene, the Companion of Jesus.* San Francisco: HarperSanFrancisco, 2004.

———. "Making Mary Male: The Categories 'Male' and 'Female' in the *Gospel of Thomas.*" *New Testament Studies* 31 (1985): 544–70. Also in *Secret Gospels,* edited by Marvin Meyer, 76–95.

———. Review of Karen L. King, *What Is Gnosticism? Review of Biblical Literature* (2004): electronic journal (http://www.bookreviews.org).

———. "The Round Dance of the Cross." In *The Gnostic Bible,* edited by Willis Barnstone and Marvin Meyer, 351–55.

———. "The Secret Books of James." In *The Gnostic Bible,* edited by Willis Barnstone and Marvin Meyer, 341–50.

———. "The Secret Book of John." In *The Gnostic Bible,* edited by Willis Barnstone and Marvin Meyer, 135–65.

———. *Secret Gospels: Essays on Thomas and the Secret Gospel of Mark.* Harrisburg, New York, and London: Trinity Press International/Continuum, 2003.

Meyer, Marvin, and Charles Hughes, eds. *Jesus Then and Now: Images of Jesus in History and Christology.* Harrisburg, New York, and London: Trinity Press International/Continuum, 2001.

Miller, Robert J., ed., *The Complete Gospels: Annotated Scholars Version.* Santa Rosa, CA: Polebridge Press, 1994.

Orbe, Antonio. *Estudios Valentinianos.* Analecta Gregoriana 99. Rome: Pontificia Università Gregoriana, 1958.

Pagels, Elaine H. *Beyond Belief: The Secret Gospel of Thomas.* New York: Random House, 2003.

———. *The Gnostic Gospels.* New York: Random House, 1979.

———. *The Gnostic Paul: Gnostic Exegesis of the Pauline Letters.* Philadelphia: Fortress Press, 1975.

———. *The Johannine Gospel in Gnostic Exegesis: Heracleon's Commentary on John.* Society of Biblical Literature Monograph Series 17. Nashville: Abingdon, 1973.

Painchaud, Louis. *Le Deuxième Traité du Grand Seth (NH VII,2): Texte établi et présenté.* Bibliothèque copte de Nag Hammadi, Section "Textes" 6. Québec: Les Presses de l'Université Laval, 1982.

Parrinder, Geoffrey. *Jesus in the Qur'an.* New York: Oxford Univ. Press, 1965.

Parrott, Douglas M., ed. *Nag Hammadi Codices V,2–5 and VI with Papyrus Berolinensis 8502,1 and 4.* Nag Hammadi Studies 11. Leiden: E. J. Brill, 1979.

Pasquier, Anne. *L'Évangile selon Marie (BG 1).* Bibliothèque copte de Nag Hammadi, Section "Textes" 10. Québec: Les Presses de l'Université Laval, 1983.

Patterson, Stephen J. *The Gospel of Thomas and Jesus*. Foundations and Facets. Santa Rosa, CA: Polebridge Press, 1993.

Patterson, Stephen J., James M. Robinson, and Hans-Gebhard Bethge. *The Fifth Gospel: The Gospel of Thomas Comes of Age*. Harrisburg: Trinity Press International, 1998.

Pearson, Birger A. *Gnosticism and Christianity in Roman and Coptic Egypt*. Studies in Antiquity and Christianity. New York and London: T. & T. Clark International, 2004.

———. *Gnosticism, Judaism, and Egyptian Christianity*. Studies in Antiquity and Christianity. Minneapolis: Fortress Press, 1990.

———, ed. *Nag Hammadi Codex VII*. Nag Hammadi and Manichaean Studies 30. Leiden: E. J. Brill, 1996.

Pellegrini, Silvia. "Der zweite Logos des großen Seth." In *Nag Hammadi Deutsch*, edited by Hans-Martin Schenke, Hans-Gebhard Bethge, and Ursula Ulrike Kaiser, 2:569–90.

Perkins, Pheme. *Gnosticism and the New Testament*. Minneapolis: Fortress Press, 1993.

Petersen, Silke, and Hans-Gebhard Bethge. "Der Dialog des Erlösers." In *Nag Hammadi Deutsch*, edited by Hans-Martin Schenke, Hans-Gebhard Bethge, and Ursula Ulrike Kaiser, 1:381–97.

Plisch, Uwe-Karsten. "Das heilige Buch des großen unsichtbaren Geistes." In *Nag Hammadi Deutsch*, edited by Hans-Martin Schenke, Hans-Gebhard Bethge, and Ursula Ulrike Kaiser, 1:293–321.

Riley, Gregory J. *Resurrection Reconsidered: Thomas and John in Controversy*. Minneapolis: Fortress Press, 1995.

———. "Second Treatise of the Great Seth." In *Nag Hammadi Codex VII*, edited by Birger A. Pearson, 129–99.

Robinson, James M. "From the Cliff to Cairo: The Story of the Discoverers and Middlemen of the Nag Hammadi Codices." In *Colloque international sur les textes de Nag Hammadi (Québec, 22–25 août 1978)*, edited by Bernard Barc, 21–58. Bibliothèque copte de Nag Hammadi, Section "Études" 1. Québec: Les Presses de l'Université Laval, 1981.

———. "Nag Hammadi: The First Fifty Years." In Stephen J. Patterson, James M. Robinson, and Hans-Gebhard Bethge, *The Fifth Gospel*, 77–110.

———, ed. *The Nag Hammadi Library in English*. 3rd ed. San Francisco: HarperSanFrancisco, 1988.

———. "Sethians and Johannine Thought: The Trimorphic Protennoia and the Prologue of the Gospel of John." In *The Rediscovery of Gnosticism*, edited by Bentley Layton, 643–62.

———. "A Written Greek Sayings Cluster Older Than Q: A Vestige." *Harvard Theological Review* 92 (1999): 61–77.

Robinson, James M., Paul Hoffman, and John S. Kloppenborg, eds. *The Critical Edition of Q: Synopsis Including the Gospels of Matthew and Luke, Mark, and Thomas with English, German, and French Translations of Q and Thomas*. Leuven, Belgium: Peeters, 2000.

Robinson, James M., and Helmut Koester. *Trajectories through Early Christianity*. Philadelphia: Fortress Press, 1971.

Rouleau, Donald. *L'Épître apocryphe de Jacques (NH I,2)*, with L. Roy, *L'Acte de Pierre (BG 4)*. Bibliothèque copte de Nag Hammadi, Section "Textes" 18. Québec: Les Presses de l'Université Laval, 1987.

Rudolph, Kurt. *Gnosis: The Nature and History of Gnosticism*. English translation edited by R. McL. Wilson. San Francisco: HarperSanFrancisco, 1987.

Sagnard, François. *La gnose valentinienne et le témoignage de Saint Irénée*. Paris: Vrin, 1947.

Schäferdiek, Knut. "The Acts of John." In *New Testament Apocrypha*, edited by Wilhelm Schneemelcher, 2:152–212.

Schenke, Hans-Martin. "Das Buch des Thomas." In *Nag Hammadi Deutsch*, edited by Hans-Martin Schenke, Hans-Gebhard Bethge, and Ursula Ulrike Kaiser, 1:279–91.

———. "Das Evangelium nach Philippus." In *Nag Hammadi Deutsch*, edited by Hans-Martin Schenke, Hans-Gebhard Bethge, and Ursula Ulrike Kaiser, 1:183–312.

———. "Evangelium Veritatis." In *Nag Hammadi Deutsch*, edited by Hans-Martin Schenke, Hans-Gebhard Bethge, and Ursula Ulrike Kaiser, 1:27–44.

———. "The Gospel of Philip." In *New Testament Apocrypha*, edited by Wilhelm Schneemelcher, 1:179–208.

———. *Die Herkunft des sogennanten Evangelium Veritatis*. Berlin: Evangelischer Verlag, 1958.

———. "The Problem of Gnosis." *Second Century* 3 (1983): 78–87.

———. "Das sethianische System nach Nag-Hammadi-Handschriften." In *Studia Coptica*, edited by Peter Nagel, 165–72. Berlin: Akademie Verlag, 1974.

———. *Das Thomas-Buch (Nag-Hammadi-Codex II,7)*. Texte und Untersuchungen 138. Berlin: Akademie Verlag, 1989.

Schenke, Hans-Martin, Hans-Gebhard Bethge, and Ursula Ulrike Kaiser, eds. *Nag Hammadi Deutsch*. 2 vols. Die griechischen christlichen Schriftsteller der ersten Jahrhunderte, Neue Folge, 8, 12. Berlin and New York: Walter de Gruyter, 2001, 2003.

Schenke, Hans-Martin, and Einar Thomassen. "The Book of Thomas." In *New Testament Apocrypha*, edited by Wilhelm Schneemelcher, 1:232–47.

Schmithals, Walter. *Gnosticism in Corinth: An Investigation of the Letters to the Corinthians*. Translated by John E. Steely. Nashville: Abingdon Press, 1971.

Schneemelcher, Wilhelm, ed. *New Testament Apocrypha*. English translation edited by R. McL. Wilson. 2 vols. Cambridge: James Clarke; Louisville: Westminster/John Knox, 1991–92.

Scholem, Gershom. *Jewish Gnosticism, Merkabah Mysticism, and Talmudic Tradition*. New York: Jewish Theological Seminary of America, 1960.

Scholer, David M. *Nag Hammadi Bibliography 1948–1969*. Nag Hammadi Studies 1. Leiden: E. J. Brill, 1971.

———. *Nag Hammadi Bibliography 1970–1994*. Nag Hammadi Studies 32. Leiden: E. J. Brill, 1997.

Schröter, Jens, and Hans-Gebhard Bethge. "Das Evangelium nach Thomas." In *Nag Hammadi Deutsch*, edited by Hans-Martin Schenke, Hans-Gebhard Bethge, and Ursula Ulrike Kaiser, 1:151–81.

Segal, Alan F. *Two Powers in Heaven: Early Rabbinic Reports about Christianity and Gnosticism.* Studies in Judaism and Late Antiquity 25. Leiden: E. J. Brill, 1977.

Sevrin, Jean-Marie. *Le dossier baptismal séthien: Études sur la sacramentaire gnostique.* Bibliothèque copte de Nag Hammadi, Section "Études" 2. Québec: Les Presses de l'Université Laval, 1986.

Sieber, John H. "The Barbelo Aeon as Sophia in Zostrianos and Related Tractates." In *The Rediscovery of Gnosticism,* edited by Bentley Layton, 788–95.

Smith, Jonathan Z. *Drudgery Divine: On the Comparison of Early Christianities and the Religions of Late Antiquity.* Chicago: Univ. of Chicago Press, 1990.

Stead, G. C. "The Valentinian Myth of Sophia." *Journal of Theological Studies* 20 (1969): 75–104.

Stroumsa, Gedaliahu A. G. *Another Seed: Studies in Gnostic Mythology.* Leiden: E. J. Brill, 1984.

Tardieu, Michel. *Écrits gnostiques: Codex de Berlin.* Sources gnostiques et manichéennes 1. Paris: Cerf, 1984.

———. *Trois mythes gnostiques: Adam, Éros et les animaux d'Égypte dans un écrit de Nag Hammadi (II,5).* Paris: Études augustinennes, 1974.

Till, Walter C. *Das Evangelium nach Philippos.* Patristische Texte und Studien 2. Berlin: Walter de Gruyter, 1963.

Till, Walter C, and Hans-Martin Schenke. *Die gnostischen Schriften des koptischen Papyrus Berolinensis 8502.* 2nd ed. Texte und Untersuchungen 60. Berlin: Akademie Verlag, 1972.

Torjesen, Karen Jo. *When Women Were Priests: Women's Leadership in the Early Church and the Scandal of Their Subordination in the Rise of Christianity.* San Francisco: HarperSanFrancisco, 1993.

Turner, John D. "The Book of Thomas the Contender." In *The Nag Hammadi Library in English,* edited by James M. Robinson, 199–207.

———. *The Book of Thomas the Contender from Codex II of the Cairo Gnostic Library from Nag Hammadi (CG II,7): The Coptic Text with Translation, Introduction and Commentary.* Society of Biblical Literature Dissertation Series 23. Missoula, MT: Scholars Press, 1975.

———. "Sethian Gnosticism: A Literary History." In *Nag Hammadi, Gnosticism and Early Christianity,* edited by Charles W. Hedrick and Robert Hodgson Jr., 55–86.

———. *Sethian Gnosticism and the Platonic Tradition.* Bibliothèque de Nag Hammadi, Section "Études" 6. Québec: Les Presses de l'Université Laval; Leuven, Belgium: Peeters, 2001.

Turner, John D., and Bentley Layton. "The Book of Thomas the Contender Writing to the Perfect." In *Nag Hammadi Codex II,2–7,* edited by Bentley Layton, 2:171–205.

Uro, Risto, ed. *Thomas at the Crossroads: Essays on the Gospel of Thomas.* Edinburgh: T. & T. Clark, 1998.

Valantasis, Richard. *The Gospel of Thomas.* New Testament Readings. London and New York: Routledge, 1997.

von Harnack, Adolf. *Marcion: The Gospel of the Alien God.* Translated by John E. Steely and Lyle D. Bierma. Durham, NC: Labyrinth Press, 1990.

Waldstein, Michael. "Das Apokryphon des Johannes." In *Nag Hammadi Deutsch*, edited by Hans-Martin Schenke, Hans-Gebhard Bethge, and Ursula Ulrike Kaiser, 1:95–150.

Waldstein, Michael, and Frederik Wisse, eds. *The Apocryphon of John: Synopsis of Nag Hammadi Codices II,1; III,1; and IV,1 with BG 8502,2.* Nag Hammadi and Manichaean Studies 33. Leiden: E. J. Brill, 1985.

Wendland, Paul, ed. *Refutatio omnium haeresium.* Die griechischen christlichen Schriftsteller der ersten Jahrhunderte 26. Hildesheim and New York: Olms, 1977.

White, L. Michael, and O. Larry Yarbrough, eds. *The Social World of the First Christians: Essays in Honor of Wayne A. Meeks.* Minneapolis: Fortress Press, 1995.

Williams, Francis E. "The Apocryphon of James." In *Nag Hammadi Codex I*, edited by Harold W. Attridge, 1:13–53, 2:7–37.

———. "The Apocryphon of James." In *The Nag Hammadi Library in English*, edited by James M. Robinson, 29–37.

Williams, Michael A. *The Immovable Race: A Gnostic Designation and the Theme of Stability in Late Antiquity.* Nag Hammadi Studies 29. Leiden: E. J. Brill, 1985.

———. *Rethinking "Gnosticism": An Argument for Dismantling a Dubious Category.* Princeton, NJ: Princeton Univ. Press, 1996.

Wilson, R. McL. *The Gospel of Philip: Translated from the Coptic Text with an Introduction and Commentary.* New York and Evanston: Harper & Row, 1962.

Wilson, R. McL., and George W. MacRae. "The Gospel According to Mary." In *Nag Hammadi Codices V,2–5 and VI with Papyrus Berolinensis 8502,1 and 4*, edited by Douglas M. Parrott, 453–71.

Wisse, Frederik. "The Apocryphon of John." In *The Nag Hammadi Library in English*, edited by James M. Robinson, 104–23.